THE
FORGOTTEN
FLIGHT

THE
FORGOTTEN
FLIGHT

Terrorism, Diplomacy and the
Pursuit of Justice

Stuart H. Newberger

ONEWORLD

A Oneworld Book

Published by Oneworld Publications, 2017

ISBN 978-1-78607-092-0
eISBN 978-1-78607-093-7

Typeset by Palimpsest Book Production Limited, Falkirk, Stirlingshire
Printed and bound by Clays Ltd, St Ives plc

Oneworld Publications
10 Bloomsbury Street
London WC1B 3SR
England

Stay up to date with the latest books,
special offers, and exclusive content from
Oneworld with our monthly newsletter

Sign up on our website
oneworld-publications.com

Contents

Prologue
The Site

I CAREFULLY REMOVED the DVD from the hard plastic jacket and slipped it into my computer. The French documentary began a sober and quiet piece, with soft music and beautifully shaded photography. The pleasant tone did not prepare the viewer for the stark pictures, wandering snapshots of debris in the desert: huge aircraft engines crushed in the sand; passenger seats in clusters of four, tilting to one side; pieces of an aircraft fuselage lying in shallow graves. The severed cockpit juts out of the landscape, its small windows and aircraft nose pointing blankly into the sky. It resembles a death mask.

Much of the television program tracks the long, harsh ride of several SUVs as they convoy hundreds of miles into the barren desert landscape, riding over endless sand dunes and dry lakes. A few camels appear in the distance, led, as they have been for centuries, by Bedouins.

At a new construction site in the sands, workers place large black rocks in designated spots inside a two-hundred-foot-diameter circle. On its perimeter, the construction crew lay down 170 panes of glass, carefully set in concrete and then gently tapped into place with a hammer. The cracked glass creates a prism, diffusing the reflected sun in countless directions. At night, it will reflect the light of the moon and the stars.

As the film continues, a number of Bedouin workers haul an ampu-
tated section of an airplane's detached wing several miles in a flatbed
truck. Working into the dark desert night, a few truck headlights guiding
their efforts, the workers dig a deep hole in the sand and then, slowly
and carefully, stand the wing on its thicker end, its narrow tip pointed
towards the heavens. It stands erect next to the circle of black rocks,
sand and broken glass prisms. A bronze plaque brought from Paris is
mounted on the upright wing as the crew and workers stand respectfully
in silence.

At this point, I click a few buttons on my computer to dial away
from the documentary and switch screen to the internet. I hit a few
more keys and a satellite map appears, showing the surface of the earth.
It takes a few seconds for the image—a photograph of the planet taken
from space, showing a circular structure spread out in the barren sands—
to come into focus. The outline of a DC-10 wide-body jet, of authentic
size, is etched into the landscape, its flight path frozen in the direction
of Paris, north by northwest.

The silhouette of black rock, light brown sand and glittering ring of
broken glass is easily viewed by anyone with access to the web.

The UTA Memorial, 25 June 2007 (courtesy of DigitalGlobe)

I stare at the screen for a long time. To me, the satellite image of the
DC-10 is much more than a web-surfing curiosity. I had devoted nine
years of my lawyering life to the very image in front of me. The story

of how a life-sized memorial in the shape of a passenger jet came to be constructed in one of the most desolate places on the planet, and into which I had been drawn, is one of intrigue and drama, of international terrorism, diplomacy and the pursuit of justice. It had begun almost twenty years before the French film crew recorded the documentary I was now watching of the construction of the DC-10 Memorial and over ten years before I had been pulled into the grip of a case that would profoundly affect my life.

Over the years, the DC-10 on my screen had made hundreds of flights in the vast blue skies seven miles above the hot dunes of the Ténéré desert in the south central Sahara, stretching from the northeast of Niger into Chad. But, as with many events that shape our lives, the story of the DC-10 Memorial began unexpectedly and was almost unnoticed.

Part I

Death in the Skies, Deals with the Devil

1989–2001

Chapter 1

19 September 1989

THE RADAR SCREEN was blank.

Flight 772 of the French airline Union de Transports Aériens—known by the large letters UTA, painted towards the front of the plane—had taken off from N'Djamena, Chad, at 12:18 GMT en route to Charles de Gaulle Airport, Paris. The DC-10 wide-body jet, a blue-and-white monster registered as N54629, was carrying 170 people, including its French crew.

The scheduled flight would take the aircraft high over the shifting brown sands of North Africa, crossing over Niger, Algeria and Tunisia. At the northern coast, the brown landscape below would morph into the shimmering blue water of the Mediterranean as the afternoon sun set on the right side of the plane. Reaching the south of France, it would begin to make a slow descent to Paris, the green manicured fields, hills and meadows coming closer into view in the fading light. The 4,236-kilometer—2,632-mile—trip would take almost five hours, not very long as intercontinental flights go, and the aircraft would undergo a fast turnaround at Charles de Gaulle before turning back to Chad and then heading due south to Brazzaville, Republic of Congo, where it would turn around again. This round-trip route between the French capital and two of France's former colonies in North and West Africa was regularly filled with French businesspeople and diplomats attending to their duties in the French-speaking posts, Africans visiting friends and family long settled in Paris, and a variety of international travelers from around the world.

Captain Georges Raveneau, the pilot of the DC-10, reported to Chadian air traffic control at 12:34 GMT that the aircraft was flying steady over Niger at the time of contact. The Chadian control asked the pilot to contact the Flight Information Center at Niger's Niamey Airport at 1:10 GMT as Niger had no radar control sites. In this vast and sparsely populated part of the world, intercontinental pilots relied on their own navigation instruments between flight control centers. For most of an hour, the DC-10 was on its own, off any local radar coverage, as it flew due north toward the Mediterranean and Europe.

At approximately 13:10 GMT flight control in Niamey expected the UTA flight to appear on screen, its air speed at almost 400 knots and altitude 35,000 feet (10,000 meters), just as it had done twenty-four hours previously. Just as it had for several years of almost daily service. But the Niamey radar screen was blank, the neon green electronic arm making its clockwise pattern over the dark background.

No sign of the DC-10.

It was late.

A few minutes later, the Niamey flight control officer initiated standard procedures, sending its frequency to the overdue aircraft, calling other flights in the vicinity to see if the plane was somehow off course, checking for unusual weather, such as the violent dust storms that were a regular feature of the North African desert. Sometimes a really big storm could foul the radar coverage.

The radar screen was still blank.

At 14:15 GMT flight control issued its first formal radio call.

INCERFA phase. Uncertainty.

Under standard international call signs, this signaled that flight control was unsure of the location and status of the aircraft.

The radar screen was still blank.

At 15:55 GMT control issued its second formal call.

ALERFA. Alert.

A heightened level of alarm and a formal call to all aircraft and ground stations.

The radar screen was still blank.

At 16:14 GMT flight control issued the most serious radio call.

DETRESFA. Distress. A signal used only if flight control believed there was a very high probability that something catastrophic had happened to the aircraft, and the 170 human beings sealed inside the pressurized cabin.

The radar screen was still blank.

* * *

TWELVE HOURS AFTER flight control issued the distress signal, a French Army transport plane carrying paratroopers from the 8th Régiment de Parachutistes d'Infanterie de Marine (RPIMA) came in low over the Ténéré. The Transall C-160 military workhorse flew on a pair of powerful turboprop engines, its wings braced high across the back of the camouflaged plane. It had taken off in the dark before dawn and flown 750 kilometers north from a French military base to cover the itinerary of the still-missing DC-10, its French commander hoping that his search came up empty and that the missing aircraft had landed on a remote airstrip to remedy some unknown problem. Any other possibility was too much to consider.

As the sun crawled over the eastern horizon, the black vastness of the desert came alive with illumination as the sand turned brighter with each passing second. Just minutes after sunrise, the entire desert was visible in every direction, as if the sun was at high noon. The colonel in command scanned the dunes, rocky outcrops and dry lake beds with his oversized binoculars, hoping only to see what rightly belonged in the desert. The turboprop engines pulled the plane in wide turns to maximize visibility, its altitude below 10,000 feet so that the spotters could focus.

Two hours after sunrise, the French paratroopers made out something on the ground that seemed unnatural. A reflection in the bright sun. They could not tell what it was, but very few things in a desert reflect sunlight. Several more reflections were then spotted only a few kilometers away.

THE PARATROOPERS HIT the hard desert sand, each just a few seconds apart. With no suitable place to land the transport plane near the desired location, six members of the regiment, with their colonel in the lead, had jumped into the sky at 5,000 feet and floated groundwards, the sun blinding their vision. The temperature on the ground was almost 100 Fahrenheit, and it was only 9:00 GMT. There was no shade or trees or villages or cars visible in any direction. Just the vast brown sands.

As soon as the troops stood up to pull in their chutes, the smell carried by the hot, light wind grabbed their nostrils, eyes and throats. Kerosene. Its strength was so overwhelming in the parched desert heat that it made some of the tough soldiers vomit where they stood.

By dawn of the next day scores of French and Nigerien soldiers had reached the desert site in all-terrain vehicles and helicopters. After further air surveillance, it was clear that debris was scattered over a huge area almost eighty kilometers long and eight kilometers wide. The perimeter extended beyond the horizon; the spotters on the plane strained to determine where the still-smoldering remnants of the DC-10 could be identified in the rolling landscape.

But from the air one could not experience the smell. Only the soldiers and sanitary squads walking under the blazing sun and in the dry, oppressive heat felt the kerosene seep into their skin. Working carefully, in teams, they began the methodical task of combing the debris to determine what had happened to the jet, loaded with fuel, when it smashed into the ground from 10,000 meters at 230 kilometers per hour.

Pieces of what had been a DC-10 were scattered in random batches within the wide perimeter. The rescue teams cautiously approached, their faces covered by cloth masks, the desert wind blowing fine sand particles into every exposed part of their faces as they examined the wreckage. As part of their training, and as the officers continued to remind them, they were required to walk almost shoulder to shoulder, their eyes focused, straight down, at the ground, scanning for any small items that had been part of the aircraft. Or its passengers.

One team discovered pieces of metal laid out in a neat pattern fifty meters by twenty meters, perhaps a slice of the aircraft's aluminum outer skin, cleanly severed from the body of the DC-10 several miles above the desert, its gliding flight down to the Ténéré a gentle and uneventful voyage until a sudden impact shattered its peaceful descent. Another found one of the three huge engines, the aircraft having had one bolted to each wing and a third mounted high on the tail. The engine was lying flat in the sand by itself, with no other debris within several kilometers. It had broken cleanly from the body of the aircraft, the factory bolts snapping miles above the earth as if removed for routine maintenance. The cylinder-like engine looked like a silver can of soda, slightly crushed by the drinker after draining its contents. It had been tossed in the sand as if at a beach picnic, the front intake wrinkled and bent, having taken most of the impact.

The blowing wind was already filling the back of the now-empty engine with sand. It was still smoldering and reeked of kerosene, the jet fuel residual coating the metal. Its insides had been gutted, like a filleted fish on the dock.

Another engine was located almost twenty kilometers away. It had not had as smooth a ride down. Stripped of its outer casing, the engine's innards lay flat in the sand like a snake's skeleton, crushed flat by the traumatic impact, the fans and flaps twisted and pulled in contrary directions. Dead and naked, it was surrounded by a few inches of sand swept in by the wind, like ripples of water on a windblown lake. The smell of fuel was strong and pervasive.

Five passenger seats were found, bolted together, the metal section leaning in the sand at forty-five degrees. Some seats were still in the upright position dictated by flight attendants at take-off; others were leaning back for a mid-flight nap. They were stripped clean of their soft, comfortable padding and covers, burned down to their metal backs, arms and bottoms, and had come to rest in a snapshot of mayhem. The passenger remains were still strapped in, the seatbelts black and stiff from the searing heat, the smell of kerosene mixing with the stench of burned flesh and organs.

The search for bodies took several days. Sanitary crews cautiously pulled the remains of the passengers from their frozen positions in their seats, gently wrapping each in a cotton shroud. Some bodies had, during the seven-mile descent through the desert air, become unseated, their free fall broken by sudden impact with the earth. Each was quickly described on a form, matched to a number and then loaded on to a helicopter. The shrouded bodies were taken from the site to the remote Nigerien city of Agadez, then to Niamey, and by military transport to Paris. A French doctor from the Medical Center of Charles de Gaulle Airport, as well as a doctor with the 8th RPIMA, inspected each shroud, a pathology formality since there was not even a remote chance that anyone had survived the crash.

The remains were then subject to autopsy at the Bourget National Forensic Science Institute in Paris, in collaboration with the 9th Office Judicial Delegation of Police. The cause of every death was listed as "polytraumatism by blast with burns and a fall from a great altitude." The autopsies listed a series of forensic details.

"Multiple shooting" of bodies by metal pieces coming from the aircraft itself.

"Traumatic lesions combining blast and bone crush."

"Brutal depressurization."

"Carbonized victims, caught fire, strong kerosene smell from bodies."

Given the extent of trauma, only 105 of the 170 passenger remains would ever be identified with certainty. Among the dead in the desert were two dogs and three apes. The manifest had not included any animals. In Africa, airport security would sometimes allow pets to be shipped for a small bribe at the baggage check-in.

AS THE RESCUE teams detailed their daily surveys, it became clear that the DC-10 had broken apart into four large pieces while in the air, with each then separately shattered into smaller pieces. After three days of intense searches on the desert floor by the French teams, the two black boxes storing the flight's operational details and cockpit recordings were located in the sand. Shipped by a special plane back to Paris, they were examined by the Investigating Magistrate of the Paris Criminal Investigation Department and representatives of the French National Directive of Civil Aviation.

The first box was the Digital Flight Data Recorder (DFDR) and the second was the Cockpit Voice Recorder (CVR). Both were closely analyzed by the In-Flight Experiment Department at Brétigny-sur-Orge outside Paris. According to the CVR, the disaster was "not due to a technical incident" and "nothing in the conversations that went inside the cockpit could lead to foresee such outcome."

The fuselage between the cockpit and the point of attachment to the wings had shattered into many pieces. It would take French investigators almost a year to ship fifteen tons of aircraft remains from the desert to an airport hangar outside Paris. In an attempt to recreate a portion of the aircraft before the catastrophe, a fourteen-meter-long section of the fuselage representing the front baggage compartment was reassembled piece by piece in Hangar HM 10 at Dugny airbase at Le Bourget Field. The investigators focused on the baggage hold, where the passengers' suitcases had been stored in-flight.

Over time, the reconstruction centered on the right front portion of the aircraft, around baggage container Number 7044 RK, position 13R. This area held the economy-class luggage. It was located in the superstructure of the aircraft between frames 595 and 1099.

THE INVESTIGATION OF the crash was assigned to Magistrate Judge Jean-Louis Bruguière, the leading terrorism investigator in France, and the huge reconstruction job had been ordered by him to determine exactly how and where the DC-10 came apart. The massive investigatory effort was the highest priority for the French government. The resources of the French State were devoted to determining the cause of the disaster, as directed by the President himself, François Mitterrand.

The first Socialist to serve as President of the Fifth Republic, Mitterrand had just been re-elected to a second term in 1988 and was quite familiar with the intricacies of criminal investigations, having served as Minister of Justice earlier in his career. A former rival of Charles de Gaulle, he had advocated that France preserve its "special relationships" with its former colonies in Africa. He had also established an "anti-terror cell" directly under the authority of the President. It specialized in illegal wiretaps of political opponents, journalists and personal rivals.

* * *

FOUR WEEKS AFTER the crash, one of the search teams in the desert found a very small piece of luggage, dark gray in color, hard shell material on the outside, the inside surface of which was covered with bits of fabric. The urgency went beyond that surrounding a normal civil aviation disaster. The forensic laboratory quickly determined that the suitcase remnant contained small pieces of PETN—pentaerythritol tetranitrate, pentrite, a common form of plastic explosive. The source of the catastrophe was immediately clear. The DC-10 had been destroyed while in flight by a bomb planted in a suitcase.

The greatest murder investigation in the history of France would attempt to determine who was responsible for what was characterized as a "terrorist undertaking." It would take years of extraordinary detective work, extensive diplomacy, complex legal proceedings and a fair amount of luck to answer the question. It would take even longer to hold anyone accountable for this act of mass murder seven miles above the Ténéré.

Chapter 2
The Prelude

MY OWN ROLE in the bombing of UTA Flight 772 did not begin until many years after the 1989 attack. But as any student of the times will remember, the events of 1989 came amid several violent years of terrorist attacks in Europe, Africa, the Middle East and Asia. The French investigators assigned to the case were very familiar with that history, and I would get to know them, and the remarkable results of their work, in due time. But when the DC-10 went down in the Ténéré desert that September, it did not take the French officials very long to uncover their first clues.

* * *

SEVERAL YEARS EARLIER, on 10 March 1984, another UTA flight running the round trip from Brazzaville to N'Djamena to Paris—a four-engine, full-sized DC-8—had a bomb explode in the baggage hold shortly before take-off from N'Djamena. That attack killed one person on board and injured twenty-three other passengers; the resulting huge fire completely destroyed the aircraft.

Although they never made an arrest for the 1984 attack, French intelligence sources had suspected that a Libyan named Ahmat Masri had handed a booby-trapped suitcase to an unsuspecting African named Abdoulaye Saleh, who had already left the plane before it taxied out to the runway. The suitcase bomb had been designed to explode while the aircraft was airborne. The timer apparently had not been properly set and went off prematurely.

THE TERROR WAVE shifted to Europe the next year. On 27 December 1985, at 9:15 a.m. local time, a coordinated attack at two major European airports struck at the heart of international air travel.

At Rome's Leonardo da Vinci–Fiumicino, four gunmen approached the ticket counters of two airlines—Trans World (TWA), one of the world's leading international carriers, and Israel's El Al. The attackers opened fire with assault rifles and threw hand grenades, killing sixteen people and wounding ninety-nine others, all of whom had the bad luck of being at the counters or nearby fast-food restaurant sipping coffee at that violent moment. The mayhem left bodies and blood all over the terminal.

Three of the gunmen were killed where they stood by Italian and Israeli security guards. Although the fourth terrorist was seriously wounded, he was captured alive by the police.

Simultaneously, and hundreds of miles to the north, three terrorists walked into the main terminal at Vienna's International Airport, tossing hand grenades at crowds of passengers waiting in line to check in to an El Al flight to Tel Aviv. Two of the passengers waiting in line were killed on the spot; thirty-nine others were wounded. One of them died a few weeks later from the effects of the hand grenade blasts. As the attackers attempted to flee, Austrian police conducted a car chase, eventually killing one of them and capturing the other two alive.

Yasser Arafat of the Palestine Liberation Organization (PLO) publicly denied any responsibility for either the Rome or Vienna attacks and a separate Middle Eastern terrorist group known as the Abu Nidal Organization (ANO) took full credit for the carnage. Only later did US intelligence determine that the ANO attackers in Vienna and Rome all held Libyan passports, which had allowed them to transit through Italy and Austria. Libya also was later accused of supplying the weapons used in the murderous assaults. Although it formally denied any responsibility, the Libyan government's public affairs office in Tripoli later hailed the attackers as "heroes."

THE TERROR WAVE continued over the next few months.

On 5 April 1986, a large bomb exploded in a West Berlin night club known as an after-hours gathering place for US servicemen. La Belle discotheque had several hundred customers inside its doors just before 2.00 a.m., the dancing, music and alcohol fueling a party-like atmosphere. The bomb had been placed under a table near the disc jockey's booth to harm as many people as possible.

Two US servicemen and a Turkish woman were killed instantly and a third US army sergeant died from his wounds two months later. Over 230 customers in the club were injured, including over fifty US servicemen. Many were permanently disabled.

But the investigators caught a break. The attackers had left what amounted to fingerprints.

SHORTLY AFTER THE West Berlin bombing, US and German intelligence sources intercepted a telex from Tripoli to the Libyan Embassy in East Berlin. The telex, from the Libyan Foreign Ministry, congratulated the Embassy on a job "well done." Apparently, the attack had been planned as revenge two weeks earlier, after the US Navy had clashed with a Libyan patrol boat in the Mediterranean in the disputed Gulf of Sidra, near the Libyan coast. Several Libyan seamen had been killed in that clash, which Libya asserted had taken place in international waters.

The La Belle bombing increased the political heat in Washington, DC for the United States to take some type of decisive action. Only three years earlier, in October 1983, the US Marine Corps had been forced to exit Beirut, Lebanon, after a suicide bomber in a truck killed over two hundred Marines at their peacekeeping encampment near the airport. This had been a humbling experience for America and its then President, Ronald Reagan, who prided himself on a tough cowboy image, even if it was a product of Hollywood. Retreating from terrorists was not the policy he wanted to pursue, and the attack in Berlin provided a chance to restore some of the image he craved.

Reagan quickly decided to retaliate for the La Belle bombing. After several diplomatic discussions failed to present a unified front, he ordered eighteen US Air Force F-111 strike aircraft based in England to join with fifteen US Navy A-6 and F/A-18 carrier-based attack planes to bomb five targets inside Libya. On 15 April 1986, this attack force flew into Libyan air space to send a message of destruction and reduce Libya's ability to support and train terrorists. Afraid of the consequences, several US NATO allies including France, Spain and Italy refused permission for the jets to fly from their base in England over their territory en route to Libya. This forced the attack squadron to fly all around the western edge of Europe and through the Straits of Gibraltar, adding 1,300 miles each way and requiring a number of mid-air refuelings.

The name of the operation was "El Dorado Canyon," the first US military strike from the UK since World War II. The actual attacks lasted about ten minutes. At least forty people in Libya were killed, including fifteen civilians, as the US planes hit targets in Tripoli and Benghazi, on the Mediterranean coast. Some of the bombs missed their military targets and the French Embassy was almost hit by a stray.

The principal target of the attack escaped serious harm. Libyan leader Colonel Muammar Qaddafi, head of the Libyan revolution and undisputed dictator since he overthrew the Libyan monarchy in 1969, had been warned by Italian Prime Minister Bettino Craxi that the Americans might attack, based on what he had heard from consultations with the US Embassy in Rome. Critically, the Prime Minister of the small Mediterranean island nation of Malta—between Italy and Libya—called Qaddafi on the phone only minutes before the attack and warned him that a large squadron of "unauthorized" military aircraft had just flown overhead. Rushing out of his family compound in Tripoli only moments before the first Air Force and Navy jets came in low from the coast, Qaddafi and most members of his family escaped injury by taking cover in a nearby shelter.

According to the Libyans, not everyone in the compound made it to safety. Qaddafi alleged that his adopted daughter Hanna, nearly two years old, was killed by the American bombs, and two of his sons were injured, but this allegation was never proven by Libya and there is no publicly available evidence to support the claim. In addition, two US Air Force pilots were killed when their F-111 was shot down over the Gulf of Sidra by Libyan anti-aircraft missiles. The Soviet-supplied weapons had only recently arrived in Libya and were put into service just days before the attack.

* * *

THE US BOMBING triggered a further escalation in tension between Libya and the West, especially the US and UK. A few days later, Libyan agents traveled to Lebanon to negotiate with Hezbollah, the Islamic terrorist group sponsored by Iran. Their goal was to "purchase" several American and British hostages held by the Shi'ite group as part of its own pattern of terror in that war-torn country. Two British hostages, Leigh Douglas and Philip Padfield, and one American, Peter Kilburn, all of whom worked at the American University of Beirut and who had been taken hostage one year earlier, were summarily executed as the Libyan agents administered gunshots to their heads. The bodies were dumped on the side of the road near Beirut. An attached note made clear they had been killed in revenge for President Reagan's military attacks on Libya, which had paid Hezbollah $1 million for each man. Years later, I would represent the family of Peter Kilburn in their own case against Libya for his murder.

The response to the attacks against Libya was not limited to inducing more terrorism. In the United Nations, the General Assembly, long a forum sympathetic to the developing world and anti-US sentiments, voted seventy-nine to twenty-eight—with thirty-three abstentions—to condemn the American military attack, which it declared violated the United Nations Charter and international law. In particular, the US and UK took the brunt of criticism. Qaddafi was especially angry at British Prime Minister Margaret Thatcher for allowing the US Air Force to launch the attack from British bases. He publicly declared that "Thatcher is a murderer ... Thatcher is a prostitute. She sold herself to Reagan." Even the normally staid British paper the *Sunday Times* noted that Queen Elizabeth II herself was upset by her "uncaring" Prime Minister.

FIVE MONTHS LATER, tension rose to even greater levels. The message President Reagan and Prime Minister Thatcher had intended to be sent—that Libya's emerging role as a sponsor of terrorism was to be reduced—apparently had the opposite effect as Qaddafi sought revenge for the attacks.

On 5 September 1986, at 6:00 a.m. local time in Karachi, Pakistan (10:00 p.m. GMT the previous night), a 747 jumbo jet loaded with over 360 passengers and crew was sitting on the tarmac, taking on a few more passengers. Pan Am Flight 73 had originated in Bombay's Sahar International Airport (now Mumbai's Chhatrapati Shivaji), its final destination New York's JFK after stopovers in Karachi and Frankfurt, Germany. The India-based cabin crew and the plane's American pilots were making final preparations before take-off and the long flight to northern Europe.

Pan Am was the leading international air carrier from the United States, a prominent role the airway had enjoyed for decades. It flew the most modern Boeing aircraft, hired the best-qualified pilots and proudly set the standard for international travel. The cabin crew on this particular flight was especially notable as one of the first non-American crews to service such a prestigious route. Several of the flight attendants came from important Indian families. As with most Pan Am aircraft, the Boeing 747-121 jumbo jet had a name—Clipper New Horizons, meant to evoke the glamor and tradition of ocean voyages.

Shortly before the doors of the aircraft were to be closed for the long flight, a white van that appeared to be an airport security vehicle drove without garnering any attention through a checkpoint and pulled up to the back of the jumbo jet, near the stairs that ran up to the exit door. Four Arab men dressed as Pakistani security guards jumped out. Two ran up the back of the plane and two to the front. They were carrying assault rifles, pistols, hand grenades and body belts wrapped with plastic explosives.

Storming up the stairs and in through the two open jet doorways, the four attackers fired their automatic weapons, running into the twin aisles of the aircraft as the stunned passengers tried to determine what was happening.

Once all four were on board Pan Am Flight 73, they ordered the flight attendants to close the aircraft doors and seal in the over 360 passengers and crew, 78 of whom were US citizens, many of dual Indian–American backgrounds. One of the flight attendants managed to alert the cockpit of the attack via the internal phone and the two pilots and flight engineer escaped through a small emergency hatch, lowering themselves down a long rope to the tarmac. By running away from the aircraft, they had prevented the terrorists from forcing it to take off, at least for the time being.

The attackers held an automatic weapon or hand grenade to the heads of several passengers and all of the people on the plane were forced to keep their hands up and heads down for several hours. No one was allowed to speak, go to the toilet or get a drink of water.

The attacker who appeared to be in charge ordered the flight attendants to collect the passengers' passports and to separate out the American ones. Suspecting that this might lead to violence, some of the flight attendants, led by one of the Indian cabin crew attendants, Neerja Bhanot, the Senior Purser, hid a number of the US passports. When the lead attacker realized what was happening he screamed that he would start killing people if the attendants disobeyed him.

To prove his point, the lead attacker grabbed a 29-year-old California resident who had only recently obtained American citizenship and dragged him to the front of the plane. He was forced to kneel at the front doorway with his hands behind his head while the lead attacker began to beat him with his automatic weapon, in plain view of many passengers. The lead attacker had also demanded that a new flight crew come on board to fly the plane out of Karachi. Unhappy with the lack of response to his demands, he ordered one of the flight attendants to open the cabin door. He then shot the Californian, Rajesh Kumar, in the head, heaved him out the open door and watched him fall down to the tarmac. Turning to the terrified passengers, he then threatened that he would kill one of them every ten minutes if the Pakistani authorities did not provide a new pilot. They wanted to fly to Cyprus, he said, to secure the release of several Palestinian terrorists. The attackers also radioed the airport authorities to warn that any attempt to rescue the passengers or storm the plane would result in a huge explosion and many deaths.

Their real intentions were different. It later emerged that they wanted to fly the plane towards Tel Aviv, crash it into an Israeli Ministry of Defense building and "destroy sensitive strategic centers of the criminal Zionist entity."

As the sun went down and the electrical power in the huge plane began to sputter, the lead terrorist ordered all of the 376 hostages towards the center. People were piled on top of each other in the seats and aisles. Two attackers stood at one end of the plane, the other two at the other end, the mass of hostages now huddled between them.

At 10:00 p.m. local time the plane's auxiliary power unit finally failed and all the internal lights went out, plunging the 376 hostages and their attackers into total darkness. As the lead attacker began loudly reciting a martyrdom prayer in Arabic—the other three joining in with cries of "Jihad! Jihad! Jihad!"—all four opened fire with their automatic weapons, throwing hand grenades into the middle of the pile of screaming, terrified hostages. The only light came from the gun flashes and explosions.

Many passengers and cabin crew died instantly, the total reaching twenty within seconds. Neerja Bhanot was killed after she flung herself across several young American children to shield them from the bullets. The only reason more people were not immediately killed was that one passenger—an expert in sports medicine and a US Navy veteran—was able to force open an emergency escape door just as the firing began, bits of the airplane's plastic cutting into his face as the bullets struck the interior wall and door.

Scores of terrified people leaped towards the shadowy outline of the doorway, clambering onto the huge wing of the jumbo jet. The scene was one of utter chaos, a mass of people desperately trying to survive the onslaught. There was no safe way to descend the huge wing, and some passengers jumped into the darkness of the night to the tarmac almost twenty feet below, breaking arms and legs as they hit the concrete. Most were covered with blood—either their own or that of their fellow passengers. Those who were able to ran towards the safety of the terminal, afraid the jumbo jet might explode at any moment.

After what seemed to have been hours but was in fact only a few minutes, the firing suddenly stopped. Pakistani special forces stormed their way into the plane, shining flashlights into the bloody massacre of the darkened 747 cabin. There were dead bodies, severely wounded passengers screaming for their lives, others moaning in pain or shouting for their missing loved ones.

Three of the terrorists were arrested immediately on the tarmac, the guns in their hands quickly identifying them as the attackers. Their leader, though, managed to slip through the net by dropping his weapon and explosive belt and pretending to be a wounded passenger seeking medical attention. He was arrested a few hours later at a local hospital where rescue workers had taken him for treatment, after passengers identified him to the authorities.

A fifth attacker had not boarded the aircraft. Instead, he had collected the others' passports and money before the attack and then watched as they drove the white security van toward the plane. As his comrades held the passengers and crew hostage, he had tried to book another flight. Before he could exit Pakistan, he also was arrested. His intended destination was Tripoli, Libya.

Years later I would represent some of the passengers (and their families) who were on Pan Am Flight 73 that fateful night in Karachi in their effort to hold Qaddafi's Libya responsible for the attack.

* * *

SURPRISINGLY, THERE WERE no attacks on the scale of Rome, Vienna, Berlin or Karachi, at least not with any obvious Libyan connection or support, for the next two years. Iran and the PLO were busy wreaking havoc in their respective spheres of influence, especially Lebanon, Jordan, Israel and Europe. Scores died in assassinations and bombings and others were taken hostage.

In the skies, a major catastrophe was the in-flight bombing of Air India 182, a B-747 jumbo jet that blew up near the Irish coast en route from Montreal to London and then New Delhi. Over three hundred passengers and crew were killed, mostly Indians and Canadians of Indian ancestry. A Sikh militant group was thought to have carried out the bombing in retaliation for Indian Prime Minister Indira Gandhi's 1984 military attack on the Sikh Golden Temple, the center of Sikhism in Amritsar, Punjab, for which she herself was assassinated that same year. Despite the unprecedented nature of this operation and loss of life, Western experts and investigators viewed it through the prism of local Indian politics and rivalries, and as such it was not considered a part of any worldwide menace.

In contrast, things appeared quiet on the Libya front. Colonel Qaddafi had enacted his vengeance against Reagan and Thatcher for their attack on Libyan soil—or so it seemed to Western intelligence experts who closely studied the enigmatic ruler.

They would soon be proven wrong.

* * *

AS EVERY INTERNATIONAL traveler knows, Heathrow Airport lies on the outer edge of London and has long served as one of the busiest and most important links in the world of international air travel. I have flown through Heathrow more times than I can remember. It connects cities on every continent and funnels hundreds of thousands of diverse passengers in every global direction. It also handles more passengers to and from the United States than any other airport in the world. On 21 December 1988, shortly before the travel crunch leading up to the Christmas break, Heathrow was, as usual, jammed with passengers and airline crews.

At the time, Pan Am was still America's leading flag carrier, in close competition with TWA. The brutal ground attack on Pan Am 73 in Karachi two years earlier was now a distant memory for most of its crews. But as a proud symbol of the United States, Pan Am had long been the target of other terrorist attacks. In 1970, a flight from Amsterdam to New York had been hijacked and diverted to Cairo, where the plane was blown up on the ground after its passengers and crew had been allowed to evacuate. In December 1973, a Palestinian terrorist group threw bombs at a Pan Am jet at Rome airport as passengers were boarding, killing 30 in the resulting fire.

For most passengers, airline hijackings and attacks were something that took place in "dangerous" parts of the world, typically the Middle

East, Africa and Asia. Air travel was different in far-flung places, and security concerns were not on the same intense level as they were in the world's hotspots, they reasoned. Terrorism and violence typically were not associated with the "civilized" environs of airports in Western Europe and the United States. The ground attacks in Rome and Vienna two years earlier had been viewed as rare events and had not reached the vulnerable aircraft. Heathrow seemed safe to the tens of thousands of passengers who passed through there every day.

IN 1988, THE demand for a direct, non-stop air service between London and New York was greater than ever. Like Heathrow, New York's JFK Airport was a principal connection hub for locations around the world, and was almost as busy, so much so that Pan Am ran three daily trans-atlantic flights between the two destinations. The holiday season in particular meant a crush of reservations, filled seats and harried crews. This time of year also signaled the vacation break for American college students spending their semester terms abroad, and catching a flight from or through Heathrow was a rite of passage for young students heading back to the US to visit family and friends.

The Pan Am 747-100 Clipper named *Maid of the Seas* was one of the earliest jumbo jets manufactured by Boeing at its giant aircraft construc-tion plant outside Seattle, Washington. It was the fifteenth 747 to come off the assembly line back in February 1970, only one month after the very first 747 entered service. Pan Am had proudly taken ownership of the first 747 jumbos in its effort to dominate the American share of the international air traffic market.

The Clipper landed at Heathrow that Wednesday at 12:00 GMT after a long flight from Los Angeles and San Francisco, California. Parked at jumbo jet stand K-14, outside Heathrow Terminal 3, it was guarded intermittently by Pan Am's own security company, Alert Security, but otherwise was only visited by the ground crews cleaning the cabin and storing the food and other items that would service the passengers on the trip back to JFK later that evening.

As was typical for Heathrow, Pan Am fed travelers through other airports in Europe and then to its London hub for the final leg back to the US. The Frankfurt flight was part of Pan Am's interconnected route, what the industry referred to as a "feeder," and for many of those on board was the first leg of their scheduled route to JFK. Almost ninety Pan Am passengers flew into Heathrow that evening on a smaller Boeing 727 from Frankfurt, West Germany, pulling into jet stand K-16, right next to the jumbo 747 as it finished taking on its fuel and supplies for the transatlantic flight. As such, they walked right off the Frankfurt plane and were directed by Pan Am personnel to board their US-bound jet in the adjacent gate. Baggage that had been loaded in Frankfurt and was to be taken to JFK was quickly transferred to the jumbo.

Pan Am's routing system meant that the Frankfurt feeder flight to Heathrow shared the flight number of the 747 getting ready to fly to JFK.

Pan Am Flight 103.

SCHEDULED TO DEPART at 18:00 GMT, Pan Am Flight 103 pushed back from gate K-14 four minutes behind schedule because of rush-hour delays. Captain James Bruce "Jim" MacQuarrie took off from Heathrow runway 27R at 18:25 GMT, heading northwest and away from the crowded London air traffic. He then steered the massive aircraft due north. The flight would follow the familiar path over Scotland before heading out over the North Atlantic.

The 747 held 243 passengers and 16 crew members, of whom 189 were American citizens. The fuel tanks located inside the massive wings were full, ready to feed the four giant engines that would carry the plane across the cold, dark ocean to JFK.

At 18:56 GMT, as the jumbo jet's engines powered the loaded aircraft towards its cruising altitude of 31,000 feet (9,400 meters), Pan Am Flight 103 crossed over the border of Scotland.

At 19:00 GMT, Captain MacQuarrie throttled back the engines to cruising power. He radioed Scottish Area Control Centre at Prestwick: "Good evening Scottish, Clipper one zero three. We are level at three one zero."

A second later, First Officer Raymond Ronald "Ray" Wagner, sitting to the right of the Captain, spoke into the number two radio with a pilot's calm, technical voice. "Clipper 103 requesting oceanic clearance."

At the same time, sitting on the ground at his air traffic control station at Prestwick, controller Alan Topp watched on his radar screen. The jumbo jet's on-board transponder signaled to Topp that it was at 31,000 feet on a heading of 316 degrees magnetic north, and at an air speed of 313 knots (580 kilometers per hour), pushing directly into a headwind.

At 19:02:46.9 GMT, Topp lost contact with the on-board transponder, its radar image going blank. He first tried to radio Captain MacQuarrie to check on the status of his transponder equipment. Captain MacQuarrie did not reply. He then radioed a nearby KLM flight to try and reach the Pan Am jet in the event that there was a technical problem with the communication radios or the transponders. The calls from the KLM pilot to the Pan Am Clipper were not returned.

At that moment, Topp saw something on the radar screen that he had never seen before. Instead of a single blip for the jumbo jet, the radar return on his screen showed four blips. Within seconds, the radar blips began to fan out more widely on the screen. Given the spacing of the blips, they were spread out over a nautical mile (1.9 kilometers). Topp's radar screen was full of dozens of smaller blips, now moving east with the prevailing wind.

Less than fifty seconds later, the British Geological Survey at nearby Eskdalemuir registered a seismic event measuring 1.6 on the Richter scale. Almost immediately, a British Airways pilot flying south from Glasgow to London radioed Scottish authorities to report that he could see a huge fireball on the ground.

His report was accurate. Almost 200,000 pounds of kerosene jet fuel, stored in the jumbo jet's tanks inside the wings of the plane, had collided with the hard Scottish winter soil and rock at 500 miles, or 800 kilometers, per hour. There was even an address that identified the precise location of the seismic event registered by the scientific equipment set up to record earthquakes.

13 Sherwood Crescent.

In a sleepy Scottish town by the name of Lockerbie.

Chapter 3

Lockerbie

IT IS NOT an exaggeration to say that the name "Lockerbie" entered the world's vocabulary from the moment Pan Am Flight 103 fell from the sky and crashed into the small market town in southwest Scotland. In the modern parlance of terrorism that has become a part of our daily lives, it resonates in the same way as September 11, or 9/11—as a shorthand reference for a notorious airplane-related act of terror. Even today, images of Lockerbie are still deeply etched into our minds. One of the most widely published photographs taken of the scene of the crash shows a Scottish policeman standing next to a portion of the plane's nose section, which lies crumpled on the ground. The name "Clipper Maid of the Seas" can be made out, upside down, below the windows of the cockpit. My own memory of this photograph from newspapers, magazines and television is vivid.

The name Lockerbie is immediately recognizable to hundreds of millions of people around the world, even those unfamiliar with the details of this tragic event. World media have employed it with such regularity that it has become a synonym for a whole series of happenings, well beyond the disaster itself. Many books have been written about Lockerbie, by family members, journalists, investigators and scholars. It has been the reason for scores of television documentaries, articles, speeches in the British Parliament, international diplomacy, acts of Congress and countless pages of newspaper copy.

Lockerbie will never be forgotten, or misunderstood. And for good reason.

* * *

SHORTLY AFTER THE jumbo jet crashed it became clear that an explosion had taken place in the luggage hold just after it had flown over the Scottish border. If the explosion had occurred just a few minutes later, the jet would have plunged into the Atlantic Ocean, and the wreckage would have been very difficult to locate. Forensic evidence is usually not available to investigators when it lies 10,000 feet below the surface of foreboding Atlantic waters. The only fortunate aspect of the Lockerbie disaster was that by hitting a small town instead of the ocean the deaths of the innocent victims could be investigated and those responsible for mass murder possibly brought to justice.

The explosion tore a twenty-inch-wide hole in the left of the fuselage, directly under the letter P in the name Pan Am on the side of the aircraft. The catastrophe caused by the bomb was immediate and the pilots clearly had no chance to save the plane, its human cargo, or themselves.

Apparently, the nose of the plane became separated from the rest of the structure within a few seconds. Because of this separation, the plane immediately lost all communication, navigation equipment and controls, which were located directly below the cockpit. The shockwaves from the explosion rippled through the skin of the plane, violently shaking the entire aircraft, causing multiple shockwaves in return. These caused the plane to split open. Part of the roof was immediately forced off the rest of the aircraft. Because the plane had reached its cruising altitude, it had full pressurization in the cabin. With the failure of the plane to maintain its structure, the huge differential between the cabin and the outside air pressure caused an effect like that of a popping balloon. Hurricane-like winds tore through the passenger cabin. Boeing had not designed the plane to survive such a catastrophic failure.

All 243 passengers and 16 crew were killed, either in the air or on impact. The passenger cabin itself was a death trap, the effects of the explosion causing unimaginable pain and torture to anyone who survived the initial blast. The control cabin crashed in a field near a church in the village of Tundergarth; the flight crew were found still strapped to their seats. According to the forensics and autopsies, Captain MacQuarrie's thumb had distinctive markings, which suggested that he had been consciously hanging on to the steering column as he rode the doomed cockpit down towards Scotland.

Citizens of the US and Great Britain accounted for the majority of the passengers, with 188 Americans and 32 British among the dead. Most of the crew were American. The number of American college students on their way home for European school term breaks was staggering. Thirty-five students from Syracuse University were killed, as were students from Colgate, Brown, Seton Hall, Hampshire College and State University of New York at Oswego. A number of the American victims lived on Long Island outside New York City. Also on board were several American passengers whose employment later gave rise to a number of conspiracy theories. The CIA deputy station chief in Beirut and an officer with the Defense Intelligence Agency (DIA), along with their bodyguards, were returning to Washington via New York, as was a Special Agent with the Department of Justice.

However, the passengers and crew were not the only victims. Eleven residents of Lockerbie were killed instantly when the fuel-filled wings and fuselage hit the ground. Several were killed instantly as they walked in the street, their bodies so vaporized there was nothing left to bury. The family home at 13 Sherwood Crescent was hit directly, pulverizing the ground and carving out a crater over 150 feet (46 meters) long. Houses were razed to their foundations; twenty-one were so badly damaged they later were demolished. Despite many months of forensic work, the authorities were unable to find the remains of any passengers who had been sitting over the wing. The fireball had vaporized them. The blast on the ground was so large and intense it reached cars passing by on the A74, the main road link to Glasgow, burning several vehicles.

To add to the ghastly scene, many dead passengers' bodies lay in the backyards, gardens and streets, to where they had fallen from the heavens. They were not moved for several days because the British forensic teams needed to piece together the crime scene, photographing and marking each victim's location to assist in the investigation.

Many shocked and grieving family members flew from the US and traveled to Lockerbie to identify their remains. Volunteers from nearby homes and villages set up round-the-clock support tents with food, coffee and companionship. In a touching gesture of humanity, the local residents were allowed to wash and iron all the scattered items of clothing that had fallen from shattered suitcases, after the authorities made sure they contained no forensic evidence relevant to the investigation.

The disaster dominated the news in both the US and UK, given the prominence of Pan Am, the importance of the London-to-New York route, and the high loss of their citizens' lives. The FBI and Scotland Yard jointly began an enquiry that was unprecedented in aviation disaster history. Many leads were pursued and a number of well-known terrorist organizations claimed credit for the bombing.

Rescuers and investigators sorted through the debris for months, and the remaining pieces of the plane were collected to determine the exact cause of the disaster. Over time, a few fragments of a hard-shell Samsonite suitcase were recovered, along with a few bits of an electric circuit board that had been part of a Toshiba cassette player. These items lost their normalcy when the investigators determined that they contained traces of Semtex. Plastic explosive.

A suitcase bomb.

* * *

THE EXPLOSION OF a second suitcase bomb in the baggage compartment of a jumbo jet nine months after Pan Am 103 crashed into Lockerbie never received the same level of notoriety. When the earth shook again from the force of an exploding jet loaded with tons of fuel crashing into its surface, this time deep in the remote Ténéré desert, there were no victims on the ground. Nor were there any passing passenger jets to observe the fireball, or supportive local villagers manning sandwich and coffee tents as grieving family members searched for any signs of their loved ones. There were no television cameras or reporters to ensure the tragedy was on the front pages and evening news broadcasts around the world.

Indeed, the tragic loss of UTA 772 and its 170 passengers and crew was only picked up as a minor story in the Associated Press and Agence France-Presse wires. I recall that the *Washington Post* had a four-line wire story about the missing UTA 772 flight on its inside pages, buried with other news from around the world. There were no photographs of the crash site. No evening news stories. No shocked family member could possibly have traveled to such a remote and barren place in the North African desert. They remained thousands of miles, and another world, away. UTA 772 might just as well have crashed on the moon.

Just a few days after French paratroopers found the debris of the DC-10 in the desert, Magistrate Judge Jean-Louis Bruguière was appointed to lead the investigation into the cause of, and possible responsibility for, the UTA 772 disaster. At first, this would be solely a French affair, relying on the great intelligence network France had developed over the decades, especially in its former African colonies. France's independent and sophisticated police and security system was very proud of its ability to develop a case and pursue suspects. Only later would France join with the US and UK in comparing the similarities between Lockerbie and Ténéré, and only when evidence was uncovered that drove the two investigations towards a common suspect.

But, at the beginning of the investigation into UTA 772, France was on her own.

* * *

EVEN BEFORE THE French investigators got down to the serious work facing them in September 1989, various groups began claiming credit for the loss of the DC-10 and its 170 victims. Less than twenty-four hours after the crash was reported in the French media, UTA's booking agent office received a call from a person claiming to represent Islamic Jihad. The caller asserted that the bombing was in retaliation for French atrocities in Lebanon committed against Shi'ite Muslims. A few hours later, another person called the Reuters news agency in London, again claiming that Islamic Jihad had carried out the "heroic" attack on the plane, and demanding the release of a radical sheikh held by the Israelis. This did not happen. Three days later, a radio station in Chad claimed that the explosion on the DC-10 was carried out by a group previously unknown to French intelligence—the "Underground Chadian Resistance." Several other calls were received over the next few days. The French authorities characterized these as coming from "strangers with questionable mental health." In the meantime, Jean-Louis Bruguière and his team began the task ahead of them.

SHORT AND COMPACT, Bruguière was the leading investigating magistrate in Paris, responsible for overseeing all major terrorism cases. In the French civil law system, which had originated two centuries previously under Emperor Napoleon Bonaparte, investigating magistrates are not really neutral "judges" resolving disputes between conflicting parties. The title is merely honorific. Instead, they are appointed by the court to lead an investigation and submit a report and evidence along with their recommendations regarding criminal charges against suspects, although they operate quite independently of the Executive branch, which in France consists of the President and the government—the Prime Minister and other ministers. The police support the investigating magistrate, as do any other branches of the government necessary to conduct the investigation, as well as branch agencies such as the intelligence and military services, as needed.

Given this independence and authority, investigating magistrates are extremely powerful figures, and Bruguière was the most powerful investigating magistrate in France. The immense scope and dimension of the UTA 772 bombing would require him to employ all of his powers and resources if he were to solve the crime.

Bruguière, coming from eleven generations of investigating magistrates, was almost at a level of nobility and born to the job. He began his career busting prostitution rings in Paris, defying well-connected and popular forces in French society. In the early 1980s he had pioneered the field of anti-terrorism in French investigative circles, forming the first anti-terrorism division in France, and was a student of Africa, the

Middle East and Asia—all breeding grounds for terrorism that affected France. Indeed, several years later he would successfully track down and arrest Ilich Ramírez Sánchez, better known as Carlos the Jackal, the most notorious terrorist in the world before a rich Saudi named Osama bin Laden usurped the title.

Bruguière was a familiar figure in the French media, and it was rumored that he encouraged and enjoyed the attention. He was pale skinned and dark browed; his hair was thin and slicked down to one side, framing his grim-looking face, his distinct Gallic nose and small mouth separated by a deep five o'clock shadow across his lip. He wore dark suits, conservative ties and white shirts; the constant presence of a pipe in his hand or mouth projected a professorial image. He traveled around Paris in a bullet-proof car with two armed bodyguards and since a grenade attack on his apartment in the 1980s had carried a .357 Magnum. This, combined with his unorthodox investigating methods, gave rise to a nickname in the French press. They called him "Le Sheriff."

But Bruguière did not work much with his counterparts at the FBI or Scotland Yard. His terrorism docket and shadowy intelligence techniques did not fit well in their regimented cultures. Rather, he was more familiar with the CIA and British MI5 and MI6 intelligence world, and they with him.

In September 1989 Bruguière was serving as First Vice President of the Tribunal de Grande Instance—the Paris Court of Major Investigations and Claims. Only days after the remains of the UTA 772 plane were spotted in the Ténéré, Bruguière got on a French military jet and made the arduous trip to the crash site.

His lead investigator was Romuald Muller, Commissioner of the Central Directorate of Judicial Police, whose offices were within the Ministry of Interior and Territorial Development. Muller was tasked with preparing periodic reports, summarizing the results of certain aspects of the investigation and organizing the massive case.

Bruguière's task was clear, but this was to be a complex investigation. First, assemble the evidence to allow the forensic experts to determine how the disaster had occurred. Second, track down every possible lead and interview every potential witness, no matter how minor their part in the story, or how many blind alleys the investigators must pursue.

Third, determine why the crime had been committed. Motive lay at the heart of every crime, especially one that hinted at international terrorism. And finally, follow the trail to those responsible for the murder of 170 people and bring them to justice, in Paris.

The greatest murder case in French history had begun, and Le Sheriff was on the job.

Chapter 4
The Plot

BRUGUIÈRE AND HIS team started with the basics.

As the soldiers, medical teams, airline technicians and forensic experts spent months tediously sifting through the widely dispersed remains of the DC-10 and its cargo in the hot, barren sands of the Ténéré, the police investigators began looking for clues, poring over the passenger and crew manifest, and files on the terrorist organizations that had been on their watch lists for some time.

Putting aside the crank calls and publicity seekers claiming credit for the attack on the plane, Bruguière's analysts pondered a few initial leads. High on their list was Hezbollah, the Shi'ite, Lebanon-based terrorist group sponsored and supported by the Islamic Republic of Iran. Hezbollah, or "Army of God," had attacked and killed dozens of French paratroopers in Beirut in October 1983 at the same time as over two hundred US Marines were killed in their barracks by another suicide truck bomber. Several French officials, professors and journalists had also been kidnapped and held hostage in Beirut. This was all part of Hezbollah's, and Iran's, efforts to influence French and Western political actions regarding Lebanon. There had even been attacks on and assassinations of Iranian dissidents on the streets of Paris, presumably carried out under orders of high-ranking Iranian officials in Tehran. Many of these were detailed in Bruguière's files.

Also under review was a splinter Palestinian organization called the "15 May Arab Organization," which had been active in the mid-1980s, bombing a Marks & Spencer department store in Paris and carrying out other terrorist attacks. By luck, a Tunisian member of the group had been arrested in his Paris apartment in 1986, shortly after the incident in the French capital. During a thorough search of his apartment, the police found a suitcase lined with a thin layer of rubber cement and pentrite. Although this arrest helped to put an end to the 15 May Arab Organization's particular brand of terror, disbanding the group's core membership, one fact became clear from interrogations of the suspect. The organization had equipped a number of suitcase bombs and passed them on to other terror groups—for a price. The French investigators determined that the pentrite found in the shattered pieces of suitcase being pulled out of the Ténéré sand was chemically similar to the plastic explosive seized three years earlier from the Paris apartment. Apparently, some of the booby-trapped suitcases had never been located. It was thought they had been sold to other terrorist groups.

To extend the murder investigation beyond the borders of the French Republic, Bruguière needed to follow a procedure that would authorize his people to operate inside other countries. The device employed for such a "courtesy" is called an international rogatory commission. Essentially, this is a formal written request by the French to another government, pursuant to treaty and diplomatic relations, to allow French investigators to interview certain witnesses or otherwise gather evidence. By granting such a request, the other country extends the courtesy of allowing the "foreign" officials to act as police within their own borders, subject to the oversight of the local authorities. Bruguière's team would send out hundreds of such rogatories during the course of the case.

AS PART OF their routine preparations, the investigators enquired of their colleagues in the French government whether there had been any significant trends, events or speeches that had stood out before the explosion that might point them towards certain lines of enquiry. A few days after the plane's remains were discovered in the desert, the General Director of the French Civil Aviation Agency contacted Bruguière.

Every three years the International Organization of Civil Aviation conducted a major assembly of the world's governments to address the topic of air transport security and terrorist attacks. This was in response to the growing threat to civil aviation around the world, especially after the Lockerbie disaster. The meeting was scheduled to take place in Montreal, Canada. Although it had been announced that a Libyan group of forty people would attend the assembly, at the last minute the delegation did not appear.

The Montreal assembly had begun on 19 September—the same day that the DC-10 crashed into the Ténéré.

* * *

IT DID NOT take long for the investigators to review the passenger and crew manifest. By May 1990, international rogatory commissions had been sent to Chad and the Republic of Congo (known colonially as French Congo). Its capital, Brazzaville, which lies directly north across the River Congo from Kinshasa, the capital of the Democratic Republic of the Congo, previously Zaire and a Belgian colony, ruled at the time by the infamous dictator Mobutu Sese Seko, was quite familiar to French businessmen, intelligence officers and diplomats. Most residents spoke French as a native tongue, and there was a large French expatriate community. Significantly, Maya-Maya Airport in Brazzaville was the originating point for the UTA 772 flight.

Bruguière decided that every victim's family, no matter where they lived, would be interviewed to determine if any leads or suspicions could be developed. Some of the first questions his investigators put to families regarded the type of luggage used by the victim, how he or she packed and whether anyone accompanied him or her to the airport. Brazzaville's importance as the originating point for the flight and the possible loading point for a suitcase bomb made it an important place in which to develop evidence. Bruguière and his team spent a month in the steamy, tropical air of the city.

After several weeks of interviews by the French team, one family appeared to provide a break in the case. Apollinaire Mangatany was a Congolese national who was listed on the UTA 772 manifest. As was the case for a number of the victims, his body was never identified. The French investigators interviewed his wife and two surviving sisters in Brazzaville, and they provided some interesting background.

Apparently, Mangatany had obtained a new suitcase right before the trip to Paris. The airport baggage records confirmed he had checked a single bag. In addition, the sisters were confused about the reasons for their brother's unexpected announcement that he was traveling to Paris. He had very little money, was unemployed, as far as they were aware, and they were surprised when the investigators informed them that he had paid for his ticket in cash.

None of his family had any idea why he had booked the flight or gone to France. They suggested that the investigators check with his close childhood friend, another Congolese man named Bernard Yanga. According to the sisters, Yanga had accompanied Mangatany to the airport that day and helped him with his new suitcase. They also noted another interesting fact. Yanga had been arrested by the Congolese police right after the DC-10 wreckage had been found in the desert.

Bruguière contacted the Congolese security services in an effort to interview Yanga, apparently the last person to see Mangatany before he went to the airport. Despite his repeated requests, the Congolese informed Bruguière that they were unable to locate Yanga and had no idea where he was.

A check on Mangatany's visa application for his trip to France revealed another puzzling clue. The Paris address he wrote down on the application for his stay, on a form he submitted to the French Consulate in Brazzaville, was nonexistent.

At the same time, the French team in Brazzaville began to hear rumors from some of their local sources—whispered conversations suggested that Apollinaire Mangatany had secretly traveled to Chad on the UTA 772 flight and had left his suitcase on the plane before it took off for Paris. He had also been in contact with Libyan diplomats located in Brazzaville for some time before the bombing.

Bruguière's team had their first big breakthrough.

FRUSTRATED THAT THE Congolese police would not acknowledge any information regarding Yanga or his arrest, the French team returned to Paris in June 1990 to develop their case. It was at this point that they caught another break.

On 11 June, a 45-year-old Congolese expatriate named Marc Mvouka was arrested at Charles de Gaulle Airport. A suspicious customs agent had found over a pound of heroin stuffed in his clothing. As he was being searched for other contraband at the airport detention facility, the police also discovered a letter addressed to the wife of General Ngouélondélé, head of Congolese State Security. Like many wealthy and connected Congolese, she spent most of her time in a luxurious apartment in one of the nicest neighborhoods of Paris. Brazzaville's tropical heat, rampant crime and poverty were easy to leave behind.

The police notified Bruguière's team of the arrest and the letter. Every law enforcement officer and intelligence agent in the French government had received standing orders from the investigating magistrate to forward any information regarding Congo to them, however irrelevant it might appear.

Bruguière himself helped interview Mvouka, who quickly shared all of his knowledge with the intense magistrate, who was now sensing even stronger leads in his case. Mvouka stated that it was known in Congolese military circles that the "victim" Mangatany had previously taken a training course in Libya for handling explosives and that a person named Yanga, one of his friends, had also been involved. He also revealed that one of the soldiers in Congo who was in charge of protecting prominent Congolese military and political figures had told him over drinks that the leader of Congolese security, a Colonel Patrice Ondele, knew all this.

The officer who had shared this information with Mvouka was not in the Congo, according to the witness. Instead, he was taking an English language course in Portsmouth, in the UK, just across the English Channel.

Bruguière and his team served an international rogatory commission on the British Embassy in Paris and within days were interviewing a young Congolese officer named Captain Jean Luc Younga, who was in charge of Congolese security for prominent officials. Without hesitation, he confirmed the information provided by Mvouka, and also noted that a person named Yanga, a childhood friend of Mangatany, had been arrested by the Congolese shortly after the DC-10 was destroyed. Armed with this confirmation, Bruguière contacted the French Ministry of Foreign Affairs, demanding that the French Republic put the full weight of its diplomatic prestige and long-time connections with Brazzaville's ruling elite to the test.

Within weeks, the pressure from the highest levels of the French government had opened the door for Bruguière. A further international rogatory commission was served on the Congo, and by July Bruguière and his team were back in Brazzaville. Remarkably, the Congolese had "re-found" Yanga after the French government put the squeeze on their most senior rulers. He apparently had been detained by the Congolese military back in January for a week of interviews.

Finally, ten months after the plane was found in the desert, the French team could interview someone who had first-hand knowledge about the crime, and Yanga had a lot of information to share. The interviews took a week.

SPEAKING IN FRENCH, Yanga told the investigators that he had been lifelong friends with Mangatany in Brazzaville and was very sad that he had died in the UTA crash. For several years, the friends had been "politically active" in groups that sought to overthrow President Mobutu, the dictator of neighboring Zaire. Mobutu's brutal regime and outright theft of billions of dollars of Congolese oil revenues was only made worse by his flaunting of his wealth, including the famous leopard-skin hats and capes that he wore on most occasions. The name of their resistance group was the Zairian Democratic Revolutionary Committee (CDRZ) and it advocated armed struggle against the Zairian regime. Mangatany had been its chairman.

Like all liberation movements, the CDRZ was constantly short of funds. Support came from a natural ally, one that shared the group's vision of ending the decades of decadent rule by Mobutu, who was also a long-time beneficiary of American and French largesse—the Libyan Embassy in Brazzaville. It also came from the group's members traveling to Tripoli for military training and other covert activities.

As an extension of its support for the group, Libya would occasionally request their assistance in other Africa-related missions. According to Yanga, three years before the UTA 772 bombing, the Libyans had conceived a plan to destroy a French airliner stopping in N'Djamena while it sat on the runway, empty of passengers and crew. The plan was intended to punish France for aligning itself against Libya in a just-ended civil war in Chad.

In late August 1989, Mangatany went to the Olympic Hotel in Brazzaville to meet with several Libyans. At that time, the Libyans proposed that Mangatany travel to Tripoli via Paris to attend a conference on young progressive leaders in Africa. The conference was being held by Mathaba, a Libyan organization responsible for political and military training of "liberation" movements from around the world. To obtain the details, Mangatany was to contact a person working at the Libyan Embassy in Brazzaville. His name was Abdullah.

Yanga later said that Mangatany told him the person at the Libyan Embassy was named Abdullah Elazragh. He had shared with Mangatany that the real purpose of his mission was to help destroy a French airplane stopping over at N'Djamena. Elazragh gave Mangatany a large amount of cash, a plane ticket for the trip to Chad and Paris, with the return leg open, and new travel clothes for him to wear. The clothes—including a bright-red tie—were intended to allow another Libyan agent in N'Djamena to recognize Mangatany at the stopover, so that he could slip off the plane and out of the airport during the panic that would follow the explosion. The day before the flight the Libyan also provided Mangatany with a suitcase for his trip.

On the morning of 19 September, the day of the fatal flight, Yanga went to Mangatany's home to accompany him to Maya-Maya Airport. It was here that Yanga first saw the new suitcase, which he described as dark, hard-sided and on wheels. At that time, Mangatany told him there was a small bomb in the suitcase, designed to go off while the plane was on the ground, and just big enough to cause damage and panic. Another member of their group, a Jean-Bosco Ngalina, was also present when Yanga showed up, but did not go with the others to the airport.

Mangatany and Yanga then took a taxi to Maya-Maya, where they saw the two Libyans who had met them at the Olympic Hotel. With them was a man Mangatany said was Abdullah Elazragh. Mangatany checked the suitcase at the ticket counter and boarded the plane.

Yanga never saw him again.

AFTER THE PLANE was reported missing and then found to have crashed, Yanga tried to contact Elazragh and the Libyan Embassy in Brazzaville for money. But the Embassy did not respond, and Yanga found out that Elazragh had left the country. He had been serving as the First Secretary of the Embassy, acting as Libyan Ambassador until a new diplomat could come from Tripoli to assume the post.

A quick check of airline records, and Congolese sources determined that First Secretary and Acting Ambassador Elazragh had left Brazzaville in a hurry on 25 September, six days after the UTA flight left the same airport. He had traveled to Zurich on a Swissair plane. The next day, he boarded another Swissair flight. Its destination was Tripoli. He had bought the ticket on 21 September.

As for the other person who saw Mangatany on his way to the airport, the French team quickly discovered that Ngalina had escaped Brazzaville for Zaire by crossing the Congo at night and bribing his way through a border station. The Congolese military shared the details of his hiding place in Kinshasa, and—a few months and a rogatory commission later—Bruguière and his team were in Zaire interviewing him. The Zairian police had picked him up.

Ngalina admitted that he had undergone military training in Libya in the early 1980s at a camp run by the Mathaba. During that time he learned Arabic, converted to Islam and learned how to handle weapons and explosives. Although he had been working with the Libyan Embassy for some time in the mid-1980s, his role diminished in 1986 when a new diplomat, Abdullah Elazragh, assumed his post. At that time, Mangatany became the principal local contact with the Embassy. Ngalina said he had seen Mangatany and Elazragh meet several times. The last time he saw them together was on Friday 15 September, outside the Ouenze Mosque after weekly prayers.

Ngalina bumped into Mangatany by accident on the morning of 19 September. His friend was holding a bright-red tie, but said he did not know how to tie it and had never worn one in his life. Ngalina helped him with the tie and Mangatany said he was traveling that day to Paris. He did not discuss the reasons for the trip.

After the crash, Ngalina mourned with Mangatany's family for three days. He never saw Elazragh again. He left Brazzaville a few months later after he got caught cheating a senior military commander in a business deal. He insisted that he had not known anything about the UTA bombing before it happened. He also insisted that he had not known the authorities were looking for him in connection with the investigation until the Zairian police had found him.

ONE FURTHER PIECE of important evidence was discovered by the French team during its visits to Brazzaville in the summer of 1990. A follow-up check with the airlines servicing the city determined that in late August, on two separate Air Afrique flights, the baggage manifest showed that there had been two diplomatic pouches, each weighing seven kilograms, addressed to the Bureau Populaire de la Jamahiriya Arabe Libyenne Populaire et Socialiste. The Libyan Embassy. They had been collected by a person from the Embassy, and there was no record of any similar diplomatic pouches ever leaving Brazzaville.

Bruguière's team was learning that the Congolese knew a lot more about these suspects, and their relations with the Libyan Embassy, than they had first disclosed. The information was coming in pieces. First, the Congolese immigration services finally compiled a list of those persons attached to the Libyan Embassy who had flown into or out of Brazzaville around the time of the bombing. They confirmed that Elazragh had left the country on 25 September, failing to pay his landlord the last month's rent, and even leaving his tailor empty-handed.

Several other Libyans with diplomatic passports and visas also had interesting travel records. The first was a man named Arbas Musbah, a 37-year-old who had arrived in Brazzaville on 24 August and left on the day of the bombing, on an Ethiopian Airlines flight just two hours before UTA 772 departed. The second was Ibrahim Naeli, a 31-year-old diplomat who flew into Brazzaville from Brussels on a Sabena Airlines flight on 23 August and accompanied Musbah on the 19 September Ethiopian Airlines flight out of Congo. A third Libyan diplomat named Abdallah Elajeli had flown into Congo on 28 August and had left one week later, again using Ethiopian Airlines. A fourth was Abdelsalam Hammouda, who remained in Brazzaville for a longer time.

Bruguière's enquiries to the French Intelligence Services came back with a full dossier on each of these diplomats. The Territory Surveillance Department, or TSD, was the French agency charged with compiling information on the intelligence services of other countries. They confirmed to Bruguière what he had suspected.

Elazragh was a 55-year-old high-ranking member of Libyan intelligence and reported directly to the top levels of the Libyan government. He was long known to French security services, having served at the Libyan Embassy in Paris during the 1970s, where he kept tabs on Libyans training as pilots at French air schools. He had even traveled to Paris in early 1989 to see a cardiologist at the American Hospital of Neuilly-sur-Seine, where he was treated for high blood pressure. Naeli was a senior officer in Libyan intelligence, a specialist in airport security and aircraft. Musbah was his assistant. They all worked for the most secret department in Libyan intelligence, and all had been under surveillance while in Congo.

Their commander was a 48-year-old Army Colonel named Abdallah al-Senoussi, second in command of Ait Al Jamahiriya (Libyan military intelligence), who was in charge of all external intelligence operations run out of Tripoli and head of security for Libya's long-time leader and dictator, Colonel Qaddafi. Senoussi was also Qaddafi's brother-in-law, their wives being sisters. They came from the same tribe, and he was widely seen as the number-two power in the regime. His biggest responsibility was to oversee the elimination of opponents of the Qaddafi government.

THE CONGOLESE FILES also disclosed some other confirmatory details. Surveillance of the Libyan Embassy showed that SOCALIB, a company formed in Brazzaville, was half-owned by the Libyan government. It was purportedly in the business of marketing precious woods for export and was run by a Libyan named Mohammed Hemmali. In fact, SOCALIB was a cover for Libyan intelligence agents working in Congo, and Hemmali was often observed meeting with Elazragh and others at his apartment.

Bruguière's team was allowed to interview a Congolese woman named Guilhermina "Greta" Araujo, the former mistress of General Ngouélondélé, chief of Congolese security. Apparently, she was also a paid informant for the Congolese government, and had offered "sexual assistance" to Hemmali for money.

Greta confirmed that she had attended a small party at Hemmali's apartment a few days before 19 September. Elazragh was at the party, along with two other Libyans who were staying there as guests, but whom she had never seen before. She told the French investigators that, at the party, she informed Hemmali that she would be taking a trip to Paris in a few days. Hemmali apparently panicked at the idea that she might be flying to Paris on the UTA flight scheduled for 19 September. He only calmed down when she told him that she was taking a different flight. When Greta heard about the UTA crash, she immediately spotted the link between her Libyan client and the bombing. She never saw Hemmali again.

ONE FINAL PART of the investigation was to determine the process for handling baggage at the airports in Brazzaville and N'Djamena. Bruguière still needed to tie down the trail of evidence that pointed towards the loading of the suitcase bomb in Congo.

At Brazzaville, the airport check-in procedures for UTA were actually handled by Air Afrique pursuant to a contract. While the personnel stressed that it was impossible for a passenger to check in a suitcase without boarding the plane, what became clear to the French team was that there was a serious lack of organization and security at Maya-Maya Airport, making it difficult to pin down precise suitcase check-ins. To make matters more complicated, the Congolese authorities tried to convince the French team that the booby-trapped suitcase had been placed on the plane later, in N'Djamena, and not in Brazzaville. The

President of Congo, another ruthless dictator named Denis Sassou Nguesso, seemingly did not want the bad publicity to reflect on his government, so he had his officials lie to the French to try to deflect the blame for operating an airport with such a lack of security.

When Bruguière and his team went to Chad to conduct a similar mission, the Chadians went to great lengths to try to convince them that the suitcase could not have been loaded in N'Djamena. Despite his suspicions that the Chadians were simply doing what the Congolese had done—deflecting the blame—at the end of this process, Bruguière was convinced that the Chadians had much better airport security, especially given the UTA bombing in 1984 and the otherwise tense political environment.

The French also learned while in Chad that a Libyan diplomat working at the Embassy had booked a seat to Paris on the UTA 772 for 19 September. However, he had never shown up at the check-in and flew to Paris the following week.

ONE FURTHER PIECE of the puzzle presented when Bruguière and his team returned to Paris. In May, the FBI forensic laboratory in Washington, DC sent the French investigators a report. Bruguière had sent a piece of some luggage for an independent forensic verification of the chemical composition of what appeared to be an explosive material recovered from the debris in the Ténéré desert. The FBI experts had put the material through rigorous testing, which confirmed Bruguière's suspicions.

They had examined what was characterized as a "dark-colored suitcase fragment," sealed in an evidence bag marked "Four/1-A." An enquiry to the manufacturer, Samsonite, confirmed that the fragment had come from their plant outside Denver, Colorado, and was an Oxford gray material used for a series named the "Silhouette" in the product catalog. Samsonite had sold thousands of such suitcases around the world, including in the Middle East.

The FBI report stated that the forensic laboratory had discovered a "PETN-based plastic explosive with a binder of cis-polyisoprene"—in other words, common glue. The sample of the hard-shell suitcase taken from Evidence Seal Four/1-A revealed a "multi-layered" chemical compound consisting of transparent glue, medium brown nitrocellulose lacquer paint, PETN explosive mixture combined with glue, more paint, and then transparent glue to seal the compound to the side of the suitcase. The forensic team noted that it looked "home-made."

The French team had previously identified these materials, but they had been confused because they had assumed that all of the plastic explosive would have been consumed in the explosion, yet PETN remained clearly visible to the chemists. The FBI supplied the answer.

According to their bomb experts, when PETN detonates it almost always leaves no residue as it is consumed by the force of the explosion. But when it is mixed with a glue or binder such as polyisoprene it will not entirely disappear into the energy of the bomb. By mixing the plastic explosive with the glue, the bomb-makers had left a trail of evidence.

As a follow-up, the FBI experts also compared some of the bomb materials seized by the French in other arrests, including the suitcases seized from the 15 May Organization suspects in Paris several years before. They were chemically identical to the suitcase fragment in Four/1-A.

* * *

BRUGUIÈRE AND HIS team were pulling their evidence together piece by piece. Police work is always a slow and painstaking process. With the UTA 772 investigation a priority for the French government, Le Sherriff would not be rushed into incomplete or unsupported conclusions. But one issue still was unclear—did Mangatany exit the plane in Chad, knowing it would soon explode? Or had he remained on the aircraft, unaware of his impending doom? The lack of a positive identification of Mangatany's remains left this subject open, but, given the large number of passengers who would never be identified, the investigators could only wonder what had happened to the man who brought the suitcase bomb onto the DC-10. This is one aspect of the mystery that has never been solved.

Chapter 5

Crossroads

BY THE SECOND anniversary of the UTA 772 bombing, in September 1991, Bruguière and his team believed they had begun to piece together how the terrorist attack had been carried out and who was behind it. Bruguière had initially become suspicious in the last months of 1991 about the possible role of senior Libyan officials in the UTA 772 bombing.

Much work remained, though, and the technical experts were still trying to reconcile critical forensic evidence to support the police work already accomplished in the field. Important, however, was the fact that at this point the case relied on the word of Congolese informants, private conversations with Congolese officials and intelligence files. Bruguière still lacked solid proof that could stand up in a French court and convict someone of murder and sabotage. However, his criminal investigation was about to begin to play out on a much larger stage.

* * *

IN OCTOBER 1991, Bruguière sent his rogatory commission requests for assistance to the United States government, seeking to compare the progress in his UTA 772 case with the status of the FBI–Scotland Yard investigation of the Pan Am 103 Lockerbie disaster. In particular, he shared with the FBI his initial findings regarding the suitcase bomb, the preliminary trail that led to Libyan diplomats at the Embassy in Brazzaville and the initial suspects he had identified.

Remarkably, the two investigations into almost identical suitcase bombings on commercial airplanes had been traveling along different paths for over two years. As luck would have it, Bruguière's request for assistance in uncovering "points of convergence" between the two disasters arrived at just the right time: the FBI and US intelligence were coming to similar conclusions and were assembling their own list of potential suspects in the Lockerbie case. Some of their clues also pointed to Tripoli.

After comparing notes and strategies, the three investigating countries—France, the US and UK—were ready to go public. On 30 October 1991, Bruguière issued four international arrest warrants for suspects in the UTA 772 bombing. Three of the names he specified had never been publicly recognized: Abdallah Elazragh, Ibrahim Naeli and Arbas Musbah. The fourth was a shocker that sent the news wires abuzz: Abdallah al-Senoussi, Qaddafi's right-hand man, brother-in-law, chief of the Libyan security and Libya's second-ranking official, was a main suspect. By issuing arrest warrants, Bruguière hoped to take the investigation to the next level. He also had France request Interpol red notices for each of the four suspects so that they would be arrested if they attempted to pass through almost any airport in the world.

The parallel US–UK Lockerbie investigation also moved into a higher gear as the French case picked up steam. Less than one month after the UTA 772 arrest warrants were issued in Paris, a Scottish prosecutor indicted two Libyan intelligence agents for their alleged role in carrying out the Lockerbie bombing. Their names were Abdelbaset al-Megrahi and Lamin Khalifah Fhimah. They were accused of putting the suitcase bomb on a flight originating in Malta, and then passing it, already ticketed, to be placed in transit on the Pan Am 103 flight from Heathrow to New York, through the airline's luggage system in Frankfurt. Unlike Bruguière's investigation, the Scottish criminal case pursued by Scotland Yard and the FBI relied heavily on circumstantial evidence. Indeed, there were no confessions, informants or security service reports directly linking the suspects to the "Malta theory." Despite their best efforts, the US and UK investigators lacked the connections and finesse that the French had gained over decades of close relations with police departments and intelligence agencies in former French colonies. Instead, they were forced to rely on more traditional police methods, forensics and intelligence from the CIA and its British partners, MI5 and MI6.

The circumstantial proof in the Lockerbie investigation would be controversial for the duration of the case, and is still. The "Malta theory" was based on a statement from a Maltese shop owner who believed he had seen the Libyan agent al-Megrahi in his store shortly before the Pan Am 103 bombing, buying clothes that later were traced to the suitcase bomb on that flight. Serious questions regarding how such a suitcase could be placed into the Pan Am baggage system without being matched to a passenger on board were never answered.

But by November 1991, the Scottish prosecutors were ready to move against the two Libyan suspects. This was all they had, and the political pressure in the UK and the US to move forward with the investigation was mounting every day. Those pursuing the suspects in both criminal cases realized that police measures alone would not bring the various suspects to justice. Nor would indictments or arrest warrants influence Colonel Qaddafi or his violent habits.

With both investigations going public with their arrest warrants, the diplomats of all three countries, working in tandem with the criminal investigators, got to work at the United Nations Security Council in New York. Since France, the US and UK all maintained permanent seats on the UN's most important body, it was decided by their governments that the Security Council would serve as the focal point for their efforts to bring pressure on Libya and Qaddafi. The first step was to convince the Council to issue a resolution to require Libya to produce the suspects to the appropriate judicial venues. The second was to force Libya to drop its support for terrorist activities. This was a major challenge, unprecedented in the history of the United Nations.

In January 1992, the Security Council unanimously adopted Resolution 731. Cast in the verbiage of international diplomacy, it essentially demanded that the Libyan state take steps to end its sponsorship of terrorism, turn over the two indicted suspects in the Lockerbie Pan Am

103 Scottish case and cooperate in both of the bombing investigations. The resolution expressly required that Libya satisfy the enquiries of Bruguière and his team "regarding Libya's role in bombing UTA Fight 772 in 1989." But the issue of compensation for the victims was only raised regarding the Pan Am 103 Lockerbie flight, at the request of the American and British governments. The French did not include this requirement for the UTA 772 victims, a difference that would create serious diplomatic problems in the future.

Two months later, to ratchet up the political pressure on Qaddafi, the Security Council adopted another measure, Resolution 748. This imposed mandatory sanctions on the Libyan regime for its refusal to comply with the first, 731. Those sanctions came into effect in April 1992 and included embargoes on arms shipments to Libya and its civil aviation. It also required that the worldwide offices of Libyan Arab Airlines be closed and that all UN members reduce Libya's diplomatic presence in their countries.

The unanimous adoption of the UN sanctions was unheard of in the great chamber, located on New York's East River. Even fellow Arab states were sickened by Qaddafi's terrorist activities and either supported the Resolutions or abstained. However, at this stage, the sanctions did not have the desired effect, and Qaddafi and his regime began a long, cold isolation from the rest of the world.

Another factor at play was that the new President of the United States was himself a former Ambassador at the United Nations and a firm believer in building an international consensus before taking action. Given his efforts to isolate President Saddam Hussein of Iraq, George H. W. Bush needed to be consistent in his approach to Colonel Qaddafi. He ordered a patient but methodical tightening of the noose around Qaddafi's neck and would not make the mistake of taking unilateral action against Libya if he wanted to truly alienate the dictator. Bush had served as Vice President to Ronald Reagan, who had used the direct military approach in April 1986. This had not stopped Qaddafi from becoming the world's most notorious state sponsor of terrorism, hence legal and economic sanctions became the weapon of choice, a path the President's son George W. Bush would later follow in his own dealings with Libya. In the end, these methods were to accomplish more in changing Qaddafi's behavior than any military jet bombing run over Tripoli.

With the Lockerbie attack driving both the US and UK in the political arena, in tandem with the French diplomatic drive regarding UTA 772, Bruguière still needed to press ahead with his search for solid evidence. He was about to find it.

* * *

ONE OF THE reasons Bruguière reached out to the FBI in later 1991 was to employ its very sophisticated forensic laboratory, considered the finest of its kind in the solving of complex crimes. He had assigned one of his assistants, Claude Calisti, to investigate certain bits and pieces of debris that had been pulled from the Ténéré desert site and brought back to Paris. Calisti reported to Bruguière that among the debris was a bag containing a very small piece of green circuit board. The French investigators could not determine how or why this piece of circuit board came to be sitting in the isolated crash site.

The FBI laboratory determined that the circuit board had suffered significant damage, which led them to believe that it had been located near the explosion point on the DC-10. Although it did not carry any trace of the pentrite explosive, it had suffered distortions similar to those observed by the FBI on debris found at the Lockerbie site. Enquiries had been made to McDonnell Douglas, the manufacturer of the DC-10 in southern California, to determine what part of the aircraft had contained the circuit board. After going through their detailed manuals and drawings of every piece of circuitry and wiring in the entire aircraft, McDonnell Douglas reported to the FBI that the green circuit board was not part of the plane. Simply put, they did not know where it had come from.

So, a piece of electronic equipment that was not part of the DC-10 had somehow found its way to the middle of the Ténéré desert. This mystery puzzled the French for some time.

The French and American forensic investigators placed the circuit board piece in a different sealed evidence bag numbered 4/4. By March 1992, they had determined that it had been manufactured in Taiwan. Two faint green letters, "TY," could be observed on it by the naked eye—the maker was a company named Tai Youn Electronics Co. Ltd.

This presented Bruguière with a legal problem. He had relied, up to this point, on the international rogatory commission requests to allow him to conduct his investigation as if he were a local official. But such commissions required that the other country he intended to visit have a bilateral treaty with France. Ever since France had recognized the People's Republic of China (PRC) as the sole legitimate representative of the Chinese nation, the independent island of Taiwan, also known as Formosa, had existed in diplomatic limbo. France did not maintain formal diplomatic relations with Taiwan and had no formal relations with the Taiwanese authorities. Thus, Bruguière could not serve rogatory commission requests to conduct his investigation in that country.

But legal and diplomatic formalities would not hinder Bruguière's investigation, especially with this intriguing piece of broken green circuit board in play. Using back-channel connections in the shadowy intelligence community, Bruguière simply arranged for a private visit to Taiwan. In May 1992, he and a small team flew to the Republic of China.

* * *

THE ACTUAL PIECE of green circuit board pulled out of the Ténéré sand was too delicate—and valuable—for the French team to carry to Taiwan. Instead, they took detailed color photographs.

Their first interview was with a Mrs. Yu Mei Chang, General Director of Tai Youn. After examining the photographs and checking her product line Mrs. Chang confirmed to the French investigators that in 1989 her company had manufactured the green circuit board in the photograph. The product was based on a subcontract she had received from another Taiwan company called Costa Electronics, which had subsequently been bought by a firm called Ming Jong.

The French then paid a visit to Ming Jong. After a quick look at the photographs of the fragments, Mr. Wolfgang Hwang, head engineer, acknowledged that the circuit board was integrated into his own products. Ming Jong had filled an order for several thousand "time-delay" products, which had household and industrial uses.

These products were called temporizing devices in the trade, or, by the lay person, timers. Mr. Hwang handed the French investigators the sole remaining timer from his company's stock, a white version that contained a circuit board similar to the piece discovered at the crash site in the Ténéré. Anxious to determine if they had finally found some solid linkage to the crime, the French disassembled it on the spot to compare it with the twisted and distorted circuit board in the picture. Although they lacked the technical expertise to say so for certain, the two appeared to be the same. They reassembled the timer product and carried it back to Paris for technical comparison. The long trip to Taiwan already seemed to have paid off.

But before leaving Ming Jong's offices, the French asked Mr. Hwang to check his records to determine if he could track where the timer products had been shipped. It did not take him long to locate the information. His biggest customer for such products was a German-owned company called Grasslin Far East Corporation, which was owned by Grasslin Corporation. It specialized in the export of temporizing devices and relied on Costa as its exclusive supplier.

The French team quickly tracked down the Taiwanese offices of Grasslin Far East, where they interviewed a Mr. Alfred Stekelenburg. He told the investigators that the Taiwanese firm simply manufactured the circuit board and resulting timer and then sold it to Grasslin, which handled all the sales. Approximately twenty-five percent of Grasslin Far East's annual sales were to the parent firm in Germany and the remainder to firms around the globe.

The evidence trail now pointed the French detectives to Germany.

* * *

A FEW MONTHS later, the French team traveled to Germany to interview officials at Grasslin's offices. They started with Mr. Thomas Grasslin, Vice President of the family-owned business. He confirmed that the German parent imported a large number of timers from the Taiwanese subsidiary. He also made it clear that all exports from the Taiwanese firm were expressly controlled and approved by the head office in Germany. Detailed records were available for the French to inspect.

Among the records were invoices, dated 1 June 1989, to a long-time customer and retailer near Hamburg called Kremser, a German firm that had purchased 101 of the very same Taiwanese timers. An interview by the French authorities with Mr. Kremser disclosed that his firm had not taken delivery of these, but instead, at Kremser's instructions, the order had been shipped directly to an occasional customer, a firm called HP Marketing & Consulting, another German firm. HP Marketing had indeed purchased and taken delivery of 101 timers in late June 1989.

Bruguière and his team had travelled around the world in their search for evidence that could definitively establish Libya's connection to the UTA 772 bombing. They could still not predict whether the trail created by a small, distorted piece of green circuit board dug out of the debris in the Ténéré sand would advance their investigation, but they continued to follow the German trail of evidence, working with the German federal police, and now joined by FBI agents looking for clues in the Lockerbie investigation.

The investigators sat down with Hans-Peter Wüst, President of HP Marketing & Consulting in his offices near the German town of Benstaben. The German police first read Mr. Wüst his rights under German law to refuse the request to be interviewed, but Wüst did not hesitate to speak with the investigators. Speaking through a German interpreter, and after explaining their role in the UTA 772 criminal case, the French team asked Mr. Wüst if he knew what had happened to the timers his firm had purchased from Kremser, and whether he had any Libyan connections. They were not expecting to hear the story Wüst was about to tell.

Wüst told Bruguière that he had personally traveled to Tripoli in 1988 and 1989, meeting several Libyan government officials during his visit. The purpose of his trip was to market and sell his products. According to Wüst, his firm developed and produced what he characterized as "jamming devices," which the German interpreters told the French and Americans actually meant radio-controlled devices for remote detonation of explosives. Ironically, these devices were marketed by Wüst as designed to "disrupt terrorist attacks" by remote-detonation of bombs. The German firm proudly noted that it was in the business of selling devices to counter terrorism.

Wüst had worked with several Libyans while employed at another company called Peter Klüver in the early 1980s. One of those he had met was a man named Issa al-Shibani. Wüst told the investigators that he thought Shibani said he worked with the Libyan transport authority. He described Shibani as under six feet tall, thin, with gray hair cut short, clean-shaven, suntanned and trim. He was in his mid-fifties and he spoke English.

Wüst continued to provide the investigators with details. On one of his trips to Libya, in late November 1988, Wüst met Mr. Shibani again, and they discussed some technical products that might be of interest to the Libyan airport authorities. Shibani asked whether Wüst could supply timing devices powered by 9- or 12-volt batteries. He told Wüst that the Libyans needed such devices to operate lighting markers along airport runways in the desert, where landing planes was especially difficult at night. The isolation of airports in the Libyan desert made battery-powered lighting even more important, according to Shibani. The Libyan customer also requested that the timers have a "fuse" of between fifty and a hundred hours and that they be waterproof.

Pressed by the French investigators, Wüst conceded that he had assumed Shibani was connected to Libyan intelligence, since airports in that country were tightly controlled by the Qaddafi regime. But that was not a big problem for Wüst, who was accustomed to doing business in non-democratic countries. As far as he was concerned, the Libyans were customers, and their request for timers to light up desert runways seemed entirely appropriate to the German businessman. As he reminded the French, his business in Libya extended back to the early 1980s, and there were no United Nations sanctions in place during any of his visits. Everything was quite legal and proper at the time.

His story continued. When Wüst returned to Germany from Libya he instructed his technicians and mechanics to design and implement a timer device that would meet Shibani's specifications. Since the Grasslin timer came with a 1.5-volt battery, they added a small device that would power up the battery to a supply between 9 and 12 volts, as Shibani had requested. A model of this modified device was shipped to Shibani in Tripoli in February 1989. Apparently satisfied with the model, the Libyan placed an order for one hundred such timers. HP

Marketing sent the order to Kresmer, which sent it to Grasslin, which had its Taiwanese subsidiary order the assembly of the hundred devices per the modification. Thus, the green circuit boards manufactured by Tai Youn made their way into Ming Jong's timers, Grasslin Far East shipped them from Taiwan to Germany, and in July 1989 Mr. Shibani received one hundred customized timer devices in Libya. The delivery was confirmed by the air carrier firm of Kuehne + Nagel.

The French investigators could not believe their luck. The German businessman had just established a clear and direct link between the debris found at the Ténéré crash site and the delivery of timers containing that very electrical component to a senior official of Libyan intelligence. Hoping to be able to rely on more than just the memory of Mr. Wüst about his Libyan customer, they asked if his firm had copies of any correspondence or paperwork to confirm the transaction. Wüst said they did not normally retain paper invoices. However, a quick check of his computers produced an invoice, Number D11521, on HP Marketing letterhead. The invoice was for one hundred "Timer Modules" priced at 76 Deutschmarks a piece, totaling 7,600 Deutschmarks. The order was shipped on 17 July 1989 and received by the customer on 25 July 1989. The customer had paid for the delivery by bank check. His name was Issa A. el-Shibani, telephone number 600799, Tripoli, Libya.

The French investigators were ecstatic. After two years of traveling around the world establishing and tracking down leads, Bruguière and his team finally had in their hands an extraordinary piece of evidence— an invoice from a terrorist. An invoice that provided a direct, evidentiary link between the bomb that destroyed the DC-10 over the Ténéré and the Libyan government.

Wüst then described one more brief trip to Tripoli in late July 1989. He had met with Shibani, who confirmed the shipment and noted he was pleased with the product. In fact, Shibani said that he might be taking a trip to Germany later in the year, and even provided Wüst with his passport number so the German could help arrange a visa for him. Wüst located his handwritten notes from that trip and provided the investigators with Shibani's Libyan passport number. Shibani never made the trip to Germany, for reasons not explained.

One more connection needed to be made. The French team had assembled a photograph book containing pictures of most of the senior officials in the Libyan intelligence services. The DST—Direction de la Surveillance du Territoire, the French domestic intelligence agency— had very good records, and Bruguière was not shy about using them in his case.

They showed the book to one of the HP Marketing technicians, Peter Steinmetz, who had traveled to Libya with Wüst on his last trip. He had no trouble identifying the photograph of Shibani as the company's customer. Bruguière knew that Shibani was the director of technical services for Libyan intelligence. As a bonus, Steinmetz also recognized a photograph of Moussa Koussa, whom Bruguière knew as the director of the Mathaba in Tripoli. Koussa had sat in on their meeting. Apparently, the most senior members of Libyan intelligence were inter-ested in buying timers for desert runways—at least, according to their German supplier.

But Bruguière knew he finally had his proof. A tiny, distorted piece of green circuit board manufactured by a company in Taiwan had made its way to Libyan intelligence just a few months before the bombing. It had been miraculously recovered from the tons of debris scattered over miles of barren desert. And he had in his hands an invoice connecting that product with a senior member of the Libyan intelligence services.

These tiny pieces of forensic evidence were all he had. But they would be enough.

Chapter 6

The First Fake-Out

ALL OF BRUGUIÈRE'S arrest warrants, letters rogatory, world travels and accumulating evidence did not go unnoticed by the Libyan government. But even with the increase in activity by the French investigators, it was the United Nations sanctions that were beginning to have a serious impact on Colonel Qaddafi's regime.

In early 1992, after the UN Security Council enacted the first sanction Resolutions, the French Ministry of Foreign Affairs informed Bruguière that it had received a message from the Libyan Ambassador in Paris— Libya was offering to cooperate in the UTA 772 investigation if it would ease tensions between the countries. In response, the investigating magistrate told the French diplomats that he would only cooperate with the Libyans if they turned over to him their entire file on the UTA 772 matter. Bruguière's years of experience had taught him not to trust a murder suspect who offered to assist the police in a case.

On 12 April 1992, the Libyans sent to the Foreign Ministry what they characterized as a formal "file" for their own internal enquiry into the UTA 772 bombing. No explanation was provided as to why the Libyan state had taken any measures to investigate the bombing of a French plane that did not have any Libyan passengers, had not flown into or over Libyan territory and, at face value, had nothing to do with Libya. The file sent from Tripoli was prepared by Mahmoud Mursi, a Counsellor at the Supreme Court of Libya. Its date—late December 1991, shortly after the issuance of the four arrest warrants by Bruguière— appeared to explain the reason for the Libyan government's investigation of the bombing.

Bruguière was not surprised by the file's contents. Mursi's report stated that he had conducted an internal investigation of the case after the Libyan authorities were informed that four of its nationals— including Senoussi, the second-ranking official in the government—had been directly implicated in the UTA bombing. Mursi noted that he had interviewed two of the suspects himself, including Colonel Senoussi and Moussa Koussa. Koussa's statement took the position that he and his Libyan colleagues previously based in Brazzaville had played no role in the crime and that they knew nothing of the plot to blow up the UTA 772 flight. Elazragh admitted he had known a Congolese man named Apollinaire while stationed in Brazzaville, but again denied any knowledge of the UTA 772 plot. Senoussi denied that he had any responsibilities for Libyan intelligence or overseas work and stated he was a simple lieutenant colonel in the Libyan Army. The final statement from one of the suspects, Mr. Naeli, proclaimed his innocence and provided what Bruguière viewed as the only surprise of his investigation—a death certificate indicating that Arbas Musbah had died in November 1990 in a "painful accident."

Bruguière immediately dismissed the Libyan "file" as a cover-up. Its existence only made him more determined to follow his leads and to find out why Libya was going to the trouble of protesting the innocence of its agents through a formal "investigation." He soon learned the reason.

The senior French intelligence chiefs in Paris told Bruguière that after a long period of silence following the UTA 772 bombing various Libyan emissaries had come to France to make hushed enquiries about the French criminal investigation. Some of these emissaries had tried to persuade the senior levels of the French government to force Bruguière to drop the entire criminal case. French and foreign lawyers, Libyan businessmen and Libyan military figures had proposed their services as middlemen on behalf of the Libyan intelligence services. The request from all of these persons was the same—to exonerate the four accused suspects, present Libya in a favorable light and, most importantly, attempt to disassociate France from the US and the UK at the United Nations Security Council. There were hints that these Libyan emissaries could arrange huge bribes as possible rewards for anyone in the French Establishment who could provide "assistance."

At Bruguière's directive, the French intelligence services sent their own message back to Libya—nothing would influence the French criminal investigation or steer it off course. This resulted in the Libyans indicating in September 1992 that they would make a "significant gesture" in order to prove their willingness to cooperate with Bruguière.

That gesture came in the form of a message. The Libyans informed DST that they were holding two booby-trapped suitcases that they had "seized" from a Libyan "opposition group" that had attempted to commit a terrorist act inside the country. The DST chief on the ground in Libya was even allowed to "inspect" these two seized suitcases at the offices of Libyan intelligence in Tripoli. He noted in his report to Bruguière that the suitcase was quite dusty and appeared to have been in storage for a long period of time. In addition, it was not kept in a sealed or secure evidence locker or other judicial custody. The French intelligence agent had insisted on seeing the suitcases and ultimately they were presented to him in an impromptu manner. The place of their presentation was none other than the office of Intelligence Chief Senoussi himself, who declared he was representing the Libyan Foreign Ministry. Bruguière noted in his report that the Libyans would regret this clumsy effort to cooperate and try to exonerate themselves.

A few days later, Bruguière received a letter from Libyan Legal Counsellor Mursi. He offered to travel to Paris and brief Bruguière in person on the results of his own "investigation" so that they could "work together" and "compare notes for complete cooperation between the French and Libyan justice." This would be done in order to "discover the truth so that justice can be done in the case of the French plane, which fell in the Nigerien desert."

In October 1992, Bruguière allowed Mursi to visit him in his Paris office at the Palais de Justice, near Notre Dame. Mursi insisted that his own interviews of three of the suspects had made clear to him that they were innocent of the murder charges, and that the fourth suspect had died. At that time, Mursi stated that a Tripoli judge had informed him of the seized suitcases as part of his "independent investigation" and that they had been seized from an opposition group and held as evidence. Mursi assured Bruguière that the suitcases had nothing to do with the UTA 772 attack, but assumed that they "might be useful to the French magistrate as evidence."

Mursi showed Bruguière several photographs of the seized suitcases. Some of the photographs revealed an interior on which there was a thin sheen of clear rubber cement covering what appeared to be pentrite explosive in white paste form.

Mursi offered to host Bruguière in Tripoli to prove his sincerity. Seizing the chance, Bruguière immediately drafted a rogatory commission for such a visit and scheduled a trip for the following week. Flying down to the south of France with his team on 21 October 1992, Bruguière boarded an armed French Navy boat and headed across the Mediterranean towards the Libyan capital. Clearances were granted by the Libyan authorities and all measures taken to allow them to dock the next morning.

At the last moment, the Libyans radioed to the French naval boat that it did not have permission to dock. Bruguière ordered the captain to make a U-turn and head back to France. No reasons were provided for the last-minute change of plan, but Bruguière had never expected the Libyans to cooperate. He had called their bluff. And they had blinked.

* * *

LIBYA'S LAST-MINUTE DECISION to force Bruguière's French warship to make a turn-about off the shores of Tripoli was not surprising to the French investigator. Almost everything that came out of Libya was irrational—such was the national character of an oil-rich country run with a firm and brutal hand for almost twenty-five years by the Brotherly Leader and Guide of the Great Revolution of the Socialist People's Libyan Arab Jamahiriya, Colonel Muammar Abu Minyar al-Qaddafi.

By October 1992 Qaddafi had become one of the world's most noto-rious and enigmatic figures. The youngest child of a peasant family, he had been trained by the Libyan military during the 1960s under the reign of Libyan King Idris I. His education had even included a short stint in England at the British Army Staff College, where many prom-ising young Arab soldiers went for their "finishing school."

But Libyan royalty, long tied to the West, was not Qaddafi's inspir-ation. He was smitten by Egypt's charismatic President Gamal Abdel Nasser and Nasser's post-colonial brand of Pan-Arabism, the goal of which was to unite all of the diverse Arab peoples into a unified nation and thus give rise to a major world power that could rival the West as well as destroy Israel. Qaddafi's admiration of Nasser and his creed was almost at the level of hero worship.

Libya's decaying and decadent monarchy, supported by a huge US payment for renting the Wheelus Air Force Base outside Tripoli, had propped up the king and his entourage for many years. On 1 September 1969 Qaddafi led a small cadre of military officers in a bloodless coup, overthrowing Idris I while he was in Greece obtaining medical treatment. The young officers immediately abolished the monarchy and set up the Libyan Arab Republic. The 27-year-old Qaddafi quickly filled the power vacuum, posturing himself as the leader of a revolutionary movement bent on defying the West, traditional Arab monarchies and the "crim-inal Zionist entity" created by the United Nations in 1948—the State of Israel.

Working quickly to cleanse Libya of the vestiges of its long-time Italian colonial heritage, Qaddafi forced almost every Italian living in the country to leave without any compensation for their homes, prop-erties or businesses. Hundreds of thousands of Italians had made Libya their home over the decades since the nineteenth century. Qaddafi's revolutionary creed highlighted the oppressive and murderous history of that colonial experience as a major blight on its population, despite the fact that the colonial era had ended with the fall of Italian dictator and Fascist leader Benito Mussolini during World War II.

At the same time as he was cleansing Libya of its Western-dominated past, Qaddafi was turning the country into a haven for almost every type of anti-Western radical group, providing weapons, training, financial support and political encouragement. He told people that he wanted to become the Che Guevara of the Middle East. With billions of dollars in oil revenues, Qaddafi did not need to ask anyone's permission to take on this revolutionary mantle.

As the head of his country's "Revolutionary Command Council," Qaddafi ruled Libya with an iron fist. His thugs killed or jailed any opponents of his regime and established an efficient and brutal police state to protect his hold on power. Always conscious of his revolutionary stripes, he refused to give himself the title of General, and even shrugged off official governmental posts. Instead, he was promoted from Captain to Colonel, along with many other senior officers. Grand titles were not appropriate for a country ruled "by the people," at least on paper and in his long-winded speeches.

The political system Qaddafi set up in Libya borrowed from a variety of sources, a blend of ingredients stirred together by the young Colonel, whose curly dark hair, slight goatee, dark sunglasses and ever-changing wardrobe of fatigues, African gowns and traditional Arab clothing were a familiar sight in news photographs. From his hero Nasser, Qaddafi took the popular strain of Arab nationalism that was sweeping monarchs and sheikhs from power. Inspired by communism and socialism, he set up a welfare state, which was easy to afford given the large oil reserves and Libya's small population. Of course, this could be best administered where the oil and other major industries were state-owned and operated, directly under Qaddafi's control. "Liberation movements" from around the world were held up as shining examples of the proper moral compass for the Libyan people. But whereas Nasser-inspired Pan-Arabism was secular, Qaddafi insisted on a fairly strict Islamic moral code, prohibiting all forms of alcohol, prostitution and gambling.

Taking a cue from Chinese communist leader Mao Tse-tung, Qaddafi scripted a three-volume tome explaining the unique blend of social, religious and political norms he wished to espouse around the developing world. His "Green Book," published in 1975, set out the Leader's personal vision, and, like Mao's Little Red Book, was required reading for anyone lucky enough to live in his new Libyan paradise. Qaddafi hoped it would help lead the masses towards his new Utopia.

To manage this vision, in 1977 Qaddafi dictated that Libya would no longer be a country on the model followed by the West for centuries. Instead, he deleted the reference to "Republic" in Libya's name and created what he called the "Jamahiriya"—a movement of the masses that did away with old-fashioned notions of government. At the head of the masses was Qaddafi, firmly directing the speed and course of every step taken by Libya and its citizens. But still he refused to take on formal posts. There was no longer a government, so he did not need to serve in any formal position. To seal his grip on power, he instructed specially trained intelligence agents to extend beyond Libya's borders their killing of opponents of his regime or the new Jamahiriya. By 1980, his assassination squads had killed Libyans in Europe and the Middle East. The Leader of the Revolution could not abide adversaries or opponents raising questions or doubts about his philosophy, or his power.

After Nasser died in 1970, Qaddafi tried to take on a leading role in the Arab world. The Palestine Liberation Organization (PLO) and its chairman, Yasser Arafat, were major recipients of Libyan financial aid, and other Arab causes—many aligned against the interests of Israel— were also on Qaddafi's list of beneficiaries. He was a major benefactor of the Black September Organization associated with the PLO, and which was responsible for the murder of Israeli athletes at the 1972 Summer Olympic Games held in Munich, West Germany, as well as the effort to overthrow King Hussein of Jordan.

But the Libyan leader's revolutionary vision was not merely horizontal, looking east and west to his brother Arab and Muslim states. It encompassed the giant continent of Africa, on which he believed Libya and his Revolution should take a leadership role. This leadership included Qaddafi's financial support of African "liberation" movements, especially against regimes supported by the US, France and the UK. But Qaddafi was not content with merely spending money in Africa. He had grand plans for Libya to expand its own territory at the expense of its neighbors. In 1973 his troops occupied the Aouzou Strip in Chad, which borders Libya to the south, from which he later launched an invasion. This border area along the Libya–Chad frontier had long been the subject of territorial disputes, originating with the Ottoman Empire and local tribes, and later made even murkier by the colonial powers of Great Britain, France and Italy. International law and history aside, the fact that the Aouzou Strip was reported to contain a large reserve of uranium deposits was not lost on the rest of the world. Qaddafi and uranium were not words the West wanted to hear uttered in the same sentence.

During several years of fighting over the Aouzou Strip, Chad's government was supported by the French Air Force, which eventually helped Chad regain its territory and even briefly occupy part of Libya. After thousands of his troops were either captured or killed, the humiliated Qaddafi finally signed a peace agreement with Chad to resolve the embarrassing loss to his southern neighbor and its French ally. The agreement was signed in 1989, shortly before the UTA 772 bombing.

The withdrawal from Chad was only a temporary setback for Qaddafi. His battles with President Reagan and UK Prime Minister Margaret Thatcher throughout the 1980s were the subjects of countless newspaper headlines, magazine articles, and even novels and movies. The air battles in the Bay of Sidra, the 1986 bombing of the La Belle Disco, and the US Air Force and Navy attack on Tripoli and Benghazi were all part of the give-and-take between the West and the man Ronald Reagan referred to as the "mad dog of the Middle East." The US broke off diplomatic relations with Libya in 1981 and shortly thereafter prohibited the import of Libyan oil into the US.

In 1984, Yvonne Fletcher, a British policewoman standing on duty, was shot and killed by machine-gun fire coming from the Libyan Embassy in London. After Qaddafi refused to waive the diplomatic immunity of the Embassy staff suspected of the murder, the British also cut off diplomatic relations with Qaddafi and expelled everyone from the Libyan Embassy. No one was ever convicted of Yvonne Fletcher's murder, but many years later Libya paid compensation to her family in a quiet diplomatic settlement arranged by the British government.

Within this atmosphere of tension, some of it resulting in military action and counter-actions by terrorists acting for Libya, it was not only Magistrate Judge Bruguière who was frustrated with the fickle Libyans and their efforts to deny and cover up any involvement in the UTA 772 bombing. The rest of the world had come to view Colonel Qaddafi, the

Great Leader of the Revolution, as a dangerous and unpredictable outcast.

* * *

THE SANCTIONS RESOLUTIONS against Libya enacted by the United Nations Security Council in early 1992 had been adopted without much opposition, even by Qaddafi's brother Arab states. Blowing up commercial passenger jets and killing hundreds of innocent civilians was simply beyond the pale even for those states that sympathized with Gaddafi's generally anti-Western and anti-Israel rhetoric. But the two Resolutions had not been enough to change Qaddafi's intransigence or to allow Bruguière and his French warship entry into Tripoli to follow through on his criminal investigation.

Qaddafi's response to the United Nations Resolutions was to stall. His agents working in France had been unable to bribe or talk their way into having Bruguière's investigation derailed, and the FBI and Scotland Yard were still pressing to prosecute the Lockerbie suspects, who, like their UTA counterparts, sat comfortably in Libya enjoying the protection of Qaddafi's police state. There was not enough pressure on the Leader to extradite his people to face criminal charges within foreign legal systems.

In November 1993, after unsuccessfully pressing Libya to comply with the earlier sanctions, the United Nations Security Council adopted Resolution 883, which this time added far stricter and more painful sanctions on Libya. These included a freezing of many Libyan assets outside the country, a ban on shipping oil technology to assist Libya in its most important industry and further tightening of the existing sanctions.

But still Qaddafi did not comply. He refused to cooperate with the investigations of UTA or Lockerbie, and his economy began to suffer severely from what became a worldwide boycott of Libya and its oil industry. Qaddafi's Libya had become a pariah state.

Bruguière and his French team would spend the next two years following up on additional leads and witnesses, all outside of Libya. The American and British Pan Am 103 investigating teams would continue their work, also outside Libya. Qaddafi would remain isolated, spending weeks at a time in his Bedouin tents set up outside Tripoli in the Libyan desert, surrounded by his female bodyguards and tightening his grip on the police state he had created.

The situation was now a waiting game. Bruguière was accustomed to waiting for his prey, and there was nowhere for the suspects to run.

Chapter 7

The Second Fake-Out

BY 1996 OVER five years had passed since the French jet had blown up over the Ténéré desert. Qaddafi and his Revolutionary Jamahiriya were feeling to the full the combined effect of the United Nations' economic sanctions and the Arab world's distancing itself from him. In France, however, a change in the ranks of elected leadership would provide Libya a chance for rapprochement.

In 1995 the French Republic had elected a new President. Jacques Chirac succeeded the ailing Mitterand in May, having risen up through the ranks of the Gaullist Party, serving as Mayor of Paris and later as Prime Minister. A critic of Mitterand's socialist approach to French government and business, the tall, smiling Chirac had won his place at the Élysée Palace through a campaign pledging lower taxes, the removal of price controls on products and business privatization. He was a well-recognized, even "presidential" figure who almost always wore finely tailored suits and his receding hair slicked back and who had presented himself as a tough law-and-order-focused leader, vowing to pursue and punish criminals and terrorists. As a civil servant familiar with the rough-and-tumble methods of French politics, Chirac had developed a reputation as a practical problem solver. It was also rumored that his role as a "fixer" was tainted by bribery and corruption, but no charges had ever stuck, and he had moved steadily up the ladder of French political life, making allies, fixing problems, building his base. Nothing would stand in the way of the ambitious, suave Chirac. His nickname was "Le Bulldozer."

One of Chirac's personal areas of interest, and of influence, was his role in maintaining close relations with dictators and military regimes in Africa and the Middle East. He was deeply involved in French military support in former French colonies such as Gabon and the Ivory Coast, and had negotiated huge oil and energy deals wherever French companies sought lucrative contracts. He had even traveled to Baghdad in the 1970s to meet with dictator Saddam Hussein so that a French company could build the Osirak nuclear reactor. That same reactor was destroyed by Israel in a 1981 military strike because it viewed the nuclear fuel as a potential source of plutonium bombs that Hussein might direct at Tel Aviv.

Given his long-time and extensive contacts with tyrants and despots in Africa and the Middle East, Chirac liked to brag that he understood how best to deal with such characters in a manner that worked to further the interests of France. Chirac was the man who could get on a plane and cut the necessary deals. Ideology was not in his dossier. He was a modern leader, unencumbered by the shackles of French philosophy and historical dialectics.

When he became President and assumed the powerful Executive authority to oversee the Fifth Republic, many of the foreign rulers he had befriended over the years believed that their own interests would now be protected by the practical and generous hand of the most powerful man in France. This new dynamic was not lost on even the most isolated despots. A certain eccentric Arab leader brooding in his Bedouin tent near the Mediterranean shores of his capital city consulted with his closest advisers and studied the developing opportunity to end his pariah status. He decided to reach out to Chirac and test the waters of the new French administration, and to drive a wedge between France and the United States and Great Britain, its allies at the United Nations, where the punishing economic sanctions had been imposed.

On 23 March 1996, the French Ambassador to Libya was summoned to the Ministry of Foreign Affairs in Tripoli. He was handed an envelope, which the Libyans requested be delivered directly to President Chirac. He was told it contained an important communication from the Great Leader of the Libyan Revolution, Colonel Qaddafi, who still had no official governmental title or office. It was sent by diplomatic courier on a plane to Paris, and the envelope was quickly in the hands of the President's staff at the Élysée Palace.

Chirac read the letter, which was drafted in Arabic, in its French translation. It was addressed directly to him as President of the French Republic, and read in relevant part:

Mr. President:

Ever since the French people elected you president, I have had the hope of seeing a rebirth of the France–Libya relations, to see them expand other horizons, and to see the cooperation between our two countries experience a rebirth for the great good of our two people and in the service of their mutual interests.

I remain confident, as I always have been, that it will be possible to reach, without great difficulty, a resolution of the matter pertaining to the accident of the UTA plane, an event that has cast a shadow on Franco-Libyan relations. I have always thought that, with the right intentions and a determination to keep this accident in the proper perspective, it would be possible to reach a solution that would satisfy the French demands while preserving the sovereignty of the Great Arab Libyan Popular Socialist Jamahiriya.

I would like to assure you that Libya is anxious to cooperate with France in order to determine the causes of the accident of the UTA plane, and make sure that the guilty parties are punished.

Libya agrees to:

Provide France all the evidence in its possession and to allow France to obtain all documents useful to the establishment of the facts of this matter.

Facilitate any contact or meeting that is necessary, as well as any other step aimed at obtaining evidence connected to this matter

Give the responsible Libyan officials the authority to cooperate with the investigator-in-charge and to respond to all of his demands.

I would like nonetheless to draw your attention to an important issue: Libyan law—like many other legal systems, including French law itself—does not allow the extradition of its own nationals to stand trial before a foreign court.

If the French judicial system—the objectivity of which we have every reason to believe in—concludes that Libyan citizens are guilty in this affair, nothing should prevent France from trying them *in absentia*, assuming French law allows such a trial. Libya will abide by all of its obligations, if all of the conditions required by law are satisfied.

Libya stands ready to greet the French investigator and his collaborators and to allow them all access and assistance during the length of their mission.

Sincerely,
Colonel Muammar Qaddafi

At first, Chirac did not share Qaddafi's letter with Bruguière or anyone outside his inner circle of advisers. This was the sort of private diplomacy he had specialized in for years. He kept things close to his chest and excluded career diplomats from processes, especially when dealing with isolated dictators. But he pondered how best to take advantage of the opening handed to him by the Libyan leader for the benefit of French interests as well as his own political agenda.

* * *

TWO MONTHS LATER, Bruguière received his first inkling that the Libyans were feeling the pressure of his investigation and the United Nations sanctions. On 28 May 1996, he received a letter from Counsellor Mursi, the same "judicial officer" who had contacted him earlier about possible Libyan cooperation in the UTA 772 investigation and who had failed to respond to any further enquiries after Bruguière's warship was turned back from Tripoli.

After checking with the French Foreign Ministry, Bruguière issued a new international rogatory commission to the Libyan legal authorities, requesting their full cooperation, not knowing if this time might be different. In early July, the Élysée Palace shared with Bruguière a copy of Qaddafi's March letter to Chirac. At first he was upset that the President had withheld such a critical communication directly affecting his investigation, but Bruguière swallowed his pride and scheduled a visit to Libya to take place just two weeks later. This time things would be different, and he would not be turned away from Tripoli at the last minute. After years of frustration and delay, Le Sheriff was hot on the trail of the suspects in his biggest case.

BRUGUIÈRE KNEW HE might only have one opportunity to visit Libya and gather evidence. On 5 July 1996, he and a large team from the anti-terrorist section of the Paris police, the DST and technical experts flew to Tripoli in order to carry out the letter rogatory commission that Libya had agreed to honor. Greeting him and his team at the airport was Counsellor Mahmoud Mursi. Bruguière had three goals for this unique trip: to interview witnesses, gather evidence and conduct technical examinations. With any luck, Qaddafi's offer to Chirac to cooperate—conditional as it was, and with the political demand that no Libyan citizens would be extradited to Paris to stand trial for murder—would help Bruguière to add even more solid proof to his already considerable folder of evidence. Qaddafi's demand that Libyan suspects not be handed over to stand trial for murder in Paris was simply the opening round of what surely would be protracted negotiations. This was to be expected. Having compiled so much evidence regarding the methods for the attack on the DC-10, Bruguière was focused on developing even more evidence to support the motive for the attack. With that in hand, he could leverage Qaddafi, and perhaps his own President, to come up with a deal that required the suspects to be brought to justice in France, at long last.

The first Libyan official to be interviewed was Moussa Koussa,

Director of Libyan Intelligence and, at the time of the UTA 772 bombing, Director of Mathaba. Allowing the investigation to be conducted in Tripoli certainly provided the witnesses with a high level of comfort, despite Bruguière's tough reputation. Speaking in a relaxed and confident manner, Moussa explained to Bruguière that Mathaba was an "ideological union of all the political parties, in all of the states." This idyllic group was designed to make it easier for opponents of non-revolutionary dictatorships—especially in Africa—to meet and be heard in order to broadcast the message of the Leader's Green Book. As an added feature, Mathaba had been unable to operate outside Libya since the imposition of sanctions by the United Nations in 1992.

But Moussa insisted to the French investigators that Mathaba was a peaceful organization and did not provide paramilitary training and weapons to members in African countries, contrary to what Bruguière had heard from many other witnesses and French Intelligence. Moussa also denied that anyone connected with Mathaba had any knowledge of, let alone a role in, the UTA 772 bombing. As far as he was concerned, Libya had always had good relations with France and the French people, particularly after the cessation of hostilities along the Chad–Libya border. This had been the path chosen by the Great Leader of the Revolution, and he had been delighted to follow.

At this point in the interview, Bruguière pulled out some files his men had collected in Brazzaville several years earlier. These included two official press releases issued by the Libyan Embassy in Brazzaville in 1987 and 1988, denouncing "French imperialist logic" and exhorting that "the Great Jamahiriya keeps the right to self-defense against the aggressions of France in Chad." He put them in front of Moussa and asked if they reflected the views of Mathaba at that time.

Moussa became very agitated and perplexed. All he could do was mumble that he was a friend of France and had never considered the French people his enemy. Satisfied that Moussa was not telling him the truth about the militant nature of Mathaba, Bruguière noted that this reaction confirmed what his five years of detective work on the UTA case had made clear to him—that the motive for the UTA 772 bombing arose from Libya's anger over the failure of its military policy in Chad, and thus was Qaddafi's punishment of France for assisting the winning side.

Several more Libyan officials reacted in the same surprised manner when the press releases were put before them. Their confidence and cool demeanor, ensured by their friendly and safe surroundings during the interrogations, quickly disappeared as Bruguière leaned towards them, his detective instincts smelling a lie.

As more officials and government agents were paraded before the French investigators in their Tripoli interviews, their stories emerged as if scripted and rehearsed at length. No one knew the Congolese man named Mangatany who had died on the plane, and whom Bruguière's investigation had made clear was responsible for checking in the booby-trapped suitcase in Brazzaville. No one who had been assigned to the Libyan mission in Brazzaville had ever heard of Mangatany. No one could recall the names of any "black Africans" who had worked with the Mathaba in Congo during the time frame. Most of the witnesses interviewed by Bruguière even said that as a policy matter they were not allowed to meet with Africans, even while stationed in another country.

This uniform line of testimony continued despite Bruguière's revelation to the Libyans that the Congolese intelligence agencies had provided photographs of Libyan diplomats meeting with Mangatany in Congo. Even Elazragh's sudden departure from Brazzaville right after the UTA 772 bombing was described by the Libyans as a long-planned rotation of diplomats, unrelated to any other events.

The Libyans then ushered into the interviews the man Bruguière had wanted to question ever since his critical discovery of the green electric circuit board leading his team from Taiwan to Germany to Tripoli. Knowing he had the forensic documentation to connect Libya itself with the timers used in the bombing, the investigating magistrate pulled out his file for Colonel Abdessalam Issa al-Shibani.

The Libyan Colonel greeted the French investigators and offered to cooperate in any way he could. Describing himself as a representative of the Technical Administration office of the Domestic Security Services, Shibani admitted that he had indeed ordered the timers from HP Marketing in Germany, and offered to produce for the French his invoices and delivery forms. He also handed them one of the Grasslin timer devices, which he explained had never been used.

Responding to the French questioners, Shibani insisted that the timers had only been used to service remote desert airport beacons, and also to set off fireworks to celebrate the twentieth anniversary of the Libyan Revolution. He only had the one remaining, and could not provide any sort of inventory of how the others had been employed. He also produced a lighting beacon to demonstrate how the desert airport system had worked. Upon inspection, it contained a Grasslin timer.

Shibani insisted in the face of Bruguière's questions that every timer he had obtained from Germany had been used for peaceful purposes or disposed of if it had failed to operate. But when the Investigating Magistrate pressed him on the circuit and timer evidence, Shibani became quite agitated, noting that he was simply a cooperating witness. He was offended that the French visitors were treating him like an accused suspect, especially in his own protective country.

In his interview, Abdelsalam Hammouda also insisted that he had never been involved in any bomb-making or military operations outside of Libya. He was a simple intelligence analyst with responsibility for overseeing the Arab Fishing Company, which he admitted served as an intelligence-gathering operation. He also acknowledged that he knew Mr. Naeli, one of the operatives who had visited the Brazzaville Embassy shortly before the bombing. Later, after making an informal request, Counsellor Mursi informed Bruguière that the telephone number called by Naeli from his Brazzaville hotel room shortly before the bombing was Hammouda's direct-dial telephone number. Mursi did not know the connection. But Bruguière was pleased that the Libyans had unwittingly provided a direct link between the actors on the ground in Congo in September 1989 and senior intelligence offices in Tripoli.

Waiting for the right moment, Bruguière enquired of Mursi whether he could gather the relevant files to demonstrate that Arbas Musbah had been killed in a road accident, supposedly in November 1990. Anxious to show his cooperation, Mursi quickly produced Libyan government documents stating that Musbah had been killed, a police traffic report describing the tragic accident and a medical expert report describing the cause of death. Bruguière, though, noted that the documents stated Musbah had been killed in December and not, as the Libyans had previously stated, in November 1990. Mursi tried to explain to the French that this was likely some sort of clerical mistake and that Libyan police were regularly making such minor typographical errors in routine reports, something he attributed to the lack of a well-educated civil service.

But Bruguière knew immediately that these documents were a fabrication. His own investigators had been able to gather documents from Athens, Greece, where a visa request had been submitted by a Libyan also named Arbas Musbah. Ironically, he had the same passport number and description as the person supposedly killed on a Libyan road in late 1990, whether November or December. The visa application was dated 1 April 1991, five or six months after Mr. Musbah had supposedly been killed.

As Bruguière revealed the existence of the Greek visa application to his Libyan hosts they all looked at each other and hurriedly promised to conduct an internal investigation of what they characterized as an "irregularity." Later, Mursi informed Bruguière that the whole thing had been a mistake. Musbah had been alive all along, and it was another person with a similar name who had been killed on the road. It was all simply a misunderstanding.

To the French investigators, this was further confirmation that the Libyans were attempting to throw them off the trail of competent evidence, and that they would not merely lie to cover their tracks, but manufacture false documents to make it appear that one of the men accused of committing mass murder was no longer alive.

NEAR THE END of their ten-day stay in Tripoli, Mursi offered to produce to the French visitors the booby-trapped suitcase he had referred to in 1992, and of which Bruguière had only seen photographs taken by the DST in Senoussi's offices. The Investigating Magistrate accepted Mursi's offer of this further "cooperation."

Bringing the black–blue Samsonite Silhouette 220 luxury suitcase to their conference room, Mursi repeated the story that had previously been provided in 1992 by Senoussi—that the suitcase had been seized from opponents of the Qaddafi regime who had planned to carry out a terrorist attack in Tripoli. This time, the suitcase had judicial seals wrapped around it, which Mursi agreed to break in order to allow the French to inspect the insides. Bruguière quietly noted that the earlier photographs had lacked any judicial seals around the suitcases and that someone had thought of this wrapping exercise afterwards to create the appearance of a formal police case.

The inside sheets and back half-strip of the lower part of the case were cut open and partly unstuck. Inside was 1.5 kilos of compact plastic explosive with a detonator, but the timing device was not present, only the remains of an electrical system with pole clips and batteries and a few loose wires. Bruguière asked Mursi if his men could take the suitcase back to Paris for forensic tests, which the Libyan was happy to allow. Anything to cooperate with his French colleagues, Mursi noted.

Once back in Paris, the French experts tested the explosive and determined that it had sufficient force to ensure the airborne destruction of a jumbo jet. The Samsonite suitcase material also matched that of the fragment found in the desert wreckage of the destroyed DC-10. Even more significantly, the explosive was identical to that seized by the French authorities in 1986 in Paris from the 15 May Organization, which had sold several of the booby-trapped suitcases before being shut down. It was also identical to the pentrite found on the DC-10 wreckage in the Ténéré desert.

BRUGUIÈRE WAS SATISFIED with the visit to Libya. The Libyans had cooperated, in their own way, in his investigation of the UTA 772 bombing, as instructed by the United Nations sanctions. They had also lied enough in their interviews and fabricated documents to the point that he was now convinced of the guilt of the suspects, as well as the senior officials of the Libyan government.

The French investigation was almost complete. Bruguière returned to Paris to prepare his report, which would reflect the meticulous detective work that would close the circle of proof to build a historic murder case. But even as the French investigators put the finishing touches to their report, events across the Atlantic were taking matters in an entirely different direction.

Chapter 8

The American Way

OTHER THAN A few special agents of the FBI who were working with the French investigators and diplomats involved in the United Nations sanctions, most Americans did not know about the progress being made by Bruguière. The explosion and crash of UTA 772 in September 1989 was mostly a buried footnote in the newspaper. As far as the American public and the press were concerned, there was only one airline bombing worthy of discussion.

The hundreds of families whose loved ones were killed on Pan Am 103 when it crashed into Lockerbie were invested in dealing with their own losses. As they completed their vigils in Scotland, worked with authorities to find any remnant of their children, siblings, parents or friends, and made arrangements for funerals and memorial services, most of them returned to the United States in an effort to rebuild their shattered lives. The death of so many students and young travelers had taken an especially hard toll on surviving family members.

Emerging from their initial grief, the Pan Am 103 family members organized themselves, working closely with the FBI and Scotland Yard to find the persons responsible for the murderous bombing. The Lockerbie investigation was one of the most intense and comprehensive criminal investigations in the history of the US or the UK. The indictment of two Libyan agents on murder and terrorism charges by a federal grand jury in Washington, DC and in the Royal Courts in Scotland was the culmination of that joint investigation. It was also extensively publicized, comprising a large portion of media over a long period of time. Everyone knew what the word "Lockerbie" signified. In contrast, the public in the US, and to a great extent in the UK, had very little knowledge of the French airliner and its 170 innocent passengers that had been destroyed in the African desert nine months later.

As a point of emphasis, many of the surviving family members were from the New York metropolitan area, the media capital of the US, which kept the Lockerbie story on the front pages. The combination of overwhelming grief and intense dedication towards finding out who was responsible ensured that the Lockerbie disaster would remain in the national consciousness for many years.

In the United States and the United Kingdom there are two legal avenues available when a loved one has been killed. The criminal justice system, firstly, had taken the Lockerbie case to great heights, with the huge resources of the US and UK governments dedicated to bringing the perpetrators to justice. Two Libyan suspects had been charged with the crime, and the career prosecutors and investigators would carry on until justice had been achieved. The fact that the two indicted suspects lived comfortably in Tripoli, protected by Libyan law and the beneficence of the Great Leader of the Revolution, was a challenge the criminal justice system had not yet been able to overcome.

Secondly, in the US—and just as much a part of the legal system as the criminal prosecution by the FBI and Department of Justice and which also came naturally to many of the Pan Am 103 family members—was civil law, which reflected a well-respected reaction to such tragedies and was supported by centuries of tradition, authority and practice.

The American legal system had borrowed much from its common-law parent in the UK, but had also expanded the scope and breadth of one very important element. This would provide the Lockerbie families with the opportunity to pour their energies into the cause of remembering their loved ones who had perished in the little Scottish town.

With the pain and grief of the disaster still fresh in their minds and souls, several hundred of the Lockerbie families filed civil lawsuits for damages against Pan American Airways.

TO SUE A commercial airline for a catastrophe that takes place outside the United States is not easy. The airline industry recognized very early in its existence that it would be bankrupt before getting started if passengers or their families could easily sue them for large amounts of money resulting from death or serious injury claims. Back in 1929, many airlines were owned by governments themselves, and thus needed international legal and financial protection. The airlines convinced a number of governments that the only way to protect them from quick bankruptcies resulting from air disasters—all too common in the early days of aviation—was to make sure that international treaties governing commercial air travel limited damages in such cases.

In 1929, only two years after Charles Lindbergh flew the first solo non-stop transatlantic flight, the nations of the world met in Poland to negotiate what became known as the Warsaw Convention, or more formally the Convention for the Unification of Certain Rules Relating to International Transportation by Air. The most important feature of the Warsaw Convention was that an international air carrier's legal liability was generally limited to damages not exceeding US$75,000 per passenger. That limitation had remained in effect for decades and was adopted by every country in the world served by international air carriers. This was especially true for the United States, which was responsible for almost half the scheduled commercial air flights in the world. Of course, the United States also had a legal tradition that favored awarding substantial damages to persons harmed or killed by a company's wrongful or negligent actions.

Recognizing that there must be a narrow exception to the $75,000 limit on damages, the countries that negotiated the Warsaw Convention put into the treaty a small provision that was rarely used and even less frequently successful. Under Article 25, a person could recover more than the $75,000 treaty limit, but only if it could be proven in a court of law that the carrier itself had engaged in "willful misconduct" and that, additionally, such willful misconduct had been the direct cause of the passenger's death. This was an extraordinarily difficult burden for any passenger and lawyer to carry. Even under this exception, a passenger could not recover punitive damages.

In early 1991, a number of Pan Am 103 Lockerbie families filed civil court claims against the carrier. They alleged that the nation's most respected and prestigious airline had operated Flight 103 in such a grossly negligent manner that it had to know that its own actions would likely cause the death of the passengers. Alternatively, they claimed that its operations were carried out with "reckless disregard" for the passengers' lives and safety. Many of the families were represented by the New York law firm of Kreindler & Kreindler, one of the nation's leading air disaster advocates for plaintiffs against airlines. Its senior partner, Lee Kreindler, had handled many air crash cases and considered the Lockerbie case the pinnacle of his long career.

The cases were brought in the federal court sitting in Long Island, the Eastern District of New York, as it is called, because Pan Am 103 had been scheduled to land at John F. Kennedy Airport in Queens, located in that federal district. Chief Judge Thomas Platt was assigned to the case from the start. A Nixon appointee with a reputation for impatience and at times intolerance, Judge Platt quickly moved the case along to trial, providing what Pan Am's lawyers believed was a procedural advantage to the families and their lawyers.

The stakes for Pan Am could not be higher, as the Lockerbie disaster had resulted in the worst loss of life and property from a terrorist act in the history of the airline. But when the case was filed, Pan Am already had begun its decline from its heyday, and the general worldwide slowdown in commercial air traffic during and after the 1990 Gulf War with Iraq had only made things worse. Indeed, Pan Am was considered such a likely target for international terrorist attacks at that time that some experienced travelers avoided booking its flights and took more inconvenient airlines to avoid potential disaster.

Even before the filing of the complaints, Pan Am took the step of filing for Chapter 11 bankruptcy reorganization to protect it from its creditors. But the civil case was allowed to proceed as part of the reorganization of the airline, as one last effort to salvage its past glory and emerge from bankruptcy as a leaner and meaner airline. The

Lockerbie claims filed in the Long Island federal courthouse represented a "bet-the-company" case. The wide public attention ensured that Pan Am's operations would be closely examined well beyond the confines of the federal lawsuit.

A civil jury trial was convened before Judge Platt on 27 April 1992. Pan Am hoped it could win the trial and emerge with its reputation intact, as this would reassure its creditors and allow it to emerge from bankruptcy, and perhaps restore the public confidence it had lost over the last few years. The insurance companies that had sold Pan Am casualty indemnity policies also worked closely with the airline's lawyers. This was a very delicate balancing act. On the one hand, Pan Am—and the insurance companies that would pay a large portion of any award—needed to defeat the claims with every legal tool at hand. At the same time, the memories of the Lockerbie catastrophe were still fresh, and the compelling human stories of grief, loss and death told by the families would melt a juror's heart.

The evidence placed before the jury revealed to the public that Pan Am was not the solid, first-class international carrier it had long claimed to be. Most of the proof centered on procedures for inspecting baggage. The families' lawyers especially focused on the fact that the booby-trapped suitcase had been allowed into the plane's baggage compartment without any accompanying passenger. The three months of trial at the federal court went terribly for the airline. Indeed, the trial revealed the fact that the airline that had long served as the public face of American international business and prestige *had* been grossly negligent.

The basic problem was that Pan Am had failed to follow mandatory safety and inspection procedures to ensure that unaccompanied inter-airport suitcases were not placed on any of its flights. To make matters worse, it had ceased its compliance with these procedures in February 1987—two years before the bombing—at its hubs in Heathrow and Frankfurt because it was too expensive and "cumbersome." It had even stopped conducting physical inspections of luggage and relied solely on x-ray machines, with the bags placed in the aircraft without even attempting to match them with a ticketed passenger. This practice was a direct violation of FAA (Federal Aviation Administration) regulations—a violation about which Pan Am had never informed anyone.

One of the most dramatic revelations at the trial was that Pan Am operations personnel in London had purposely not even informed the flight crews that it had ceased these luggage security procedures. Thus, the pilots assumed—incorrectly—that their safety systems had continued to comply. According to the testimony and evidence put before the jury, Pan Am operations managers at Heathrow instructed gate agents not to advise pilots of unaccompanied luggage because it made crews "jittery."

To make matters even worse, this was not the first time someone had attempted to place an unaccompanied bomb-laden suitcase on a Pan Am flight. As recently as 1983, a plane getting ready to fly from Rome to New York had averted a similar catastrophe when, at the last minute, authorities were informed of a bomb and determined that the ticketed passenger had not boarded the flight. Similarly, in June 1985 an Air India 747 flying over the North Atlantic on its Montreal–London–Delhi route had been blown out of the skies over Irish airspace, killing several hundred people, because an unaccompanied interline suitcase had passed through its system. As with Pan Am 103, that suitcase bomb would have been discovered had Air India matched it to an empty seat.

The evidence got even worse. In 1986, Pan Am had commissioned a security study by a leading Israeli expert who concluded that Pan Am's security systems at Heathrow and Frankfort were quite vulnerable to a terrorist attack. The Israeli study specifically noted that x-ray machines were not reliable, were not a substitute for physical inspections, and were a particularly weak link in the airline's system where interline bags were concerned.

Proof of negligence piled up. In July 1988, the FAA had issued a security bulletin warning airlines of a high threat of a terrorist attack in retaliation for the downing of an Iranian Airbus A300 jumbo jet in the Persian Gulf by the US Navy. Acting on battle alert during the long-running Iran–Iraq War, the USS *Vincennes* guided missile cruiser had accidentally shot it down, mistaking the commercial jet for an attacking plane. All 290 passengers on board were killed, including scores of children. Iran's Islamic Revolutionary Government screamed for revenge. Shortly after this threat was circulated, the FAA issued a separate security bulletin to Pan Am, warning that a raid on a terrorist group had uncovered a bomb built inside a Toshiba radio cassette player—the same type of bomb later found in the Pan Am 103 wreckage. The security bulletin pointed out that such bombs were difficult to detect by the use of a normal x-ray machine, as used at Heathrow.

But the most damaging evidence of neglect of passenger safety—later characterized as "outrageous" by the federal appellate court—was a December 1988 FAA security bulletin to Pan Am. That bulletin advised the airline that the US Embassy in Helsinki, Finland, had received a telephone call warning that a Pan Am flight from Frankfurt to London on the New York interline connection would be bombed. This warning was received only fourteen days before the Lockerbie attack. It also repeated the warning about a Toshiba cassette bomb detonation device. Despite all these clear warnings and signs of potential trouble, Pan Am had continued to allow unaccompanied interline baggage to make its way on to the US-bound flights through Heathrow, its main European hub. It did not even alert its x-ray technicians—the last line of defense— to these warnings.

As if cursed with bad luck, combined with bad evidence of its own woefully negligent operations, the record in the trial revealed that the Helsinki security bulletin to Pan Am had been placed under a pile of papers on the desk of the security officer responsible for the doomed flight. It was only discovered by him the day after the disaster. Sadly, in an effort to make it appear that he had properly noted the alert, the security officer apparently arranged for the document to be backdated so that government investigators would be led to believe that the security warning had been disseminated. Chief Judge Platt found this evidence too much to bear. He instructed the jury that such backdating was evidence of Pan Am's "conscious guilt" on its part for its role in the disaster.

The best Pan Am could muster as a defense was that it had instituted an internal security program in May 1986 during a sharp decline in air travel due to other terrorist attacks. The "Alert" system was found by Judge Platt and the jury to be neither related to security nor a program. Instead, it was ruled by the judge to be a "misleading public relations ploy designed to make would-be passengers feel more secure."

On 10 July 1992, after a hotly contested thirteen-week trial, the jury issued its verdict. Employing a special verdict form to record its decision, the jury found that Pan Am had engaged in "willful misconduct" that directly led to the cause of the crash.

The families and their lawyers reacted with very mixed emotions. Although relieved that some measure of responsibility for the death of their loved ones had been apportioned, there was a tremendous lack of satisfaction with the process of suing Pan Am. Despite the large awards—ranging up to $9 million per family—the families felt empty. Pan Am would appeal, of course, and the legal proceedings would drag on for several more years. But hundreds of family members felt that the hard-fought and successful trial against Pan Am was simply not enough to provide them with any psychological closure. Their grieving did not give way to relief or finality. This was just about money, much of which would go to their lawyers and towards the huge costs of prosecuting the case. There actually was a sense of disappointment that the lawyers had been able to prove in court how careless and uncaring Pan Am had become. The most prestigious airline in America had slipped from its position at the apex of the industry into a grossly negligent and sloppy operation that had contributed to the deaths of hundreds of passengers.

But what hurt the families the most was that the disaster may well have been averted had Pan Am simply followed existing security rules designed to safeguard its passengers from this very type of attack. Pan Am's own negligence had allowed terrorists to kill their loved ones. If the airline had done its job properly, the word Lockerbie might never have become a synonym for international terrorism.

At the end of the day, what mattered most to the families was that the killers were still free and living comfortable lives on the shores of Tripoli. All the money from Pan Am and its insurance companies was not going to hold them—or the leader of the Libyan Revolution—accountable for killing 270 innocent people.

THE MIXED EMOTIONS of the families would not fade away. In 1994, as the Pan Am lawyers prepared to argue their appeals against the verdict, some of the Lockerbie families and their lawyers decided to file another civil case before Judge Platt. This time, they would sue the government of Libya for damages, alleging that it and its agents had been directly responsible for placing the suitcase bomb on the 747. They simply could not accept that the murderers remained free, or that the government responsible for planning the bombing would not be held to account.

Compared to suing Libya, the court case against Pan Am had been child's play, even considering the huge hurdles posed by the Warsaw Convention. Kreindler and his team had overcome those hurdles with great assistance from the self-inflicted evidence of Pan Am's gross indifference to safety and had obtained a large award that was now to be argued before the Federal Court of Appeals in New York, known as the Second Circuit. They had done so mostly through factual evidence and testimony. Once the damning FAA security bulletins had been obtained by their lawyers in pre-trial discovery, the Lockerbie families had a fighting chance of convincing a jury to issue a verdict in their favor— this was a "triable case," as the lawyers would say. The pending appeal would simply review the factual record and determine if Judge Platt had made any serious errors of law or evidence.

But bringing a claim for damages against Libya, or any other foreign government, was not something that would turn on how much evidence of negligence Kreindler and his team might collate. It did not matter how far the FBI and Scotland Yard had proceeded with their investigation. Nor did it matter that the two Libyan agents charged with the bombing—still living in their Tripoli homes—were under indictment in Washington and Scotland. The criminal evidence could be stacked up in a pile, but one insurmountable hurdle would remain—a legal doctrine known for several centuries as foreign sovereign immunity. In short, courts only allow a civil suit for damages to proceed against a government if the government expressly allows such a claim. Taking its foundation from English common law and constitutional principles, the law had long observed that "the King can do no wrong." Thus, for two hundred years US constitutional law had held that suits against foreign sovereigns could not be brought in the US courts, unless expressly allowed.

But who had the constitutional authority to allow such suits? Under the US Constitution, the federal courts historically played no role in international issues or foreign relations. That business was left to the other two political branches of the US government—Congress and the President. In 1976, Congress enacted for the first time a series of laws that allowed, under very narrow circumstances, suits against foreign governments. The Foreign Sovereign Immunities Act (FSIA) was intended to allow commercial and other special claims to be litigated in the American courts. But it said nothing about suing terrorist states for damages incurred in airline disasters over Scotland.

Recognizing that US law would not likely allow the case against it to proceed, Libya quickly engaged a Washington lawyer named Bruno Ristau to appear on its behalf. Ristau had spent a career with the US Department of Justice litigating foreign and international claims and was an expert on sovereign immunity issues. After retiring from government service, he had developed a reputation for defending rogue states in the American courts. His nickname was "Attorney for the Damned."

Because immunity is a pure question of law, Ristau filed for Libya a motion to dismiss the entire case. He argued that even if every allegation of the complaint against his client were true and correct, US law required dismissal immediately as a matter of law—foreign sovereign immunity was determined by Congress and the President, and they had drafted the FSIA in such a manner as to only allow a very narrow class of commercial cases to proceed. State-sponsored terrorism was simply not included.

Judge Platt also took on this newly filed case against Libya. Despite his sympathies for the Lockerbie families, who had spent an emotional three months in his courtroom proving their case against Pan Am, he had no choice under the law. In 1995, he granted Ristau's motion and dismissed every claim against Libya. Whatever crimes Qaddafi and his regime had committed—even to the point of mass murder—the federal courts could not hear the claims by the Lockerbie victims' families. The courthouse door was shut tight against any effort to hold Libya accountable for the bombing.

The families were heartsick at this ruling. Despite the fact that the Second Circuit Court of Appeals had upheld the negligence verdict against Pan Am in every respect in September 1994, they felt a sense of emptiness. A very large amount of money—over $500 million—was going to the families and their lawyers as a result of the jury award and appeal against Pan Am. The American system of civil justice had accomplished a substantial financial success for them, despite the challenges posed by the Warsaw Convention.

Yet the murderers remained free, and Libya congratulated its American lawyers for keeping it out of the morass of civil litigation that now brought the once-proud Pan Am to its demise. Indeed, Pan Am at this point was being dismembered by its creditors in bankruptcy, and other airlines were buying up its once-profitable routes, including the coveted New York-to-London path. As the once-mighty Pan Am wound down its operations, Lockerbie being its death blow, the families began to look outside the legal arena to try to pursue Libya in a manner that would hold it accountable.

Chapter 9

A Change in the Rules

ON THE MORNING of 19 April 1995, just a few minutes before 9:00 a.m. Central US time, a yellow Ryder rental truck pulled up to the drop-off zone next to a large federal office building in downtown Oklahoma City. A tall thin white man in his late twenties with a short haircut and military bearing got out of the truck, locked the door and walked to another car sitting nearby. After getting in the car and driving a few blocks, he tossed the truck keys out the window and headed out of the city for the interstate highway.

A few minutes later, an explosive cocktail of ammonium nitrate fertilizer, nitromethane and diesel fuel sitting in the Ryder truck exploded with the force of five thousand pounds of TNT. The blast was heard over fifty miles away across the flat Oklahoma prairie. It destroyed several hundred buildings, shattered windows, burned parked cars and set off secondary explosions from fuel tanks. It instantly destroyed the front one-third of the Alfred P. Murrah Federal Building and left a crater eight feet deep and thirty feet wide.

By the time authorities had cleared the rubble it had become clear that the Oklahoma City bombing was the worst terrorist attack ever carried out on US soil, until 11 September 2001. Almost 170 people were killed, including many children playing in the day care center on the first floor. The collapse of the building crushed the life out of most of the victims. Downtown Oklahoma City resembled a war zone. The American heartland had been targeted for attack and the nation was stunned. The world could not believe it. Television pictures made the city look like war-torn Beirut.

At first, the FBI speculated that the attack was carried out by a drug cartel—the Drug Enforcement Agency had an office in the building. It also theorized that an Islamic fundamentalist group might have been responsible, given that in 1993 a truck bomb planted by Muslim terrorists had detonated in the basement of one of the World Trade Center buildings in Lower Manhattan. The media quickly descended on the bomb site and reported various theories of international terrorism, with countries from Iran to Libya to groups not yet named being blamed.

Prior to the Oklahoma City bombing, the largest single loss of American life in a terrorist attack had been Lockerbie. The criminal investigation initiated by the FBI and state officials in Oklahoma City would be even more intense than the Lockerbie case. But all the grand terrorism theories and international intrigue were for naught. The plot had been carried out by a former US soldier named Timothy McVeigh and his friend Terry Nichols. They were sympathizers of an American militia movement and had planned the bombing as revenge for the federal government's law enforcement "campaign" against other militias, especially the deaths of groups in Waco, Texas, and Ruby Ridge, Idaho. Evoking the Revolutionary spirit, they had carried out the attack on the anniversary of the Battle of Lexington and Concord in the American Revolutionary War. McVeigh was arrested shortly after the bombing for driving the getaway vehicle without a license plate and was held because the police found a gun in the car.

The destruction and death that McVeigh and Nichols inflicted on the people of Oklahoma City was enormous. Families buried their dead, nursed the injured and began to rebuild their proud town, watching with great interest as the federal and state criminal investigations moved forward. Their options were quite limited. They did not have anyone to sue. There was no large corporate entity at which they could point a finger for negligence or from whom they could obtain damages. There

were no insurance companies ready to issue l.
was found liable. Certainly, there was no foreig.
to seek damages. The killers were Americans. The,
military, which is supposed to protect Americans from
they who had been attacked, their families shaken to the
not supposed to happen. All the families had to cling to wa.
investigation and the hope that a jury would convict the ....s of
murder and then execute them under Oklahoma and federal law. But
they also knew that a criminal case could take years, and with appeals
and other court challenges even a death sentence might be delayed for
decades. There could be a long time to wait for justice.

* * *

ONE THOUSAND MILES east of Oklahoma City, the nation's capital swirled
in never-ending waves of intrigue, partisan maneuvers and policy as
President Bill Clinton jousted with his Republican counterpart House
Speaker Newt Gingrich on every issue under the sun. It was great theater,
and the stakes were high at all times.

Gingrich and the Republican Party had seized the conservative mantle
and employed every opportunity to portray the Arkansas Democrat–Yale
Law–Georgetown College–Rhodes Scholar President as soft on crime
and on those evil international forces that threatened America's security—
Iran and Libya, and other countries that used terrorism as an
extension of their foreign policy. Gingrich was a master at putting
together legislative packages that appeared to be based on common
sense and normal American sensibilities. Appearing tough on crime
was central to his strategy. Blaming liberal judges for criminals being
on the streets and not in prison was easy to proclaim and difficult to
disprove. One of Gingrich's favorite issues was the exceedingly long
time it took for death penalty cases to work their way through the
courts. He and his staff were also aware that the federal courts had
little trouble dismissing any effort by Americans to sue foreign terrorist
states for damages, no matter how egregious the violations of law and
cost in human lives.

After Judge Platt dismissed their case against Libya, the Pan Am 103

...rbie families had come to Washington with their lawyers and lobbyists to explore how they might convince Congress to open the courthouse door and allow them to sue Qaddafi's state. It was a tough sell. They had already obtained a very large jury award against Pan Am, and the public record made clear that their legal rights, as well as their financial interests, had been protected by existing legal procedures and rights. The system had worked for them—perhaps not perfectly, but close enough. Pan Am and its insurers were held to account and were compelled to pay huge amounts of damages. Even the most sympathetic legislators had a hard time finding a way to accommodate the Lockerbie families.

Also pushing back against the families' request were the career lawyers and diplomatic policymakers at the US Department of State. They made it clear to Congress that making such a radical change in the law would open up a Pandora's box of problems for the United States government and its ability to deal with foreign nations, even those engaged in terrorism. Congress already had implemented several laws that provided presidents with the authority to impose sanctions on rogue states such as Libya and Iran, and several—Reagan, Bush and Clinton—had implemented these, including the international sanctions against Libya issued by the United Nations.

Of course, President Reagan had ordered the bombing of Libya back in 1986 for the attack on La Belle in Berlin. That was the way to deal with state sponsors of terrorism, the diplomats and lawyers repeated. Their arguments were based on two centuries of constitutional law, diplomacy and international legal norms. These arguments made sense. No other country allowed its citizens to sue foreign governments for supporting terrorist activities. Such things were not the business of domestic courts and judges. Passing such a law would severely compromise the President's ability to direct foreign relations, not to mention interfere with the Department of State's historic role as the chief diplomatic agency for the US government.

But the Department of State lawyers and diplomats briefing members of Congress did not anticipate that the mass murder of Americans in the country's heartland by a former American soldier would overcome all their strong and convincing arguments. The Oklahoma City bombing had changed the political landscape, and Newt Gingrich was not going to allow the opportunity to advance his and the Republican message—that they stood stronger than President Clinton and the Democrats on fighting crime and terrorism—to pass.

GINGRICH HAD PACKAGED his national agenda under the banner of a "Contract with America." To support the posturing, he and his Republican troops would put forward publicly that they wanted to address one of the conservative movement's biggest complaints—that criminals convicted of murder and sentenced to death could avoid the ultimate punishment through what appeared to be endless appeals and liberal judges reviewing their cases. It was not unusual for death row inmates to spend twenty years in prison after conviction, raising every sort of legal and factual challenge.

The Oklahoma City families relied heavily on their own representatives in the House and Senate to express their frustration, fears and grief. They appreciated that one of the largest criminal cases in the history of the nation would take time, patience and resources. What they wanted Congress to do was make sure that if McVeigh and Nichols were convicted and sentenced to death, they actually would receive their punishment without delaying the process for decades. That might provide them with some closure and a sense of justice.

At the same time, the Lockerbie families were making their rounds on Capitol Hill, trying to convince Congress that Libya should be held accountable in a federal court for blowing up the 747 over Scotland, pushing back on the legal and policy arguments put forward by the State Department as to why that was not a good idea. They had some support from a few other families who had also tried to sue Iran in federal court in Washington for supporting terrorist activities in Lebanon, Israel and the Palestinian territories. Like the Lockerbie families, they had been frustrated that Iran also had hired Bruno Ristau to defend the cases, and that the federal courts—although entirely sympathetic to their plight—had been forced to dismiss the cases. Foreign Sovereign Immunity was an absolute bar to hauling Iran and Libya into a US court. The door was tightly closed.

As with most major accomplishments in Washington, it took a

coincidence of events, alliances and personalities to achieve any type of positive result in Congress. As they represented the biggest constituencies for advocating the rights of American victims of terrorism, the Lockerbie and Oklahoma City families carried tremendous political weight and sympathy for their cause. In addition, geopolitical factors were in harmony: the Lockerbie families had the attention and support of the mostly liberal and Democratic legislators from New York, New Jersey and Connecticut to carry their arguments; the Oklahoma City families had the mostly conservative and Republican Oklahoma members of Congress act as their champions. This was a political match made in heaven.

The families and their lawyers worked together to construct a political compromise that met their goals. From the perspective of the Oklahoma City families, it was most urgent to obtain federal legislation that would ensure that any death sentence for McVeigh and Nichols would be carried out without the decades of delay typical in sensational murder cases. The first trial of McVeigh and Nichols would likely be in federal court, with the state prosecution having to wait until the federal courts had finished their business. Obtaining "reform" under federal law was their principal objective.

The Lockerbie families had a narrower objective. They merely sought an opportunity to bring their claim for damages against Libya into federal court so that, as with their victory over Pan Am, the party ultimately responsible for the act of mass murder would be held accountable in a court of law. They sought a small amendment to the Foreign Sovereign Immunities Act—the addition of a "terrorism" provision that would allow the door of the federal court to be opened so they could put forward their proof of Libya's responsibility for the bombing.

What emerged from these joint efforts was a rare creature in the otherwise tumultuous environs of Washington in early 1996—broad bipartisan support in both the Senate and the House for passage of the aptly named "Anti-Terrorism and Effective Death Penalty Act." Democrats and Republicans joined together to support the bill, both sides of the aisle attempting to satisfy important and highly visible—and vocal—constituents who would loudly applaud their efforts. Democrats were relieved that they had been able to garner joint credit for the legis-lation and thus deprive Gingrich of sole credit. And as the bill was sent to the White House for the President's signature, the Lockerbie and Oklahoma City families both felt relieved that their alliance in Washington would comfort them in their still-prevalent grief.

The handsome, eloquent President with the soft southern drawl was also happy to share the limelight with the families when they gathered to watch him sign the bill on the White House lawn on 24 April 1996. Like his colleagues down Pennsylvania Avenue, Bill Clinton appreciated the political opportunity to be associated with the Lockerbie and Oklahoma City causes. In his remarks, Clinton paid homage to "all of the family members of Americans slain by terrorists and to the survivors of terrorism," specifically thanking the Lockerbie and Oklahoma City families, as well as other victims who had lost family members and children in Israel.

One person he asked to join him at the signing was a young member of his own staff, who was serving in a very junior capacity on the National Security Council. Andrew Kerr had been living in Beirut when his father, Malcolm, was assassinated by Iranian-backed members of Hezbollah while emerging from an elevator on his way to his office as President of the American University of Beirut. Andrew had been a 15-year-old boy when his father was killed, and he had sworn that he would somehow seek vengeance for his murder. The legislation his boss was signing in front of him might open the door to allow his family to pursue those responsible. A few years later, our law firm would handle Andrew and his family's case against Iran.

THE LEGISLATION THAT had been passed by a large bipartisan margin and signed with great fanfare by President Clinton received great coverage in the national press. It promised to limit greatly the time and manner in which prisoners could drag out their appeals and other challenges to death penalty convictions through the time-honored prac-tice of habeas corpus petitions in federal and state courts. This was a "tough-on-criminals" law, and that message went out forcibly. The Department of Justice would sort out the consequences of this law if it obtained a guilty verdict and death penalty in the Oklahoma City bombing case.

But over at the Department of State in Washington's Foggy Bottom neighborhood, the "anti-terrorism" portion of the hybrid bill was causing the professionals who managed the daily challenges of the country's foreign policy serious concerns. Obviously, the Lockerbie families and their lawyers would quickly file new lawsuits against Libya for large damages claims, throwing open the federal courthouse door. Other American victims of Libyan and Iranian terrorism would also contemplate filing suits, and the State Department's long-stated concerns about how such a process would impact their ability to manage foreign relations was the subject of much debate.

The law had only added a few small provisions to the Foreign Sovereign Immunities Act, but they were of enormous importance. In short, any country listed by the Department of State as a "state sponsor of terrorism" could be sued by American victims of terrorism. To the new law, Congress added a new "terrorism exception" to immunity, sweeping aside centuries of sovereign immunity that even rogue nations had enjoyed. Terrorist acts included "torture, extrajudicial killing, aircraft sabotage, hostage-taking" or even providing support for such activities. Since Libya had been listed as a sponsor of terrorism since 1979, it automatically could be sued. Iran had been added to the list in 1984, and so American victims could now immediately begin suing Iran in federal court as well.

The other significant addition to the new law was that anyone who was able to obtain a court award against a terrorist state could then enforce that judgment by trying to seize commercial assets of that country anywhere in the US. This was a huge change in the law, and the State Department was extremely nervous about the consequences.

As the diplomats had noted to Congress, the new law might create a conflict between the families suing Libya and the US government itself, since three separate presidents had insisted—through the UN sanctions and other measures—that Libya pay compensation for the Lockerbie attack directly to the US government on behalf of the families. This had been the traditional method for asserting international claims between countries. Now Congress had put that authority in the hands of families, their lawyers and federal judges who would preside over these cases.

A new legal era had arrived for the President and his diplomats. It would have far-reaching consequences and open up a new chapter in my professional life that would eventually lead me to become deeply involved in the UTA 772 bombing, as well as several other terrorism cases, over the next twenty years.

* * *

IN PARIS, BRUGUIÈRE and his team were not concerned with the political developments and intrigues taking place in Washington. Oklahoma City was a purely domestic issue of little concern to the French. France did not allow lawsuits against countries—the doctrine of sovereign immunity was well established, and not likely to change. The French and African families whose loved ones were killed when UTA 772 exploded and crashed in the Ténéré desert did not dream of public litigation against Libya or huge damages awards from Qaddafi's treasury. That was for the Americans and their silly approach to justice. Nor were any lawsuits planned against UTA since the chance of prevailing under the Warsaw Convention standard was so small, and UTA's insurance carrier had already paid some small amounts to the families.

In addition, France had not demanded compensation from Libya as part of the United Nations sanctions—it had merely insisted that Qaddafi cooperate with Bruguière's investigation. Gaddafi's letter to President Chirac made clear that none of the Libyans charged with the UTA 772 bombing would be extradited to face murder charges in Paris. At least that was his position in the diplomatic Kabuki dance.

After the French investigators had returned to Paris from their visit to Tripoli, Bruguière had decided to add two more international arrest warrants to his list in January 1997. It was clear to the investigating magistrate that Issa al-Shibani had been directly involved in procuring the bomb and timer materials shortly before the DC-10 went down in the Ténéré desert and that Abdelsalam Hammouda had acted in Brazzaville to coordinate and follow up on the plot. Thus, Shibani and Hammouda were the subject of fresh arrest warrants. Although it was clear that Moussa Koussa had played a role in the plot through his oversight of Mathaba, whose agents had carried out the conspiracy in Brazzaville, Bruguière could not directly tie Koussa to the crime. A warrant for him would have to await more evidence.

Now there were six prominent Libyan officials and agents subject to French arrest warrants—Senoussi, Shibani, Hammouda, Naeli, Musbah and Elazragh. Bruguière knew that Qaddafi was not simply going to hand them over to the authorities in Paris for a murder trial. This would require a diplomatic solution, something he could not directly control given the obvious fact that he was really charging the Libyan State—and, by implication, its leader—with carrying out the killing of 170 people. But issuing the arrest warrants would ensure that all six suspects remained inside Libya—comfortably, of course—since any effort to travel would trigger the Interpol red notice, their arrest in any other country, and their extradition to Paris to stand trial.

Bruguière continued to be patient. Eight years had now passed since the destruction of the DC-10. He knew that more time would be needed if he were finally to arrest these suspects and bring them to justice. His team continued to prepare their case—they did not know any other way. But they could not have predicted the political events that were to take place.

Chapter 10

The Getaway

THE PASSAGE OF time appeared to provide Qaddafi with some room to maneuver even within the confines of his isolation. By early 1998, the United Nations sanctions had been in effect for almost six years. Despite the hardships and inconvenience these penalties placed on his regime, Qaddafi had avoided the most draconian sanction—an international ban on exporting and selling Libya's vast oil and gas reserves. Too many countries depended on Libya's most valuable natural resource; thus, billions of dollars in revenues continued to pour into its treasury. This took out much of the sting of the sanctions. He might have been a brutal despot and sponsor of terrorism, but Qaddafi's bank accounts made him the ruler of an incredibly rich country.

Even the existing international sanctions were difficult to enforce. Many of the countries that had supported the UN in 1991 and 1992 votes had lost interest in or patience with the Great Leader's antics. He had been publicly rebuked for his terror in the 1980s, but the world's business must go on, and almost a decade had passed since the Lockerbie and UTA bombings. Despite the continuing efforts of the US and UK to keep Libya on the front burner, the fact that there were no further major terrorist actions directly attributable to Qaddafi's regime made their advocacy difficult to carry.

On the criminal front, the US and UK prosecutors were losing hope that the two Libyan agents charged with the Pan Am 103 Lockerbie bombing would ever be brought to justice. Qaddafi did not appear willing to surrender them, despite repeated demands. But the Leader knew that he had to find a reasonable way out of his isolation. A deal of some sort might be possible, but the terms might be difficult for him—or the Americans and British, for that matter—to accept.

In Paris, Bruguière felt that President Chirac was not doing anything to press Qaddafi about the six Libyan suspects in the UTA 772 criminal case. The French President was happy to allow his American and British counterparts to take the leading role in the criminal sphere. He had sent quiet messages to Qaddafi in response to the Leader's 1996 letter seeking a rapprochement. Chirac was also biding his time, looking for an opening that would provide him, and France, with some advantage. The unified front that France had put forward in the early 1990s with the Americans and British to isolate Libya was no longer in his interest. French oil companies were anxious to exploit the lucrative oil and gas fields under Qaddafi's control. Business was business, and French diplomacy under Chirac fully appreciated this reality.

Bruguière knew that, left to his own devices, Chirac might not support his efforts to bring the men to face justice in France. Employing his own approach, in January 1998 he formally sent his files for the entire UTA 772 investigation to the Paris Prosecutor's Office, which would prepare the criminal murder indictments against the six suspects.

By June, the Prosecutor had completed the process, and the Paris criminal case for the murder of 170 people on board UTA 772 commenced. The Court of Appeals of Paris issued the indictments at the direction of the prosecutor. Bruguière knew that Chirac and his political appointees could not stop these judicial efforts and hoped it would influence Chirac to pressure Libya to produce the suspects for trial before the diplomatic deals were done and the suspects placed beyond the reach of the criminal process.

The lengthy criminal indictment of the six Libyans listed the name of each of the 170 persons who had died on the DC-10, including that of Mangatany, the unsuspecting African who probably had been killed by his own Libyan handlers as he traveled to Paris with the booby-trapped suitcase. As Bruguière figured, Mangatany did not know he was going to die on the flight, but instead was misled to believe the bomb was being brought to Paris for some other attack. Such a "double game" was a Libyan trademark. It also was convenient for the Libyans, as the link to them was supposed to be cut when Mangatany perished in the crash. Only the thoroughness of Bruguière's investigation, and some luck, had thwarted the Libyan plan to cover its tracks.

Qaddafi saw that he could reduce the international pressure on his regime by continuing to drive a wedge between the Americans and British and their French ally. Quietly reaching out to Chirac, he made clear that a political deal would reap France large economic benefits, at the expense of the American and British oil companies that also desired to return to Libya after so many years of fractured relations. Seeing that Chirac would not press him on the criminal front, Qaddafi continued to insist that he could not surrender the Libyans charged with the UTA 772 bombing. Ironically, he knew that the French Constitution prohibited the extradition of French citizens living in France to other countries, so he had his lawyers in Libya and Paris construct an argument that Libya would respect French law in this area, which of course meant that Libya similarly could not, and thus would not, extradite its own citizens to Paris to stand trial. French law was fair, he noted, and so Libya would respect it.

Accepting Qaddafi's position, Chirac agreed that France would not press Libya to surrender any of the suspects charged with murder. But to save face, he wanted Qaddafi to agree that Libya, as a sovereign government, would respect whatever legal process was carried out by the French courts. So long as the suspects could remain in Libya, the Leader was happy to oblige the French President's request.

All of these discussions were conducted through the most secretive channels. Bruguière and the Paris prosecutors were informed only after the fact. Once they learned that the French President had agreed that the suspects charged with the greatest terrorist attack on France in history would remain free, they were extremely upset. Years of international investigation, interviews and painstaking detective work were being undone by Le Bulldozer. Chirac was seeing the bigger picture, his aides informed Bruguière and the prosecutors. Restoring French–Libyan relations was paramount. It was good for French business interests, especially the giant French energy company Total, and a deal would open up routes to other potential trade—many French workers would benefit from the orders for goods and services. Chirac prided himself on coming up with practical solutions.

The families of those killed on UTA 772 were also stunned by Chirac's "deal with the Devil." They had watched Bruguière and his team put the case together piece by piece and had patiently waited for the slow wheels of French justice to grind their way towards the conviction of those persons responsible for the deaths of their loved ones. They had hoped that they would be able to participate in a murder trial in Paris, since under French law victims of the crime and their families could join in the case with the prosecutor, examine the evidence and otherwise bear witness to the pursuit of justice.

As Chirac's political deal was announced there was an even greater disappointment for the UTA 772 families. It was decided that the prosecutor's office would proceed with the trial of the Libyan suspects, but without their presence. The accused would be tried in absentia, six empty chairs signifying their symbolic response to the murder charges. The Libyan government would not object to this procedure—after all, it was consistent with French law—and at least Chirac could then say he had brought the UTA case to closure for all parties concerned. The families would see the vast array of evidence presented in a formal courtroom setting before a panel of judges, the investigators and prosecutors could demonstrate the quality and importance of their years of dedicated work, and the resources devoted to the biggest murder case in French history would not go to waste.

This was Chirac's plan—to balance all the competing factors and come up with a practical solution. French Justice would be served, he proudly stated.

Those charged with the responsibility to carry out French justice were aghast. A trial in absentia would be a farce worthy of the Paris Opera. Bruguière and his team could not believe that the nine years they had devoted to the case would come to such an unsatisfactory and embarrassing end.

* * *

QADDAFI NOW HAD put in place the first half of his plan. With Chirac willing to drop any demand that Libya turn over the six suspects charged with blowing up the DC-10, he turned to the issue of what to do about Pan Am 103 and Lockerbie. Dealing with the British and Americans would be more complicated than cutting deals with the pliant Chirac.

The biggest problem for Qaddafi was that the Lockerbie prosecutors were demanding that the two Libyan agents charged with putting the suitcase bomb into Pan Am's interline system be turned over for a trial. In contrast to Chirac, neither the US nor the UK could politically afford to drop the criminal case or conduct a trial that was little more than a farce. Indeed, that was the principal basis for the United Nations sanctions back in the early 1990s.

The Libyans had dropped subtle hints that they might be willing to consider allowing the two suspects to be tried in some sort of neutral court, but these feelers were never clarified when the diplomats pressed for confirmation. Ironically, one of the biggest concerns for Qaddafi was that the two suspects charged with the Lockerbie bombing might face the death penalty if convicted in an American court of law. The 1996 Anti-Terrorism and Effective Death Penalty Act, by its literal title, was enough to convince the Libyans that US-style justice posed far too great a risk, for the accused as well as the Qaddafi regime itself. The Leader could not afford to surrender the men if there was even a remote chance they might be executed, or turn state's evidence and confirm the Libyan role in the crime. Even a despot has to worry about losing face with his own people. The recent legislation enacted by Congress in response to the Oklahoma City bombing made such a deal impossible.

With the US legal system eliminated as an option, the Libyans floated subtle suggestions that they might consider allowing the two suspects to be tried in a special Scottish court, but not within the UK itself. One suggestion raised by the Libyans was the creation of a special Scottish court sitting at The Hague, Netherlands, which traditionally served as a neutral forum for international courts and arbitrations. Indeed, the International Court of Justice was located in The Hague, and Libya had brought claims in that venue to complain that the United Nations sanctions themselves were in violation of international law. That case had not produced any positive rulings for Qaddafi, but neither was this a hostile venue. Still, the Libyans were vague about what they were willing to do even in The Hague.

From the perspective of the US and UK, Libya's subtle suggestions were not fully understood, and many diplomats believed they were just another bluff by the Leader, buying more time to see how events played out. But the allies were running out of realistic options and were concerned that if they did not come up with some sort of solution the criminal trial of the two Lockerbie suspects might never occur. Moreover, the political pressure from the Pan Am 103 Lockerbie families and the tremendous media attention they continued to generate made such an outcome too painful to bear.

After quietly clearing the possibility with the Dutch government, the US and UK decided to call Qaddafi's bluff. They proposed that a special Scottish criminal court sit in The Hague to try the two Libyan suspects for the Pan Am 103 Lockerbie murders, under Scottish law. To make the proposal even more palatable to the Libyans, they also made clear that the court would only consist of three professional judges—there would not be a jury. This would push the emotional temperature of the trial even lower and help ensure that the evidence was reviewed in a professional and low-key manner. It might even increase the chances of an acquittal, given that the Pan Am 103 evidence—in contrast to Bruguière's dynamic proof of Libyan responsibility for the UTA bombing—was thin and mostly circumstantial.

To host the trial, the UK and US proposed that the special court sit in an abandoned US Air Force base called Camp Zeist, about forty miles from The Hague. The United Nations would issue the necessary resolution to make sure that this unique creature of Scottish law and procedure would not be subject to Dutch law—the notion of independent Dutch judges reviewing the proceedings was unacceptable to anyone involved in putting the process together. To accommodate the Libyans further, the allies also promised that the UN sanctions would be lifted if Libya actually produced the two suspects for the trial. This was the closest Qaddafi had yet come to stepping out of isolation.

The proposal was discussed, negotiated and revised by all the parties for much of 1998 and into 1999. Qaddafi was still playing for time. He wanted the French process regarding UTA 772 to move along before committing to anything in the Pan Am 103 Lockerbie arena. Divide and conquer was the Leader's approach to reign and life.

IN ACCORDANCE WITH Qaddafi's plan, in Paris, the trial of the six Libyans moved forward—it was to be in absentia and without any chance of actually bringing them to justice. The French and African victims considered it a farce.

Convening a special three-judge Court of Assize, or criminal court, the French prosecutors presented the mountain of evidence and testimony gathered by Bruguière and his team over the last nine years. Participating alongside the prosecutors were a number of prominent French criminal and human rights lawyers, acting for several dozen UTA 772 victim families. Taking advantage of their rights as victims to review the evidence and ask questions of the investigators on the record, the lawyers were able to pass along to their clients some of the more critical evidence that uncovered the Libyan plot to blow up UTA 772.

Given the large number of French citizens killed on the DC-10, several victims helped form and support an organization for terrorist victims and their families—SOS Attentats. This was important, since the evidence submitted by the prosecutor was not generally available to the public, even in a public trial. No one was allowed to review it unless party to the case—prosecutor, judge, victim and defendant, through their counsel. Reporters and others could not access the court file. SOS Attentats would make sure it kept a complete set of the criminal court file, especially Bruguière's remarkable forensic evidence and reports. This would become an essential ingredient in my later efforts in the US to hold Libya accountable for the UTA 772 bombing.

By March 1999, the Avocat Général prosecutors had finished presenting their case against the six absent defendants. The three judges and their staff had taken the time to review the record of almost ten years of first-class detective work. Their written verdict convicted all six Libyans of murder and they were each sentenced in absentia to life imprisonment. The written verdict set out the facts assembled by Bruguière's investigation and carefully summarized how each of the six accused Libyans had played a prominent role in placing the suitcase bomb on UTA Flight 772.

In compliance with French law, the verdict was posted in the court-room of the Court of Assize in Paris, as well as on the front door of the Paris town hall. For centuries, criminal convictions had been posted in this manner so that all would know of the result of French justice.

Pursuant to French law, the victims who had participated in the trial through their counsel were awarded civil damage judgments against the six convicted men. This reflected the moral and economic damages the victims suffered from their untimely death at the hands of Qaddafi's agents. When the francs were added together, the total was the equivalent of approximately $31 million.

The French press widely reported the verdict, although it received scant notice beyond France and a few of its former colonies in Africa. Chirac's government spoke reverently of how the murder verdict and associated civil awards vindicated the rights of the victims and established a fitting closure to the biggest terrorist attack in French history.

By September the Libyan government had sent a wire payment to the French Trésor public—public treasury—for $31 million in full payment for the civil damages against the six convicted men, just as Qaddafi had promised to Chirac. The French government applied almost half the funds to cover court and administrative costs. The rest would be distributed to the families who had participated in the Paris trial. None would receive checks anywhere approaching the type of recoveries already obtained by the Pan Am families from their New York case.

* * *

HAVING SUCCESSFULLY CONSTRUCTED a face-saving method for resolving the UTA 772 criminal charges in Paris without so much as lifting a finger and in an amount that, for him, was pennies, Qaddafi was ready to accept the US–UK proposal for resolving the criminal charges against the two Libyans charged with the bombing of Pan Am 103. Just weeks after the Paris Court of Assize issued its murder convictions in absentia, his diplomats put their signatures on the Pan Am 103 Lockerbie criminal deal.

With the closure of the French proceedings and increased pressure at the United Nations to move ahead with Libyan rapprochement with the West, Qaddafi wanted to ensure that any deal regarding the two men charged with the Lockerbie bombing would be limited to a proceeding solely against them as individuals and not the Libyan State. Qaddafi wanted a guarantee that the Libyans would be returned to Tripoli if they were acquitted and he insisted that international observers sit in on the trial so that he could assure his own people that any biased or improper procedures would be quickly reported.

Critically, Qaddafi demanded that any agreement to produce the two Libyans to the special criminal court in The Hague would not be used to challenge the legitimacy of his own regime or the sovereign rights of his country. Based on the knowledge gained from his own thirty years in power, he suspected that, once surrendered, the suspects might lose some of their revolutionary zeal and implicate other Libyan officials in the Pan Am 103 Lockerbie plot, including their Leader. He even was concerned that they might succumb to pressure under torture to confess "falsely" their crimes and turn on him. Qaddafi assumed that all government officials would behave like him if given the chance. He had survived for thirty years using that very logic and practice.

Once the deal was finalized to Qaddafi's satisfaction, the Scottish authorities made the final arrangements for the trial at Camp Zeist. Qaddafi insisted that the two Libyans travel from Tripoli to the Netherlands on a United Nations plane, accompanied by security agents of the United Nations, so that he could say that they had voluntarily traveled to the court and surrendered on their own behalf. The UN personnel then handed the suspects over to the Dutch authorities, who turned them over to the Scottish police so that the UK formally took custody of them for trial.

The actual trial began on 3 May 2000. All the witnesses and evidence supporting the charges were brought to The Hague for presentation to the special Scottish court. The men stood trial for killing the 259 passengers and crew of Pan Am 103 as well as 11 unsuspecting people 30,000 feet below the explosion of the suitcase bomb. Consistent with the political deal with Qaddafi, the Scottish prosecutors focused their evidence and arguments on the role the individuals played in carrying out the plot. They made sure to stress that Libyan government agents played an unspecified role in the bombing. However, the murder charges did not require that they prove as an element of the crime that anyone other than the two suspects was responsible. The government of Libya was not on trial; neither was Qaddafi or his regime. So was the deal between all the concerned governments and the United Nations.

Defended by very competent Scottish and English lawyers, the Libyans chose not to take the stand in their own defense, an absolute right under Scottish and common law that could not be held against them by the judges. Instead, the defense lawyers attacked the credibility of the forensic and documentary proof linking the suspects to the bomb. They did not deny that a sinister plot had been carried out by someone intending to commit mass murder, but they attempted to impeach the prosecutor's witnesses and raised doubts about the sufficiency of the evidence against the accused Libyans. They also raised the specter that other terrorist groups from the Middle East had every incentive, and opportunity, to place a bomb on Pan Am 103.

As with the UTA families and the Paris trial of the six absent Libyans, many Lockerbie families attended the Scottish trial in the Netherlands, sitting in the courtroom for months as the evidence was slowly and methodically presented and challenged. The US and UK governments also set up a television feed of the trial so that the victims could watch the proceedings back in the US and UK. But they could only sit and observe. Scottish law did not allow them to participate, in contrast to the UTA 772 families, whose lawyers actively participated in the Paris trial.

After eight months of testimony and legal arguments, the Scottish judges issued their decision on 31 January 2001. To the shock of the families and prosecutors, one of the Libyans, Lamin Khalifah Fhimah, was found "not proven" guilty of any charges. He was quickly escorted out of the court complex and flown back to Libya within hours of the verdict. The second suspect was found guilty of placing the suitcase bomb into the baggage flow at Malta's airport, for transit to Frankfurt and then Heathrow. The judges noted that the Libyan government had some involvement in the plot, but did not make any specific findings or conclusions that held Qaddafi and his regime responsible. It simply stated that the plot "was of Libyan origin."

The court did not mention any other Libyans who might have been involved. The Leader's name was never noted. They were also unable to articulate any motive for the bombing. The Scottish court then sentenced the second Libyan to life imprisonment, recommending he serve at least twenty years before any consideration of parole, pardon or release.

Abdelbaset Ali Mohmed al-Megrahi, the only Libyan who would ever be convicted of the Pan Am 103 Lockerbie bombing, was taken to Scotland to begin his prison sentence. His lawyers noted an appeal, and under Scottish law it would take some time for the appellate court back in Scotland to review and analyze the verdict. The defense lawyers vowed that his conviction would be overturned, based on the thin, circumstantial evidence against him and the many violations of law and procedure in the trial.

As predicted, Libya announced to the world that an innocent man had been convicted by a prejudiced court. But world opinion did not respond to Qaddafi's call, as it was considered Libya's own decision to allow the trial in The Hague, and any problems with the verdict would be reviewed on a full appeal. And, as everyone noted, one of the two suspects had beaten the charges and had safely returned to Libya. On the face of it, the unique trial had been conducted in a fair and transparent manner.

The split verdict left the Lockerbie families even more dissatisfied with the customized ad hoc criminal justice system that had been arranged by the politicians and diplomats. The US and UK governments were left with half a loaf, as the release of one of the two suspects demonstrated that the circumstantial evidence they had spent years collecting and organizing was thin gruel when examined by experienced and professional judges. But they had at least one conviction, if it would withstand review on appeal. With the second criminal trial now concluded, Qaddafi had achieved a fairly high measure of success.

Fhimah, who had been returned to Libya after he was released from the Scottish trial, was considered a national hero, and Qaddafi vowed to pursue Megrahi's appeal so that he too could safely return home. UTA 772 was now wrapped up after a farcical trial in Paris, and for no more than a token payment to the French Treasury, and his regime itself had emerged unscathed from the Scottish procedure. Qaddafi basked in the manner by which he had extricated himself and his government from years of economic and legal sanctions. His status as an outcast was coming to an end—he and his regime had not been held accountable for two of the most hideous acts of murder in aviation history.

The Leader had run the gamut of international sanctions, criminal trials and diplomatic condemnation. Vast revenues continued to flow from what seemed like unlimited supplies of oil and gas. The world was slowly welcoming Qaddafi back into the fold, holding its nose at his terrorist past and tolerating his eccentric behavior. It was also buying his limitless supply of oil.

The Great Leader of the Revolution was back on the world stage. He had skillfully solved his most serious political and legal problems through guile, patience and wealth, which had kept him in power for so many years. He genuinely believed that his problems were now behind him.

But Qaddafi did not appreciate that this was only the end of Act One. Act Two, and my own immersion into this saga, was about to begin.

Part II

The Journey for Justice

2001–2013

Chapter 11

Gemini

MY PLANE WAS in its final approach, the pilot gently guiding the Alitalia Boeing 737 low across the Mediterranean, the bright September sun reflecting off the cobalt-blue waters. Suddenly, the Italian landscape—golden fields and green cypress trees—came into focus outside the window as the aircraft descended towards Rome's Leonardo da Vinci–Fiumicino Airport.

As the aircraft pulled up to the gate, I sensed that the flight attendants were more tense and businesslike than normal. The cabin door opened and I walked out to the jetway. As I exited ahead of most of the other business-class passengers, I noticed several Arma dei Carabinieri—Italian armed police. They had black metal machine guns slung over their shoulders and crisp blue military caps tilted down over their brows, their grim faces closely examining each passenger walking off the plane.

Although I was normally oblivious to such things—my mind focused on the details of getting my bags, hailing a taxi, meeting my appointments in Rome over the next few days—it seemed that many of the people walking through Rome's airport were quiet, even reserved. This was not my memory of how Italians acted in their daily lives, their boisterous personalities an animated blend of talk, gesture and emotion.

I had been in Italy just a few months before, on vacation with my family, and had expected a repeat of that holiday atmosphere. Perhaps it was because the summer season had passed, I thought, and this is more what Rome is like when it gets back to business. I hauled my bag and briefcase out to the taxi stand, the intense Italian sun beating down. The smell of diesel fumes, the sounds of horns and engines, the voices of dozens of Italians jostling for rides and suitcases … this was more what I had experienced as a tourist.

Nodding to a dispatch supervisor, "Roma" my destination, I threw the bags into the trunk of a small Fiat taxi and slipped into the back seat, the hot leather and humid air causing my shirt and slacks to stick to the seats. The driver slammed his door shut, yelled out something in rapid-fire Italian to the dispatcher and floored the accelerator, despite the jumble of traffic and parked cars and buses. Now I felt that I was back in Rome. They drive like maniacs here. All the time. I groped for a seatbelt, but could not get my hand on one as they were jammed under the seat. Typical.

Sliding out of the dispatch line and onto the service road that led to the six-lane A-91 roadway to Rome, thirty kilometers away, the taxi driver was twisting the radio station dial. He switched from station to station in search of something. Even while busy with the radio, the driver was on his mobile phone, speaking rapidly to someone, in competition with the Italian voices on the radio. The volume was up high and the Fiat was filling with hot air as its speed picked up to over eighty kilometers an hour. I was tired after getting up early in Brussels, fighting my way to the airport, the jet lag of several days in Europe still throwing me off. I had spent several days in my law firm's Belgium office after flying in from Washington and was eagerly looking forward to several days in Rome to work on one of my cases. We were taking a video deposition of an important witness while enjoying the pleasures of the Eternal City.

As the taxi slipped in and out of lanes, the driver seemed to be getting overly excited, his radio blaring while he yelled into the phone tucked under his chin, one hand on the steering wheel, the other working the manual stick shift. Just as I was getting comfortable in the back seat, the air blowing in nicely through the open windows, the driver turned around and looked me straight in the eye.

"Americano?" he said in a heavy accent.

"Yes. Si," I replied, very anxious as he devoted only a limited portion of his attention to the high-speed traffic on the multi-lane highway. Other drivers were swerving in and out of lanes, cursing at each other, cigarettes dangling from their lips.

"Terrible, terrible," he said.

I did not understand what he meant, except that being an "Americano" was something terrible—a strange thing in a country usually quite welcoming to us!

"American. Si. Si," I replied, not sure what he was trying to say. He seemed distraught at this point; the radio spilled out words I could not understand.

"Terrible, terrible," I thought he said again. At least something that sounded like terrible.

He pointed to the radio as we raced along the highway, trying to get me to understand the voices. I was clueless, except that the radio voice sounded alarmed, or excited. Maybe it was a football match against some rival. Or perhaps some sort of Italian political debate.

"Terrible, terrible," he said over and over again.

Then, as he realized that I did not understand him, or the radio, he freed his right hand from the phone and stick shift to pick up a napkin on his seat. While driving at high speed, he started to draw something on the napkin as he pressed it against the steering wheel. He was intent on demonstrating something important. I was scared to death he would entirely forget to drive and have us both wind up in a twisted pile of metal on the side of this busy highway.

After fumbling with the napkin and a pen—the road was seemingly forgotten, and I tightly gripped the door handle—the taxi driver turned toward me and handed me a drawing.

"Gemini," he said. "Gemini."

On the napkin was a drawing of what looked like the Washington Monument, and so I assumed he was asking if I was from Washington.

"Si, yes," I replied. "Yes, I am from Washington." I was certainly curious how he would have guessed where I was from.

"No, No, No," he said, frustrated at his inability to communicate in English and my lack of any practical Italian. He took the napkin back, then drew another Washington Monument alongside the first, and handed it back to me.

"Gemini, Gemini," he said, half turned toward me and half attentive to the traffic.

"No, there is only one monument," I replied. "Uno, uno, just one."

"No, no," he insisted, pointing to the radio and the rapid on-air Italian voices.

I was clueless.

"Gemini, Gemini," he kept repeating. He did not know any other words in English. "America, terrible," he said as we sped into the outskirts of Rome, modern buildings and ancient city walls coming into view as we slowed down in the congested streets.

We arrived at my hotel and he handed me the napkin again.

"Terrible, terrible," he said. "Gemini, Gemini."

I quickly paid him in euros, grabbed my bags and pushed my way through the hotel's revolving door and into the cool, air-conditioned lobby. I walked up to the desk and presented my American passport and American Express card—the usual routine in foreign travel.

"Welcome to Roma, Signor Newberger," the desk clerk said in impeccable English, a slight Italian accent coming through. "We are so sorry for the terrible news from America."

Now I was really stunned—the hotel clerk said something terrible had happened in America. I had no idea, having been stuck on a flight from Brussels to Rome and lacking access to a television or radio.

"What are you talking about?" I asked nervously, now concerned that something might have happened in Washington, given my driver's drawing of the Washington Monument on his napkin.

"The planes, Signor. The planes. What a terrible thing," the clerk said.

I grabbed my key and went directly to the second floor to find my room. I opened the door, threw the bags down and immediately turned on the television. I was panicked. Nothing frightens a person more than the unknown. I flicked the channels, finally hit the familiar English voices of CNN and stared in disbelief at the screen. Here I was in a very nice hotel room in Rome, one of the most serene and historic cities in the world, on a beautiful and sunny afternoon, but I was watching in horror as the newscaster described again and again the jet planes smashing into the two World Trade Center towers in Lower Manhattan. The violence was repeated on loop, along with scenes of some sort of bombing or crash at the Pentagon. In Washington, near my home and family.

Gemini. The twins of Roman mythology. The taxi driver had been trying to tell me about the twin towers.

As I sat on the edge of the bed in my hotel room it became very clear there had been some sort of terrorist attack. The driver had not meant "terrible," I thought. He meant "terrorist." I picked up the phone and tried to call my wife at our home in Northern Virginia, but all overseas lines were jammed. On 11 September 2001, we were still wedded to landline telephones and television sets. These were the days before smartphones, convenient laptop computers and Blackberries. After over an hour I finally got through to one of my law firm partners in our London office. He told me that our firm's principal office in downtown Washington had been evacuated and everyone was fighting to get out of the city. Another attack might hit soon, and our offices were across the street from the National Headquarters of the FBI. My own office looked directly across Tenth Street at FBI Headquarters. My colleague did not have much more information at this point, but two jets had struck and destroyed the twin towers in New York, some sort of jet had crashed into the Pentagon, and apparently another plane was unaccounted for and might be headed for CIA Headquarters in Northern Virginia. My home was one mile from Langley, the massive CIA facility.

I really needed to reach my wife. My older daughter was in college in Philadelphia, but my two younger kids went to school near our home, and the CIA Headquarters. But all the phones to the United States were jammed. It was just me and CNN.

* * *

I HAD TRAVELED to Rome to conduct a videotape deposition of an important witness in a case I was handling at the federal court in Washington. The witness's name was Reginald Bartholomew, and he was the top executive for Merrill Lynch in Europe, Africa and the Middle

East. But my taking his testimony in Rome had nothing to do with his firm, or commercial or banking interests.

Bartholomew had served as the United States Ambassador to several countries—Spain, Italy, Lebanon—during an illustrious career in the Foreign Service. He had also held several important posts at the Department of State in Washington. I needed to record his testimony on video to show at a trial I was presenting the following month. Ironically, the federal judge in the case, Thomas Penfield Jackson, had been Bartholomew's roommate at Dartmouth many years earlier.

The subject of his testimony was his service as the US Ambassador to Lebanon in September 1984, when his Embassy was blown up by a suicide bomber driving a truck laden with explosives. Several US citizens were killed and many more injured. Bartholomew had been sitting in his office on the top floor of the East Beirut Embassy Annex, as it was called, the main ambassadorial building in the west of the city having been destroyed by another suicide truck bomber in April 1983. The bomb went off just as he was sitting down with the British Ambassador to discuss the never-ending intrigue and violence of Lebanese politics.

Bartholomew had been badly injured in the bombing. He had been pulled from under a huge cement slab by US Marine guards as dust, fumes and death consumed the building. But he had escaped with his life, something the Hezbollah attackers and their Iranian sponsors had not wanted. His testimony would be straightforward and riveting. Sitting in his well-appointed Merrill Lynch office preparing for the deposition, we both acknowledged the irony that the twin towers in New York also had collapsed in "pancake-style" from the force of the suicide explosions. Just like his Embassy back in September 1984.

I had brought a case against Iran for the family of one of the Americans killed in the September 1984 Embassy Annex bombing. Michael Wagner, a young Navy technician from a Christian family in rural North Carolina, had thrilled his family with stories of the exotic world of Beirut and the life the US Navy had allowed him to enjoy in overseas posts. That is, until he was killed by a terrorist bomb, destroying his family and his future.

* * *

AT THE TIME I arrived in Rome on 11 September 2001, my legal career had taken several interesting turns. I was in my mid-forties, a partner at Crowell & Moring, one of Washington's finest litigation firms, where we represented some of the most prestigious and successful corporations in the world. I had come to Washington in the early 1970s to attend college at George Washington and then law school at Georgetown, the city's premier training ground for young lawyers. After having the honor of clerking for one of the city's most respected federal judges, Harold H. Greene, I eventually joined the United States Attorney's Office, where I had the time of my life. I tried all sorts of cases and argued many appeals in the US Court of Appeals for the DC Circuit, considered the second most important court in the land after the US Supreme.

I had been recruited to Crowell & Moring to help build out their litigation practice, especially given my experience as an Assistant US Attorney and federal law clerk. At first, the cases were the usual mix of corporate, commercial and insurance disputes around the country that pay the bills, and the salaries, of big law firms. But shortly after I left government service and joined the land of billable hours, I began to get calls from unique clients about unique cases, usually requesting pro bono representation on some esoteric legal issues. One of those was a 1991 case under the Freedom of Information Act against the State Department to declassify the still-secret correspondence between President John F. Kennedy and Soviet Premier Nikita Khrushchev during the October 1962 Cuban Missile Crisis. The plaintiffs, my pro bono clients, were a professor at American University named Philip Brenner, who specialized in Cuban–American relations and politics, and a newly minted public interest group called the National Security Archive, which focused on compiling detailed records of historical events for scholars and journalists.

I had spent many years representing the State Department, the CIA and other federal agencies while in government and knew my way around those bureaucracies as well as the federal courthouse where such disputes usually wind up. After a bit of maneuvering, we were able to get the documents declassified, and, as a benefit, I was invited to travel to Cuba to participate in a conference about the events that had almost caused a nuclear war. Spending several days with Fidel Castro, Robert

McNamara and a bunch of Russians discussing the details of a historical event demonstrated to me that life at the big law firm might not be so boring after all.

This is where my non-traditional law practice began. A few years later, in 1994, I was asked to handle another pro bono case for a journalist who had spent seven years as a hostage in Lebanon as part of the infamous Iran–Contra crisis under President Reagan and the first President Bush. He wanted to find out what his own government had been doing during his long captivity and had heard that I might be able to help him out—free of charge, of course. I arranged for him to come down from New York where he was teaching a journalism course at Columbia and feel out the possibilities of working together. After a fun meeting in which we both realized that each was as big a smart ass as the other, I agreed to handle the matter and file a Freedom of Information Act case.

His name was Terry Anderson. This initial meeting with him was the first step in a long journey that would take me around the world, representing victims of terrorism, for the next twenty years.

* * *

IN LATE 1996, as I was handling Terry Anderson's case in Washington federal court under the Freedom of Information Act, he called me. I was on a fishing trip with some friends down in North Carolina's Outer Banks. Terry told me that he had been getting phone calls from several lawyers who wanted to represent him in a lawsuit against Iran under a new law recently enacted by Congress and signed by President Clinton. I had vaguely heard something about this new federal law, but was quite skeptical about Terry—or my law firm—chasing windmills. One big pro bono litigation on his behalf against our own government seemed like enough for the time being. Suing Iran was a whole different matter. And I did not want to push my luck at Crowell & Moring, who had been very supportive of my pro bono efforts while I otherwise was building a successful—meaning profitable—practice.

I told Terry that I thought he would be wasting his time pursuing such a case; since the law was untested, Iran might not show up to defend, and the chance of collecting on a court award was almost zero. Of course, I was talking to a man who had lived a tumultuous life, first as a US Marine in Vietnam, then as a hard-charging war correspondent for the Associated Press in South Africa. He then landed in Lebanon as Chief Middle East Correspondent, where he had been kidnapped in March 1985 outside his Beirut apartment and held as a hostage for almost seven years. His story was well known, and the brutality and torture of his captivity had been the subject of his book *Den of Lions*.

Terry had been the longest-held and most famous of the Lebanon hostages. Since coming home in December 1991 he had taught at Columbia, written books, made speeches and otherwise lived a very safe and rewarding life. He was co-chair, with legendary anchorman Walter Cronkite, of the Committee to Protect Journalists in New York, and was setting up a charitable organization of former Vietnam veterans to build schools in that country as a positive force in this beautiful but sad nation.

He agreed a lawsuit against Iran would not be worth his time at present, given how well his life was going, but said he would call me back if the prospect seemed more promising. I told him that sounded fine to me. This was the first advice I gave any client about the 1996 amendments to the Foreign Sovereign Immunities Act and its "terrorism exception." It was clearly not going to be the last.

ALMOST TWO YEARS later, Terry called me again. This time, he noted that Congress had passed another law that indicated there might be an opportunity to collect some money on a court award against Iran, at least according to the lawyers who continued to call him about filing a case on his behalf. He was the poster child for such a case, and lawyers around the country were offering to represent him free of charge.

I told Terry that I would research the new law and get back to him. Without much effort, I reviewed what Congress had done in 1998 to make a possible collection on such a case feasible, particularly the new statutory language that called on the Justice and State Departments to assist anyone in collection efforts if he or she obtained such a court judgment. With this new law in hand, I discussed things with my law firm, whose skepticism was not surprising. No one had ever won such a case and the investment of time and costs might be very large indeed. Fortunately, Crowell & Moring was doing very well, I was very busy with many other billable and profitable matters, and the firm's management agreed to humor me and approved my handling Terry's case.

So now what?

Suing a foreign country is never easy, even under ideal circumstances. Suing the Islamic Republic of Iran on behalf of a famous hostage, and for millions of dollars in damages, was an entirely new concept. After enlisting a few young associates to do some legal research and fact gathering, and with several more intense days with Terry to make sure we had the full story, we filed a complaint in Washington federal court in late 1998. Of course, the United States and Iran had broken off all formal diplomatic relations in 1979 after Iranian students stormed the US Embassy in Tehran and held a large number of Embassy employees as hostages for over four hundred days. That crisis had helped humiliate President Jimmy Carter and clear the way for the election of Ronald Reagan in 1980. The hostages were released at the very moment Reagan took the oath of office in front of the US Capitol under a deal in which the Algerian government had acted as an intermediary.

Thus, the "Algiers Accords" not only allowed for their release, but the Iranians made sure the agreement provided that the American hostages held in Tehran could not bring any claim for damages against Iran under international law—a waiver of American rights that both President Carter and President Reagan quickly and quietly agreed to as part of the deal. The Algiers Accords also set up an arbitration court in The Hague where the billions of commercial and property claims between the US and Iran arising from the 1979 Islamic Revolution could be sorted out over time. On that basis, the rights of Americans who had been tortured, beaten and held prisoner at the Tehran Embassy were disregarded and waived by their own government, but companies that had lost large sums and property to Iranian government expropriation could recover their losses in the special arbitration venue at The Hague. This political approach to national priorities—commercial and property interest versus those of terrorism victims—would come back to haunt me many years later.

With the complaint filed and a press release issued—Terry was, after all, a well-known figure—we began the slow and arduous process of having the complaint actually served on Iran through diplomatic channels. The lack of an Iranian Embassy in Washington, combined with the special protection afforded sovereign countries from normal lawsuits, required us to have the federal court send the complaint—in both English and Farsi, Iran's first language—to the Department of State. In turn, State sent the complaint to the US Embassy in Berne, Switzerland, where it was then taken to the Swiss Ministry of Foreign Affairs. Switzerland had agreed to act as a liaison country for both the US and Iran and would transmit official communications between countries that did not otherwise speak to each other or carry out any sovereign business.

The Swiss then sent the complaint via diplomatic courier to their Embassy in Tehran, and from there it was directed to the Iranian Ministry of Foreign Affairs for the "official" service of process under international law. The entire process was then put into reverse by the Swiss, who drafted a diplomatic note—in Farsi, German and English—certifying that the service of process had been accomplished, which was then transmitted back to the US Embassy in Berne, and by courier to Washington. The Department of State then submitted all this paperwork—on high-grade paper and wrapped in the fancy seals and ribbons, all part of diplomacy—to the Clerk of the federal court in Washington.

With this act, Iran was now a defendant in the case of Terry Anderson v. Islamic Republic of Iran. This lumbering process had taken almost eight months. Now the lawsuit could commence. But would Iran appear to defend? We did not know. Prior to the passage of the 1996 terrorism exception amendment to the FSIA, Iran had appeared in court by hiring the former Department of Justice lawyer Bruno Ristau, who would raise a host of jurisdictional defenses that required the federal court to dismiss the case. Ristau had done so in several cases against Iran, Libya, North Korea and Iraq, and this was, of course, how the Lockerbie families' case against Libya had originally been dismissed. I fully expected the same response in Terry's case.

But the sixty-day period in which Iran had to appear and submit a defense expired. Nothing happened. No lawyers, no motions to dismiss, no filings of any sort. We quickly requested that the judge assigned to the case enter a default against Iran, hoping that might stir things up. There had been a small number of other cases brought against Iran under the new 1996 law, and they also had obtained a default. But none were as notorious as Terry's case, so we decided to press ahead.

The Judge hearing the case was well known. Thomas Penfield Jackson was in the middle of hearing the US government's antitrust case against Microsoft, and also would become quite familiar to the American populace by presiding over the criminal drug trial of Washington's flamboyant and incorrigible "Mayor for Life" Marion Barry. A Harvard-trained lawyer and Navy veteran whose father had established a respected law firm in Washington, Judge Jackson was right out of Central Casting. He was a veteran trial lawyer and Reagan appointee who loved being in the courtroom; his deep voice and silver hair atop a well-fed physique gave him the look of a real jurist. After a series of preliminary motions and scheduling issues, he set down the Terry Anderson case for trial by spring 2000. To do so, he declared a one-week break in the Microsoft trial that was dominating headlines across the country.

Without a defendant and counsel at the defense table, this was a rather one-sided affair. But the law anticipated such circumstances and did not allow the plaintiff a free ride even when the defendant chose not to appear. Instead, the plaintiff in such a case was required to present evidence "satisfactory to the court" in order to obtain a judgment on the merits and the measure of damages. Terry described his experience as a hostage, and his wife, Madeleine, related how her husband was kidnapped while she was pregnant with their first child. Their teenage daughter Sulome did not meet her father until he was released, when she was seven.

Terry and I knew that the chances of collecting on any judgment would turn on more than just an award from Judge Jackson. There still was no realistic method for collecting on an award, and Congress and probably President Clinton would need to take further action to help Terry and the small number of other people who had Iran lawsuits. So the first thing we did was turn up the media heat at the trial.

On the second trial day, we brought in Dan Rather, at the time the best-known television network anchorman in the country and the successor to Walter Cronkite at CBS Evening News. An old friend of Terry's, Dan had agreed to appear in the case and describe for Judge Jackson how Terry's years of captivity had seriously undermined the ability of news organizations, including CBS, to cover sensitive hotspots such as Lebanon. He spoke for over two hours, answering every question I had been able to think of in his office up in New York during our prep, the Judge totally engrossed and impressed with his testimony and its impact. I noticed that a number of spectators had come into the courtroom to hear Dan Rather testify, word having got out that a celebrity was on the stand.

To round things out, I also brought in Gene Roberts, the former managing editor of the *New York Times* and *Philadelphia Inquirer*, who also helped run the Pulitzer Prize Committee for journalism. Roberts was one of the most respected print journalists in the country, and another good friend of Terry's. His testimony, like Rather's, made clear that the impact of Terry's captivity went far beyond the personal lives of this one family.

Finally, I called Ambassador Robert Oakley, the former director of counter-terrorism for the US government and an expert on Iran's role in kidnapping and holding hostages such as Terry. His testimony left no doubt that the Islamic Republic of Iran was responsible for this and most other terrorism in Lebanon.

A few months later, Judge Jackson issued his judgment. I was in New Orleans for a court hearing when I heard from one of my associates that the ruling had been received at our office. Terry and his family were awarded almost $40 million in compensatory damages against Iran for his kidnapping and seven-year ordeal. Judge Jackson's published opinion not only described the horror of Terry's years as a hostage but also the harm to American journalism that Iran and its agent, Hezbollah, had caused. The ruling was picked up around the globe thanks to a strong storyline by the Associated Press, Terry's former employer, and a photo taken outside the Washington federal courthouse of me, Terry and his daughter Sulome. I received phone calls and e-mails from people who saw the photo on the front page of their newspapers as far away as Asia.

Yet even with a court award in hand and the accompanying world-wide publicity, we did not know how to collect any money. We had to get creative.

* * *

ONE OF THE "leftovers" from the 1980 Iran–US settlement that came out of the Algiers Accords was that the Pentagon and Treasury were still holding almost $400 million in Iranian government funds. These had been paid by the late Shah of Iran for military equipment that was never delivered because of the Islamic Revolution and collapse of relations between the two countries. It had been sitting in government accounts for over twenty years as the arbitration proceedings in The Hague crept along.

Knowing such an action might stir the pot, I requested that Judge Jackson issue a writ of attachment on those foreign military sales (FMS) accounts to satisfy the Anderson award. He gladly agreed, and within a few days Terry, my partner Karen Hastie Williams and I were sitting in the ornate meeting room of the Secretary of the Treasury, next to the White House. Deputy Treasury Secretary Stuart Eizenstat was surrounded by over a dozen lawyers and aides from State, Treasury, Justice and the Pentagon. Terry was praised as a national hero and role model. But after the compliments were concluded, Eizenstat soberly stated that there was nothing the US government could do to help Terry satisfy his court judgment. The United States would fight us in court on the writ of attachment. The writ would not be enforced because, Eizenstat asserted, only Congress could waive the immunity of the US government. This was money held by the President, he made clear, and it was to be used as a bargaining chip in any future negotiations with Iran, not to pay default judgments such as Terry's.

So, after all our efforts, the government was going to oppose our strategy to make Iran pay for its support of terrorism. It was as though they were defending Iran itself. Terry's famous temper flared and he did not spare the Deputy Secretary or his staff. I could tell they were embarrassed. But policy was policy, law was law, and human emotions were clearly not going to carry the day. We left the Treasury building and mapped out our next move.

* * *

CAPITOL HILL IS nothing like a federal courtroom. The two bodies of the Senate and the House of Representatives are a swirling vortex of coalitions, allies, causes, speeches and favors. The legislative process, as German Chancellor Bismarck observed, is like making sausages: a lot of ingredients, a lot of blood, a lot of things you do not want to know about when it is served. This is how laws are made.

We learned that the 1996 FSIA law that had allowed the terrorism lawsuits to proceed was the result of a coalition of families from very different parts of the country who had suffered unspeakable losses of life and loved ones—the Pan Am 103 Lockerbie families in the New York metropolitan region and the Oklahoma City families. The Lockerbie families had filed their own lawsuit against Libya up in New York, but that did not have much effect on our cases against Iran. In contrast to Iran, Libya had chosen to defend the Lockerbie case, and was mounting a serious jurisdictional defense, as far as I could tell. Iran was absent in our case and we needed another ally. It did not take long to find more than one.

A small group of families with claims and court cases against Iran came together. The family of Alisa Flatow, a young American student from Massachusetts' Brandeis University, killed by a terrorist attack on a bus in the Gaza Strip, had also filed a case; the federal judge hearing their claim, Royce C. Lamberth, had issued a thorough and comprehensive ruling in their favor. I knew Judge Lamberth quite well, as he had been my boss in the US Attorney's office before going on the federal bench, and my oldest daughter would later serve as his law clerk. Over the next few years he would issue some of the most important judgments and rulings about Iranian terrorism. The Flatow award was his first.

A few other hostages who had been held for less time than Terry in Lebanon also brought claims. But the number of people with Iranian judgments was very small. The large and well-organized group of Pan Am 103 Lockerbie families was pursuing a different path up in New

York federal court, so was not of assistance to our cause. Lockerbie was also in its own orbit—this was the one terrorist attack that everyone knew about.

Luckily, the allies we needed on Capitol Hill came forward. They were from Florida and all had Spanish names—the families of Cuban Americans killed by Castro's Air Force when their small plane, which had been searching the Florida Straits for refugees from Cuba floating on rafts, was shot down in cold blood. Their organization, Brothers to the Rescue, had supported a terrorism case against Cuba, which also was on the State Department's list of terrorist states, and had obtained a large judgment from the federal court in Miami. The families also were having a difficult time collecting on their judgment—as with the Iranian FMS account at the Pentagon, the US government would not release frozen Cuban assets. The group had hired a Washington lobbyist to assist them in their efforts.

Joining forces, the victims of Iranian terrorism, including Terry, and the Cuban victims convinced a bipartisan group of Senators to enact a law that would direct the President to release frozen assets—both Iranian and Cuban—to pay at least those judgments that had so far been issued by the federal courts. I was sitting in the Senate Gallery with Terry and my partner Karen when the Justice for Victims of Terrorism bill was enacted. With a unanimous vote of approval of the Senate bill in the House the next day, it was sent down Pennsylvania Avenue to President Clinton for what we hoped would be his signature.

But our experience with Secretary Eizenstat and his government lawyers made us nervous. We knew that State had serious concerns about releasing any frozen Iranian assets, which they hoped to employ as leverage in the arbitration process at The Hague. The law we had worked hard to just get passed by Congress—bipartisan and unanimous, a feel-good for all concerned—was contrary to anything State had dealt with in the past. It was a direct disruption of State's, and the President's, authority to conduct foreign policy. President Clinton might heed advisers' warnings and veto the bill, perhaps causing Congress to pause before pushing it forward again.

Fortunately for all the victim families, President Clinton had a keen ear for political rhythms and, rejecting the advice of his own State

Department, signed the bill into law. The political winds were too strong to resist, and Clinton had, of course, signed the 1996 law—with much fanfare and ceremony—that had allowed these lawsuits to be pursued in the first place.

By early 2001, things were looking pretty good. We had obtained a new law that required the release of substantial funds, and the historic Anderson judgment against Iran was then paid, in full, within a short time. Terry and his family received a huge amount of money, as did the other families of the victims who also had obtained judgments. My law firm was quite pleased with the result—several years of hard work, serious investment and uncertain prospects had paid off—and was doubly pleased to read a front-page article in the *Washington Post* describing Terry's victory and collection in his case. His being so well known had drawn attention to his case on the Hill and at the White House, and the media gave his story the royal treatment.

Right after the *Post* article appeared, I started to get calls from people who wanted to hire Terry Anderson's lawyer. It was one of these new terrorism cases that had brought me to Italy.

* * *

SITTING IN THE ornate Merrill Lynch office in Rome, right after the 11 September attacks, I pondered the path that had brought me to Ambassador Bartholemew's deposition. We had collected the money for Terry's award back in March; then calls from other victims of terrorism had begun to pour in. The case for Michael Wagner, killed in the Beirut Embassy Annex in 1984, was one of the first. Indeed, it had come to my firm early enough to be added to the list of cases that would be paid out of the frozen foreign military sales (FMS) Iranian assets authorized by Congress and President Clinton. Thus, I put all my energies into making sure we gathered as much proof as possible to convince the presiding judge to award the Wagner family a large amount of damages for the tragic loss of their son. Ambassador Bartholemew's deposition was a key piece of evidence to convince Judge Jackson to award to the Wagner estate and family.

But unlike the Wagner family's case, most of the terror victim cases coming in had missed the chance to be included in the Justice for Victims of Terrorism Act. One involved the killing of another American hostage in Beirut by Libyan agents. In December 1984 Peter Kilburn, the librarian of the American University of Beirut, was kidnapped by Iranian-backed Hezbollah terrorists and was purchased from Hezbollah by Libyan agents for $1 million. Apparently, Libya and its ruler, Colonel Qaddafi, had sought to purchase and then kill an American hostage. This cold-blooded act of murder was in retaliation for President Reagan's decision to launch the military attack on Tripoli as punishment for Libya's bombing of the La Belle Disco in Berlin. I was preparing a case against Iran for Kilburn's kidnapping, and against Libya for his murder, but did not know how the Qaddafi regime would respond to the Libya portion of this hybrid case. This was my first case against Libya, and, as I was well aware, it was very different from the well-known Pan Am 103 Lockerbie case pending in New York. The proof and evidence of Libya's responsibility for Kilburn's murder was going to be difficult to gather.

The other large case being organized by my firm was on behalf of the American victims killed and injured in the earlier, and even more deadly, US Beirut Embassy bombing of April 1983. It was this event that had led to the opening of the Embassy Annex, which in turn was blown up one year later when Bartholomew served as Ambassador. A group of survivors from the 1983 Embassy bombing had read about the success of our action for Terry Anderson in the *Post* article, and many other victims were joining them in the case. As we met and discussed how best to proceed, some of these new clients mentioned that the former Ambassador in Beirut and his Deputy Chief of Mission (DCM), both of whom had survived the bombing, were available to assist our efforts.

Anne Dammarell had been terribly injured in the April 1983 attack and she ultimately became the lead plaintiff in the case that would bear her name. Anne mentioned that the former DCM in Beirut had lost his wife in a separate terrorist attack several years later. It had to do with an airplane crash, but she could not recall the specifics. Something to do with Africa, she noted.

Chapter 12
Chief of Mission

THE IMAGES OF the 11 September World Trade Center and Pentagon attacks were familiar to anyone with access to a television, computer, newspaper or magazine. Among those studying the violent and chaotic scenes from New York and Washington was the Great Leader of the Libyan Jamahiriya. In contrast to most world leaders, though, Qaddafi's interest in the events of 11 September were quite personal.

Long before the suicide flights struck the Twin Towers and the Pentagon, Al Qaeda had been the opposing side when it came to the Qaddafi regime. Despite his observance of fairly strict Muslim customs and habits, including a nationwide ban on alcohol, Qaddafi's cult of personality was anathema to the fundamentalist doctrine of Osama bin Laden and Al Qaeda. In the late 1990s, Qaddafi had offered the US his quiet assistance in the efforts to locate the members of this terrorist group and share intelligence that his own organization had been able to gather. Renegade groups like Al Qaeda were considered a threat to his regime, and his life.

Khalid Sheikh Mohammed Ali Fadden, one of Al Qaeda's principals who later planned the 11 September attacks, first became involved in terrorism in the United States in 1993, when his nephew and several associates drove an explosive-laden truck into the parking garage of one of the World Trade Center towers. The bomb had killed several civilians, injured hundreds and caused the entire building to be evacuated. But the terrorists' goal of collapsing this symbol of Western decadence had failed—the tower's structural integrity had not been adversely affected. Eight years later, the 11 September Al Qaeda attack finished the job.

In 1998, Al Qaeda attacked the US Embassies in Kenya and Tanzania, employing suicide truck bombers to inflict huge losses of lives and property. The tactics were copied from the attacks on the American Embassies in Beirut in 1983 and 1984, both of which were now familiar to me as active cases. A few years later, I would represent the families of the Americans killed in the Nairobi Embassy bombing in a suit against Sudan and Iran.

So, Qaddafi had closely studied the 11 September attacks. In keeping with the dictum that the enemy of my enemy is my ally, he had come to believe even before 11 September that Al Qaeda was a major threat to his regime, and his own life.

Several members of Al Qaeda had been arrested by Libyan security forces, but Qaddafi's offers to the West to cooperate in the hunt for bin Laden prior to 11 September had been rejected. President Clinton and his advisers had been overwhelmed by political and diplomatic pressures to compel Qaddafi to turn over the two accused Lockerbie suspects for trial. Working alongside a regime that had killed so many Americans and which had not cooperated in enquiries into the horrific bombing over Scotland was simply too much for the US government to bear. Hence Qaddafi's offers of assistance regarding Al Qaeda were rebuffed. Even though their interests in fighting Al Qaeda were overlapping, only when Lockerbie was resolved could the US do business with the Libyan regime.

But Lockerbie was not the only issue that troubled the Americans and the West when the subject of Qaddafi and his position in the world order was discussed. President Clinton and his advisers had also learned another dark secret about Qaddafi—one that in their view caused them even greater concern about the Great Leader's intentions in cooperating with the West.

* * *

THREE THOUSAND MILES to the east of Tripoli, a Pakistani nuclear scientist named Dr. Abdul Qadeer Khan—or A. Q. Khan, as he was known—was working quietly in his offices outside Islamabad. With the support from the highest levels of the Pakistani government and military, Dr. Khan had helped oversee the development of that country's atomic bomb, probably with a boost from its ally China. In May 1998, a nuclear device was exploded in an underground test center in a remote part of the country. Pakistan had proudly achieved some measure of strategic parity with its neighbor and bitter rival, India, which had exploded its own nuclear device many years before.

Like many Pakistanis, Dr. Khan had left India as a young boy in 1952, after the former British Indian Empire was partitioned into two predominantly Hindu and Muslim states—India and Pakistan. The intense rivalry and occasional warfare that erupted between the two new countries—immediate enemies because of religious differences—was a simmering concern for world leaders, but was still generally considered a regional affair, even with the introduction of nuclear weapons in each country's arsenal. Indeed, Pakistan's successful launch of a low earth orbit satellite in December 2001—from a Russian rocket facility in Kazakhstan—was still viewed as an escalation of regional tensions.

But intelligence gathered by the West since the late 1990s hinted that Pakistan's entry into the "nuclear club" was not confined to the regional theater. The evidence, closely guarded by senior intelligence agencies, indicated that Dr. Khan and his team had shared their nuclear capabilities with several states that were of great concern to the West. The sources revealed that Dr. Khan had been selling his nuclear secrets to North Korea and Iran. The notion of two of the most dangerous nations in the world acquiring nuclear weapons was terrifying to the West and its allies in the Middle East and Asia. Such a proliferation of nuclear weapons would directly alter the balance of power in these sensitive parts of the world, where Western allies such as Japan and Saudi Arabia would be under the threat of a nuclear rival without any counterbalance of their own. Dr. Khan's apparent willingness to share such technology with North Korea and Iran was simply beyond anything the rest of the world could tolerate.

But the nuclear threat was not the only dire concern. It was suspected that members of the military and intelligence services in Pakistan were sharing certain information with the Taliban, who had taken over Afghanistan and who were allied with the Pakistani government, at least prior to 11 September 2001. Western intelligence had heard rumors that the Taliban, and possibly Al Qaeda, had requested from the Pakistanis that they share some information about nuclear devices and radiation—or "dirty"—bombs. In the post-11 September world, this nightmare kept the world's leaders awake at night.

Dr. Khan apparently had embarked on this black-market venture because of his anti-Western views regarding the nuclear trigger. He also wanted to demonstrate that his colleagues could construct a "Muslim" bomb, something of great pride beyond the borders of Pakistan. Not purely motivated by political or religious conviction, however, he had accepted large amounts of cash and real estate for supplying nuclear information to his buyers. This had made him rich.

The intelligence was creeping out slowly. The possible acquisition of nuclear technology by Iran and North Korea from Dr. Khan gained the attention of the most senior government officials around the world. As part of that intelligence, it became clear that he had another prominent cash-paying customer. Apparently, the Great Leader of the Jamahiriya had paid Dr. Khan a vast sum of money to help initiate Libya's own nuclear program. Qaddafi's threat to the West had been bad enough when it focused on the bombing of commercial airliners, attacks on airports and general support for terrorism throughout the world. The notion that the Colonel would be able to threaten his neighbors, or Europe, with a plutonium bomb sent the threat warning from Libya off the charts.

* * *

IN MARCH 2002, I read on the front page of the *Washington Post* that the conviction and sentence of the Libyan agent convicted of blowing up the Pan Am 103 Lockerbie flight had been affirmed by a Scottish Court of Appeal. At that time I had begun working on a single Libya matter, the Kilburn murder in Beirut. But my interest in all things Libya and the country's relationship to terrorism was now a part of my work, however tangential information might appear. It sounded to me as if the criminal process in this notorious case was winding down and would soon be over.

Clearly, many Lockerbie family members expressed very mixed feelings when the appellate ruling was announced. As widely reported in the press, the Lockerbie families were somewhat satisfied that the Scottish Court of Appeals had upheld the conviction of one of the indicted bombers. But this was far from what they wanted, or needed, for closure's sake. The second Libyan suspect had been acquitted and set free because of very thin direct or forensic evidence tying him to the attack. Even the appellate decision upholding the conviction of Megrahi was up for debate, as the prosecution's evidence against him was not much stronger. Libya announced that it would pursue more appeals on behalf of Megrahi, whom it characterized as an innocent Libyan citizen. Libya itself continued publicly to deny any responsibility for the Lockerbie bombing.

The families' lawsuit against Libya in the New York federal court under the 1996 FSIA terrorism law had accomplished some important jurisdictional rulings. But a trial on liability—in other words, was Libya directly responsible for the bombing?—was years away, and it was difficult to predict the outcome given the prosecution's thin evidence from the criminal case in Scotland and The Hague. Of course, the families had received large payments from the bankrupt Pan Am and its insurance carriers. But by all public accounts, there was great angst and emptiness in their hearts. They felt they were not progressing in their quest for justice.

Such was the climate in April 2002 when I received a phone call that would pull me into the center of what I had been reading about in the newspapers.

OUR OFFICES AT Crowell & Moring sit on the top floors of a sturdy building on Pennsylvania Avenue, directly across from the US Department of Justice, FBI Headquarters and other government buildings. One can look east towards the huge white dome of the Capitol, its marble congressional buildings flanking the national symbol of democracy. Along Pennsylvania Avenue, I can look at the National Gallery of Art, the National Archives and other famous landmarks. At the end of Pennsylvania Avenue, on what was known as "Jenkins Hill" before it was purchased by the new government in the late 1700s, sits the Capitol itself.

Behind the huge white dome is the Library of Congress—designed by Thomas Jefferson and based on the style of the Paris Opera House, which he had greatly admired while serving as the US Ambassador to Bourbon France—the dome of which is clearly visible behind the Capitol's. I sometimes can see military jets beyond the domes as they take off and land at Andrews Air Force Base in nearby Maryland. It's a great view: iconic Washington institutions clearly visible from the window of my office, which is filled with art and plaques reflecting my years of government and private law practice.

I was sitting at my desk one day, admiring this vista, when the phone rang. I take my own calls, so picked up the receiver.

"Hello, is this Stuart Newberger?" a male voice asked.

"Sure," I replied. "Who is this?"

"Hi. My name's John Metzger. I'm a lawyer in Florida. I have a client here in Palm Beach of long standing. He's interviewing law firms to handle a possible case against Libya for blowing up his airplane back in 1989."

I receive calls from lawyers around the country on a regular basis, so this type of conversation was not unique. Over the past few months I had received several calls for other terrorism cases, although I turned down many of them when the details showed that the matter was not worth pursuing. At first, I did not know what Metzger was talking about.

"I'm not sure I know what attack you are talking about. This isn't connected to the Lockerbie bombing, is it?" I asked.

"No. This isn't the Lockerbie case. This is the French case. You may not remember it, given that all anyone ever talks about or reads in the press is Lockerbie. My client owned a DC-10 that blew up over Africa in September 1989. Almost two hundred people were killed. His plane was a total loss. He's been closely following the criminal cases in Paris that have been going on for some time. But no one has been brought from Libya to France to stand trial. There doesn't appear to be a lot of money floating around to compensate him for the plane. He got some insurance, but hardly enough to cover the losses. And he thinks this may be a good time to look into a legal claim against Libya. He heard about a recent law allowing lawsuits against terrorist countries. We found out about the Lockerbie families case in New York. But we don't know how to handle something like this. Are you interested?"

Metzger's enquiry stirred my memory. As I sat at my desk, considering a response, I quickly typed search terms into my computer, trying to find information about the French case. I vaguely recalled the incident, and some very minor press reports about it. But even a voracious newspaper reader like me could not recall much about the French bombing—coverage was all about Lockerbie.

Stalling the conversation with Metzger as I searched, I read the bullet points of information popping up on my screen. It was coming back. I juggled the phone with one hand, the keyboard with the other. "UTA Flight 772. Flying from Chad to Paris. September 1989. 170 persons killed when plane was destroyed by a suitcase bomb. Criminal case in Paris. Libyan agents involved. Sometimes referred to as the French Lockerbie," I read to myself.

"Yes," I said to Metzger. "I recall the attack. Were there any Americans on the flight who were killed? Is your client, or his company, American? That's important if you want to try something here in the States. I thought this was a French matter."

"My client is an American. His company is American. One of the largest aircraft leasing firms in the world at the time. They'd leased the plane to the French UTA airline. It has since been acquired by Air France. I think there were a few Americans on the plane, but I'm not sure how many. My client has tried to stay in touch with some of them [the families]. None of them have filed any type of case against Libya or anyone else, as far as we know. And it's really difficult to sue a French airline in France. The Warsaw Convention limits damages a great deal. But I don't have much on that. I'm just calling around to identify lawyers who might be able and interested. Are you?"

"Well, I might be. But there's a lot to look into before any competent lawyer can advise your client about any sort of claim."

"Great. Can you meet him next week? In your office? He wants to move fast."

* * *

ONE WEEK LATER, I greeted a tall, handsome man in his late fifties in the reception area of my firm.

Douglas Matthews was born to be a pilot. His father had served as personal pilot to General Eisenhower in Europe when he commanded NATO, and he had grown up in an Air Force family, mostly in Europe. After graduating from the US Naval Academy in Annapolis, Maryland (where he was a two-time All-American athlete), Matthews chose to become a naval aviator, eventually flying F-4 Phantom fighters off the deck of the USS *Kitty Hawk* aircraft carrier. He flew 155 combat missions over North Vietnam in the 1960s, earning commendations for his flight skills while watching some of his young comrades crash and die in the horror of war. With an honorable discharge in hand and a proud military record, Matthews followed many of his colleagues into civilian air employment. He started as a test pilot for a business jet factory and then joined Delta Airlines as a pilot, eventually working his way up in seniority to captain wide-body jets.

It was during his career as a Delta pilot that Matthews saw a business opportunity that would open doors well beyond the not-inconsiderable duties and salaries of senior airline captains. In the 1980s, airlines realized that they could take advantage of finance and tax vehicles to greatly lower their costs and increase their profits. Their single biggest expense, of course, was the high-priced and hi-tech jetliners manufactured by Boeing and Airbus. The lawyers and accountants figured out that the best way to operate the airline was for the company not to own its aircraft. Instead, they would arrange for aircraft finance companies to own the planes, with the backing of international banks, and the airlines would lease the planes under long-term contracts. This greatly reduced their overhead and liabilities. It also created a very lucrative business for those firms that could work with banks to purchase large numbers of jets and then lease them to airlines around the world. The value of jets was rising every day as the demand for international travel rose. And the waiting time for a new jet was so long—many years in some instances—that a company owning jets and leasing them could charge huge premiums to the airlines, who were desperate to service the growing international field.

Two giants had emerged in this field: General Electric and International Leasing Finance Corporation of California. But there was room in the industry for another player. Matthews had been approached by several airlines and banks and, with some start-up cash, had formed Interlease, a company that by 1989 owned a fleet of almost a hundred aircraft. His customers were the leading airlines of the world. He no longer needed to fly Delta runs between Atlanta and London. The aircraft leasing business was booming, and by the late 1980s Matthews was a billionaire, flying himself around the world on his private jet to negotiate deals. He lived in the largest home in Atlanta—bigger than the showcase home of media mogul Ted Turner—had another house in Aspen next to movie stars, and dined with Prince Charles in London, with whom he played polo. He was living the life.

That is, until 20 September 1989, when he received a phone call in London while negotiating a deal to lease several 747 jumbo jets to British Airways. One of his customers, the French airline UTA, reported that a DC-10 wide-body jet was missing over North Africa. Terrified at the possible loss of life in a horrific crash, the former pilot immediately called his financial manager in Atlanta to make sure his insurance carriers were put on notice of a potential loss of a plane valued at over $40 million. To his shock, the financial manager had neglected to renew one of the two insurance policies for the missing aircraft Interlease had leased to UTA. The DC-10 was lacking over $10 million in property insurance.

Matthews shook my hand with a firm and confident grip. He was in good physical shape, had a military bearing, wore a beautifully tailored suit and had hair nicely groomed over his tanned face. He was extremely personable. And he got right down to business.

"Glad to meet you, Stu. I hear you can deliver. I want to sue Libya and recover the damages for my DC-10. Interested?"

His smile made clear he already knew I was ready to handle the case.

ONCE WE GOT comfortable with each other, Matthews and I decided that the best way to proceed was for him to contact the seven American families—out of 170 victims—who had lost a loved in the UTA 772 explosion and crash. Since 1989, Matthews had continuously assembled information on the disaster, and had extensive files. It was unclear whether Interlease could bring its own claim against Libya for property and commercial losses, but having at least one of the American family members in the case would boost our chances of success. It was also unclear whether any of the families would want to even hear about, let alone join, Doug's venture. Matthews had made some minor contacts years before, when the French courts were conducting their trial in absentia, but he had no idea what the American families would want to do, or whether they would even talk to him. He also had no idea how to locate all of the victims' relatives.

Since my law firm was not in the business of soliciting clients, Matthews embarked on a national tour to speak personally with each of the seven families. He was armed with a package I had prepared so that they would be able to understand the background of the case and the legal and factual challenges, plus a rough outline of my possible litigation strategy. He also took along a draft "Joint Prosecution Agreement" so that any one of the relatives who decided to sign up could share in the joint enterprise—in other words, my firm would bear all the risk of fees and costs and anyone who enlisted with Matthews and the case would share in any type of settlement or recovery. If we were successful, the families, Interlease and my law firm would all take a piece of the recovery. If unsuccessful, my law firm would be out several million dollars in fees and costs. It was a risk, for sure. But the risk appeared to be worth taking.

* * *

EVEN BEFORE MATTHEWS contacted Robert Pugh, the former Ambassador was familiar to me and my law firm. I just did not recall him at the time.

As my team was putting together the case for the over ninety people who were preparing to sue Iran for blowing up the US Embassy in Beirut in April 1983, Pugh had been on a few conference calls with me and some of the other survivors of that terrorist attack. He had been serving as the number-two official at the Embassy, the Deputy Chief of Mission (DCM), when the Hezbollah suicide bomber had driven a truck up to the Embassy entrance, bringing down the entire front of the building and killing scores of Americans and non-Americans who worked at the post.

Pugh was a former Marine who had enlisted in the Foreign Service and had served tours in Turkey, Iran (before the Shah was deposed), Greece and London before his Lebanon assignment. Serving as the DCM in such a hotspot was a solid path for an officer to obtain a coveted Ambassadorial post. And Beirut's years of civil war, PLO invasion, Israeli invasion, Syrian intervention and warring factions certainly made for a fast-paced and intense experience. The Embassy was the vital nerve center of American diplomacy and intelligence—not just for Lebanon, but for the entire Middle East.

Pugh had just eaten lunch and was sitting in his top-floor office in Beirut when the huge bomb exploded a few minutes after 1:00 p.m. local time. Security teams had recently installed Mylar—a strong polyester film—across the plate glass windows looking out on Beirut. The adhesive did its job, as instead of shattering the windows into thousands of deadly bullets that would have caused severe injury or death, the explosive force popped the entire plate glass out of the frame in a single sheet. Despite the dust and debris all around him, Pugh escaped without a scratch.

In the next room, his boss, Ambassador Robert Dillon, was lying under a blanket of rubble, the drywall of his office across him like a fallen kitchen table. His American flag was draped over it, as on a military coffin. Pugh and some Marine guards lifted the drywall off the Ambassador, using the flag pole as a lever. Incredibly, he was unhurt except for a few small scratches. Sadly, their staff had not been so lucky.

Bodies and partial bodies were scattered throughout the remains of what had been a hotel before it was converted into the Embassy. The entire front of the building had collapsed. Survivors, many critically injured, screamed and moaned in the dust and heat. With the elevators broken and the stairs torn away, those who had survived the blast gingerly climbed down through the rubble to the street, where ambulances, security guards, Lebanese police, firemen and other emergency responders did their best to assist them.

As the second in command in the Beirut Embassy, Pugh had to concern himself with the immediate task of coordinating the rescue of survivors and the handling of the dead. But this was not just an office building. Large amounts of classified papers and files had been kept in its file cabinets and safes. Some of these were of the most sensitive nature, containing highly secret intelligence and diplomatic information. Pugh and a security officer tried diligently to identify and gather all of these files, some of which were being blown by the hot breeze into the street below.

Recognizing the extraordinary task before them, Pugh and Ambassador Dillon decided to divide their duties. The Ambassador would take on the "outside" work, meeting with the special envoy of President Reagan who was flying in that night from Washington, touching base with the Lebanese authorities and taking on the sad but necessary official duty of escorting the dead to the airport for transport back to the United States for burial. Pugh would take on the "inside" work of making sure the Embassy came back to life and functioned as the outpost for the US government in this violent and uncertain city.

Assisting were some of the US Marines stationed at the barracks they had set up near Beirut Airport, where President Reagan had posted them to serve as a symbol of America's determination to stabilize Lebanon. Six months later, an even bigger truck bomb would explode there, killing over two hundred Marines and scores of French paratroopers nearby. Years later, Judge Lamberth would issue a series of court judgments against Iran, in the billions of dollars, to the families of those Marines killed and injured in the attack. But in April 1983, six months before this fateful day, the Marines' job was to assist Pugh in the ghastly job of putting the Embassy back together again.

Pugh's wife, Bonnie, provided him with the support he needed to carry on during the sleepless nights and grueling days after the Embassy bombing. As a "foreign service wife," she had accompanied Pugh on his postings, and as the wife of the DCM she played a critical role in trying to pull together the Embassy family in the aftermath of death and destruction. She worked so closely with the US Marines attached to the Embassy as guards that she was regarded by many as a second mother.

The life of a foreign service spouse was not all it sounded, especially for the generation serving overseas during this unpredictable era. Daily life was a combination of numbing routine and unexpected turmoil. Many families left their children in school back in the States if the post was inhospitable, and every two years the officer was rotated to another post. And so the cycle repeated for the next two or three decades.

In 1984, after Pugh finished his tumultuous tour in Lebanon, he and Bonnie enjoyed a tour in Washington, where he taught at a senior State Department program and they enjoyed the swirl of diplomatic life in the nation's capital. As expected, he finally was appointed an Ambassador by President Reagan, to the North African nation of Mauritania for a full tour, and then received a second ambassadorial post in recognition of his excellent service. Less important posts were typical for career officers who lacked political clout at the White House, but any post was considered a prize, and acting as the President's representative in any sovereign country was the height of an officer's career.

Chad was very much a developing and remote country when the Pughs arrived to take over the Embassy. There were not that many Americans there, and those that lived there were mostly oil workers, Peace Corps volunteers, diplomats and intelligence officers. Relations with its neighbors were always a flashpoint for the Chadian government. Libya and Nigeria were big players in Africa, and their relations with Chad were always fodder for the Ambassador and the Chadians.

In September 1989, Bonnie Pugh was heading back to the States to plan the last few details of the wedding set for their daughter, Ann, who lived in Charlottesville, Virginia. Pugh would finish up some work at the Embassy and follow Bonnie home right before the wedding. He accompanied her to the airport in N'Djamena as she boarded the flight to Paris and her connection to Washington. At the foot of the stairway on the hot desert tarmac, Pugh kissed his wife and watched her walk up the stairs into the DC-10 jet.

He would never see her again.

AFTER AMBASSADOR PUGH signed the Joint Prosecution Agreement the other six American families also agreed to sign up with Matthews. Given his status and profile, it was decided that Pugh would serve as the lead plaintiff in the case, in which he would sue Libya on behalf of his late wife's estate as well as on his own behalf. The other families also brought their claims on behalf of their departed loved ones, a diverse mix of oil rig workers, accountants and a young college girl finishing a hitch in the Peace Corps, along with the former Ambassador's wife.

Matthews worked fast. It only took him a few weeks of flying around the country to meet with all the families, whom he had tracked using private investigators. The group was brought together over a dozen years after the DC-10 had been blown out of the sky. They had never met, and did not know each other—the doomed victims on the plane were the only connection—and none could predict how their new journey would conclude. It would be several more years before they actually gathered together for the first time. But events in the other air terrorism case—the Lockerbie bombing—would provide clues as to what they might expect.

* * *

ONLY DAYS AFTER Matthews finished organizing the seven American families into a litigation group, the newspapers and evening news disclosed a significant development that immediately caught our attention.

In May, Kreindler & Kreindler, the New York law firm that was taking the lead in the Pan Am 103 Lockerbie case against Libya, disclosed that they had been secretly negotiating with the Libyan government for a possible settlement. According to news reports broadcasted around the world, Libya had offered the Pan Am 103 Lockerbie victims $10 million for each family, totaling almost $2.5 billion if the deal went through. But there were serious problems with the terms, which was why the settlement discussions had been leaked to the press.

With its vast oil wealth, Libya had structured its offer in a way that would assist Qaddafi's efforts to have the United Nations and the related (and more stringent) US sanctions lifted. The reported offer would put all the money in an escrow, to be released in three stages. First, each family would receive $4 million when the United Nations Security Council lifted its international sanctions. Second, each family would receive an additional $4 million when the United States lifted its own economic sanctions. Third, each family would receive a final $2 million when Libya was removed from the State Department's list of states that sponsor terrorism.

In short, a staggering amount of money was on the table. But the strings that Qaddafi's government attached to the purse caused tremendous heartache for many of the families who would benefit from the payment. They felt it placed them in the awkward position of taking Libya's side in its effort to re-emerge as a member of the civilized world. By taking Qaddafi's millions under this formula, the families who had been devastated by the suitcase bomb that caused the 747 to crash in Scotland would find themselves in a position they had never imagined. They were being asked to make a deal with the Devil—the Devil who had killed over 250 of their loved ones, and was using his vast supply of oil monies to buy his way back into respectability.

Chapter 13

The Turnaround

THE LOCKERBIE FAMILIES were not the only ones struggling with how to deal with Qaddafi's $2.5 billion settlement offer. In Washington and London, diplomats and government lawyers were trying to determine what to do in the face of this "private diplomacy" between Libya and the Lockerbie families' lawyers. Apparently, the settlement discussions had been kept secret even from the American and British governments.

For starters, the United Nations sanctions had called for Libya to pay "appropriate compensation," but to whom, and how much, was left to the ambiguities of international diplomacy. As the two governments were well aware, the sanctions called for more than the payment of compensation: an end to the support of terrorism, for example, was a key element of US foreign policy in dealing with Libya.

But what really surprised the government officials was the linkage Qaddafi included in the proposal. By staggering the $10 million payments, Libya was playing hardball. It was employing its oil wealth to incentivize the Lockerbie family lawyers and tempt the families to pocket monies in addition to what they had already collected from Pan Am and its insurers. It was a clear pressure tactic, intended to influence the United Nations, and then the United States, into lifting the various sanctions that had isolated Qaddafi in the first place.

Clearly, there was tension among the Lockerbie families, many of whom were very concerned that if they accepted the staggered payment terms they would become Qaddafi's advocates to lift the sanctions, and as quickly as possible. Other families saw it differently—they believed this was the best way to bring Libya back into the fold of civilized countries. The tension even among the various families was obvious, and divisive.

From the perspective of the two governments, a decision was made at the highest levels—including President George W. Bush and UK Prime Minister Tony Blair—that they would not interfere with the ongoing negotiations between the private lawyers for the Lockerbie families and Libya. Since compensation for the Pan Am 103 Lockerbie disaster was an essential part of the United Nations sanctions, the governments would treat any family financial recovery as a priority. They would not press Libya to reimburse the two governments for the huge costs of the criminal investigation and trial in The Hague. Another decision the two governments made was that the Pan Am 103 lawsuit against Libya in New York would be allowed to settle on behalf of all the Lockerbie families—even the non-Americans who, under the Foreign Sovereign Immunities Act, lacked legal standing to recover a judgment against Libya. Diplomacy would trump the legal technicalities, as a package deal in a single case was viewed as the best way to move forward with the anticipated Libyan deal.

On a more sensitive level, the American and British diplomats faced a different dilemma. Should they sit back and let private civil lawyers play the role always taken by the US Department of State and the British Foreign Office as the sole spokespersons in discussions with a foreign government? Especially one as notorious and isolated as Qaddafi's Libya. This was a highly irregular process, one they did not easily embrace in light of decades of practice and professionalism. But facing the practicalities, and considering their lack of alternatives, they swallowed their pride. Kreindler and his associates in New York could proceed to finalizing the historic settlement. The two governments would not get in the way. But, to keep their options open, the US government made clear to the Lockerbie lawyers that any decision to lift sanctions against Libya would not be influenced by the legal settlement.

Qaddafi's plan to leverage—buy—his way out of isolation was building up a new head of steam.

* * *

WITH PUBLIC REPORTS of a possible multi-billion-dollar settlement in the Pan Am 103 Lockerbie case, Doug Matthews and I decided we had to move fast to get the UTA 772 litigation organized and filed. The seven American families who had lost their loved ones on the UTA 772 flight read the newspapers and watched network television. They saw the large sums being publicly discussed in another, more notorious, aircraft terrorism case in New York. We all had an expectation that an American lawsuit arising from the UTA 772 bombing—with Interlease and the American families out front—might create momentum for a similar settlement with Libya.

In June, I flew from Dulles Airport in northern Virginia to Charles de Gaulle Airport in Paris, caught an early morning taxi and pulled up to the grand entrance of the Ritz. Matthews already was waiting in the lobby to greet me, having come over to Paris a few days earlier to lay the groundwork for our first joint visit regarding the case. Despite the loss of much of his aircraft business over the years, he still had a billionaire's tastes. Gulf sheikhs and movie stars wandered through the lobby of one of the world's most beautiful and famous hotels. Over a wonderful morning omelet in the bar, we mapped out our first steps. Matthews had already made a number of calls and arranged several meetings. There was a lot of catching up to do. Thirteen years' worth, to be exact. The constant media attention regarding the Pan Am 103 Lockerbie settlement that Qaddafi had put forward was a continual drumbeat accompanying our mission.

MATTHEWS AND I stood up from a small table in a cafe located in the 6th Arrondissement district. The woman walking towards us had a pronounced limp, made even more noticeable by the heavy effort she was making to shuffle through the crowded restaurant. Leaning on a wooden cane, she nodded at Matthews as she gratefully sat down on a chair he pulled up for her at our table.

Dressed in modest clothes, at least by Parisian standards, Françoise Rudetzki placed her books, large handbag, mobile phone and satchel on the table. Although only in her late fifties, she had the look of someone who had aged too quickly. From what Matthews had explained earlier, this was no surprise to me.

Madame Rudetzki was the daughter of a Jewish Parisian tailor who had attended excellent schools and obtained graduate degrees in public law. She had served as a government lawyer in the French Ministry of Industry early in her career and later became a business executive. In December 1983, she and her husband were at dinner in a restaurant called Le Grand Véfour in Paris, where they had regularly dined for almost ten years, a custom many locals followed. In the middle of dinner, a terrorist bomb had exploded, and she was seriously injured. The limp was one of the attack's legacies. She had undergone numerous operations to try to repair her crushed legs. She had also contracted the HIV virus through the many blood transfusions following her surgeries. She later titled her autobiography recounting her struggle as a Jew in France, her crushed legs and her terrible disease *Triple Peine— Triple Trouble*.

We were meeting Rudetzki because, in 1986, she had been inspired by her injuries to form the first French group for civilian terrorist victims, the SOS Attentats, *attentats* meaning attacks in French. Her sad, removed expression hid the passion and energy she had shown in persuading the French government formally to recognize the victim group and accord it official governmental status, an unprecedented move in the French legal system, especially since it allowed the organization to intervene as an interested party in criminal proceedings. Using that very status, embodied in Section 2–9 of the French Code of Criminal Procedure, SOS Attentats had participated in the UTA 772 murder proceedings pursued by Judge Bruguière and the French prosecutors in 1999. The organization's objectives were clear and easy to understand: to obtain justice for all victims of terrorism carried out in France, or against French citizens abroad; to "end impunity" for terrorists and fight to ensure that no terrorist should be allowed to escape legal proceedings; and to assist victims in legal cases. Significantly, Rudetzki's organization opposed the death penalty even for terrorist killers. In seeking justice, SOS Attentats did not seek revenge. This in itself was a remarkable step forward in the world of victimization.

As we ordered coffee and reviewed her role as an observer in the UTA 772 criminal proceedings, Rudetzki's heavy French accent, deep voice and serious face explained in halting English why she was interested in helping Matthews and me in our efforts across the Atlantic Ocean.

"We have not been able to hold anyone accountable for the DC-10," she said. "Qaddafi is laughing at the French for letting him off the hook for mass murder. A few of his petrol-euros and a welcome to French companies in Tripoli is all it took for our President Chirac to forgive him for this crime. We are very frustrated. No one even talks about the DC-10 case outside of France. All we read about is Lockerbie. Lockerbie. Lockerbie. I feel for those families, of course. But it is not Qaddafi's only crime. And it is incredible how much of a fortune Qaddafi is probably going to pay to the Americans to make that go away. Compared to what the French and African victims received for the DC-10, it is a disgrace."

Matthews and I looked at each other. We knew we had found someone to help us put the Washington case together.

The next day, I took a taxi from the Ritz over to the 7th Arrondissement. Stepping out of the cab, I gazed up at the gold dome of Les Invalides, the Baroque basilica modeled after Michelangelo's Saint Peter's in Rome, built at the direction of the Sun King Louis XIV at the height of French dominance of Europe in the seventeenth century. The dome reflected the bright Paris sun.

Walking across the broad green field towards the building, I pushed through a side door that Rudetzki had instructed me to approach in order to reach her offices. Entering a marble-lined foyer, I noticed a long line of tourists following a guide with an umbrella. I followed them briefly to get my bearings and figure out how to locate the offices of SOS Attentats hidden away in the vast interior of Les Invalides complex. Originally used as a military hospital and soldiers' retirement home, it was now a maze of French military history museums and monuments. Although it was itself a replica of the huge Saint Peter's, Les Invalides' own beauty was so admired that San Francisco City Hall was copied from its design.

As the tour group turned a corner, they came to a sudden stop in a grand round hall in Saint Jerome's Chapel. A huge dark gray sarcophagus, the final resting place for a dictator from another era, rested in the center of the room. The self-proclaimed Emperor Napoleon Bonaparte's remains had been brought back from his exiled grave in Saint Helena in 1840 to be laid in a place of honor. I had never visited the tomb before. My only recollection of this particular monument was an old black-and-white photograph of Adolf Hitler gazing at it after the Germans had captured Paris in 1940—a twentieth-century dictator contemplating a nineteenth-century French predecessor and his failed efforts to conquer all of Europe. I briefly considered that this might be an omen, given that we were now trying to chase a North African dictator, albeit in a court of law rather than on a battlefield. But such fanciful thoughts were quickly extinguished. The tour group moved on to another historic crypt and I was left to find my way to Madame Rudetzki's rooms.

Turning around another corner, I spotted Rudetzki opening the door to her office, the ever-present satchel over her arm as she leaned on the cane for support. The French government had supplied SOS Attentats coveted office space in Les Invalides as part of recognizing its official status as the representative for terrorist victims. She motioned for me to come over and I followed her into a side room off the main hall. We entered a cluttered bureau—loose files, books, boxes and papers scattered all around. The air was musty and cold, the windows covered in grime that filtered the daylight into a soft brown haze. Rudetzki seemed unaware of the chaos and dust as she hobbled around looking for something to show me. She seemed possessed, almost in a trance, as she scanned shelves and filing cabinets.

"Here they are," she said in her heavy French accent. "All the files from the murder case at the court. We get all the files since SOS is a party."

Pulling open a number of cabinet drawers, she lifted several court jackets from their jammed holders. We counted over thirty large, bulky folders filled with exhibits, reports and witness statements. This was the entire, unabridged criminal record of the French investigation of the UTA 772 murder case. I knew instantly that here was quite a catch. In France, the files in a criminal case were never made available to the public and were only shown to the accused, and their lawyers, in the courtroom. This was quite different from in the United States where the courthouse clerk's office would make available to anyone—journalist, curiosity seeker, investigator—anything in a case file.

"Everything in the case is here," she said, a weak smile on her pained face as she leaned on her cane. "But it cannot go with you to the States, I am sorry. It cannot leave Paris, by law. They are very strict in these things. But you will want to look at this one."

She selected a folder stuffed with reports, charts and what appeared to be witness statements and almost twelve inches wide from a shelf.

"This has the best summary of the case," she said. "It is Judge Bruguière's report. He spent years putting this together."

Of course, the entire file was in French, and my command of the language was limited to ordering wine and perhaps an appetizer from a menu. Accepting that this was the motherlode of the French criminal proceedings, I scanned the thick Bruguière report to see if anything jumped out. It did not. The previous day, when Rudetzki told me and Matthews about her files, I had hoped we could copy a few documents. I had not imagined that she would have the entire criminal proceedings in her office. I pulled out my cell phone and called my partner Emmanuel Gybels, who was fluent in French, in our law firm's Brussels office and asked him if someone could get on the train to Paris the next day and arrange for a service to copy the entire file. I wanted every page and every piece electronically copied by a local vendor, as I knew we might not get an opportunity like this again. Gybels made arrangements with Rudetzki on the phone and the plan was set. The entire file would be copied at night and put on a DVD. We would have the best evidence on the planet to use in our Washington-based case to prove how Libya and its agents had blown up the UTA DC-10.

After locking up the office and its treasure trove of files, Rudetzki asked me to follow her out of Les Invalides and towards a row of towering buildings. Walking at a fast pace, considering her limp, she directed me to a monument right outside, in a quiet garden nestled near the building we had just left. She pointed at a very tall bronze statue in a modernist style, similar to a sculpture by Henry Moore. The figure it depicted was holding its head in its hands, a death mask-type face staring into space.

This was the memorial to terrorist victims that Rudetzki had been able to compel the French government to construct on what is considered sacred ground. President Chirac himself had come to the dedication in 1998, kissing Rudetzki's hand in grand style as his congratulation for her achievements. She had recoiled from the gesture, knowing how Chirac had befriended Qaddafi and forgiven the murder of 170 innocent persons in the African desert. A photograph of the event that I later found on the Internet made clear that Rudetzki was appalled at Chirac's empty gesture.

"French Justice," she was saying. Her face was solemn and grave, lost in thought, as she leaned on her cane in the fading summer light. "A statue instead of justice."

* * *

THE NEXT DAY, with the French criminal files in the process of being copied and on their way to my Washington office, Matthews and I walked from our hotel on the Place Vendôme to the Left Bank. Rising in front of us as we stood on a bridge crossing the Seine, taking up an entire city block, was the massive gray fortress of the Palais de Justice— the Palace of Justice. The stone towers and conical roofs loomed forebodingly over the river. Here was a true medieval castle in the heart of ancient Paris.

The Palais de Justice was extraordinary. It had been built on what had been the grounds of one of thirteenth-century King Saint Louis's palaces. Before this, it was the area where Roman governors lived, when Paris was just a muddy town in the province of Gaul. The only part of that former royal residence that remains is the famous Sainte-Chapelle, a beautiful gothic gem with stained glass that King Saint

Louis built to house what he thought were the remains of the Crucifixion. As Matthews and I walked to the entrance of the building, we saw the long line of tourists lining up to visit. Saint-Chapelle was only open at odd hours.

The Palais de Justice itself was also the location of what had been the oldest prison in France. Much of the stone structure that had previously housed notables such as Queen Marie Antoinette and the Revolutionary figure Robespierre—until they lost their heads on the guillotine—was still standing, and was now used for many of the local courts. We were heading for the offices of the Paris Court of Appeal. Matthews had been able to use his contacts to arrange an interview with the most critical player in the UTA 772 investigation. His cooperation was essential if we were to go after Libya in our case in Washington.

Even after we navigated our way through the metal detectors and security posts, finding our way to the meeting was not easy in the labyrinthine complex. The Palais was not really a single building, but a number of separately built sections, with additions that had, over the centuries, been blended into a maze of hallways, stairwells, nooks and crannies that lacked any meaningful signs or directions, even in French. Every time Matthews made an enquiry in his own passable French, we received a different lecture as to how and where to turn and climb in order to reach our destination. At least twice, we circled back to the same spot, unable to figure out where to go next. Once we even wound up back outside, only to find that we had taken the wrong turn twice.

Finally, we climbed a series of dark wooden stairs and crept along a dark, windowless corridor smelling of dust, French cigarettes and sweat. At the end of the corridor was a plain wooden bench. It was empty. Beyond the bench was a thick steel door with no window or door knob. As we approached, it opened, and two burly men with close-cropped hair and leather jackets came out, rushing quickly past us and down the hall. Right behind them was a woman in her forties, a smile on her face as she nodded that we should follow her through the steel door.

"Messieurs Matthews and Newberger?" she asked, already knowing the answer. She pronounced Doug's name as if it were two words— "Matt Hews"—and mine in a style I had never heard—"New-ber-jay."

"Come this way please," she said, and we followed her down a corridor lined with files, padlocks sealing every cabinet and safe. "The judge will be out soon from his meeting."

Matthews and I sat down on two hard steel chairs next to the woman, one of the secretaries, as she went back to her computer screen. There was no art on the walls, no plants to spruce up the office, just files. Lots and lots of files. I was accustomed to such offices after my years in the US government. It was the sign of a busy agency that had neither the time nor the budget to bother with frivolous decoration.

The door suddenly opened and a short, compact man with a large nose, dark eyes, gray hair slicked to the side and wearing a rumpled gray suit, white shirt and blue tie came out to greet us. He was obviously busy and distracted by what must have been an important meeting. Right behind him emerged two more very bulky men in leather jackets. They did not smile or even acknowledge us. They nodded to the man who was clearly their boss and with deadly serious looks on their faces rushed out of the office. I made a mental note to myself that I should run in the opposite direction if I ever saw these two tough guys in a dark alley. As they passed us in the crowded office space, I saw that one had a large pistol strapped to his chest in a holster. I felt confident that he knew how to use it, and had probably done so on occasion.

"Come in, come in, gentlemen," the boss said to us in a very heavily accented English. "I have been waiting for you."

SITTING DOWN BEHIND his cluttered desk, Investigating Magistrate Judge Jean-Louis Bruguière of the Paris Court of Appeal motioned for us to take seats across from him. Behind him was another wall lined with file cabinets and safes, locks and bolts across them all. He pulled out a worn pipe and began to light a ball of tobacco. He looked like a professor about to deliver a lecture to an eager class.

"So, you will make a case in Washington for the DC-10?" He obviously had been prepped by whatever contacts Matthews had used to get us the appointment with one of the most secretive and guarded persons in France. "But a civil case, no?"

Matthews took the lead, as we had discussed on the way over.

"Yes, Judge. Mr. Newberger's firm has a lot of experience in seeking civil damages against terrorist countries like Libya and Iran. We want to prove that Libya blew up my airplane and murdered everyone on board. Including the seven Americans who were killed. We have organized them into a group to file the case together. We hope you will be able, I mean the French authorities will be able, to assist us in the case."

Bruguière pondered this for a moment, puffing on his pipe and looking towards the wall behind us. His face was a little ashen and pallid, with a five o'clock shadow of beard and a light sheen of sweat across his forehead. He leaned forward and put down the pipe.

"Mister Matthews," he began. "I spent over ten years of my life investigating the Libyans for blowing up the DC-10, your DC-10. It was the biggest case I ever handled. And I have handled all the biggest ones, for sure." He smiled at his fame, and his reputation. "I never had such a case. But after years we found the evidence that made it a solid case. Not just with confessions. We have those in many cases."

Sure you have, I thought to myself. And I doubt the confessors had any fingernails remaining by the time your thick-necked, leather-jacketed associates were through with them.

"No," Bruguière continued, looking me straight in the eye. "We had a miracle. In the desert. A true miracle that never can happen in a case. We found the circuit board for the bomb. In the sand of the desert. In the middle of nowhere. By luck. And after much work, we connect it with the Libyans. Right to their security chief in Tripoli. The best evidence. Better than in Lockerbie. My FBI and Scotland Yard friends, they do not have such evidence, for sure. It was the greatest thing I have ever done in my whole life. We have the proof of the murders—170 people dead. And we have the proof. Solid, as you Americans say."

Bruguière sat back and re-lit his pipe. His sense of pride was obvious. We had read about the forensic proof he and his team had been able to uncover to nail down the responsibility of the Libyan security services for putting the plastic explosive suitcase on the flight. We still did not have the evidence in our hands, but the files I had been shown by Madame Rudetzki the prior day would shortly fix that problem.

And then, in an instant, Bruguière's face turned stern; his smile disappeared and his expression darkened.

"But my President, Monsieur Chirac, he make the deal with Qaddafi.

All the killers, they stay free. Our oil companies come back to Tripoli and beat the Americans to the money. But all my work, all my evidence, it is not to be used to bring the killers to justice. I am just a judge. I am no politician, or a diplomat. But I did not understand this. And I still do not. It cannot be this way. Qaddafi, he is the killer. He killed the people on the DC-10. This is very hard. Very hard to understand. We have many, many people here in Paris, they do not understand this. It is not right."

Matthews and I sat still as we absorbed Bruguière's words. This was the most powerful investigator in France. He had spent a decade of his life tracking down the killers of the 170 people on the UTA 772 flight. And he and his team had done the impossible. They had ultimately found conclusive proof that the Libyan government, at the highest levels, had carried out this act of cold-blooded mass murder. Better proof than in the Lockerbie case, as he said. But their President, with the stroke of a pen, had forgiven everyone responsible for the worst terrorist attack in French history. Just for some oil. And to get to that oil before their American competitors could.

"You see, Mister Matthews"—Bruguière leaned over and looked him dead on, lowering his voice and speaking with conviction—"the French, Mister Matthews, they never forget."

* * *

BACK IN THE States, Matthews and I pushed hard to get the complaint prepared and filed. For his part, Matthews touched base with the American families to brief them on our trip, the cooperation we had obtained in France and the coordination for filing, and publicizing, the federal case.

In Washington, I worked with a team in our Brussels office to review and translate at least the more important parts of the French criminal file, which was now on my desk in the form of several shiny discs. It was clear that Judge Bruguière's massive report was the backbone of the French investigation. Our colleagues in the Washington office lifted critical facts from the English translation and placed them in the draft complaint, which was coming together. One of my partners, Laurel

Malson, a former Justice Department lawyer and experienced litigator, oversaw the drafting and helped edit the massive pleading as the factual recitation was laid out in detail. This was the first time such evidence had been disclosed outside the French murder proceedings and Bruguière's report had never been disclosed publicly, or released to the press. The amount of detail was fantastic, and the complaint was beginning to read like a combination of a legal thriller and fast-paced novel of international intrigue, a meeting of Johns le Carré and Grisham.

We also made a tactical decision. The complaint would actually have two central themes. The first, as with other cases under the Foreign Sovereign Immunities Act, was directly against the Libyan government for sponsoring the UTA 772 attack. The second was against the six Libyans who had been convicted of murder, in absentia, in Paris, and who still were living in freedom and luxury in Tripoli. For that claim, we relied on an arcane federal law, under Title 18 of the US Code Section 2337, that provided for damages against individual terrorists. We also included a claim for property damage and commercial losses for Interlease in addition to the claims by the estates of the seven murdered Americans and their family members. We requested billions of dollars in damages. Given the media reports of the Pan Am 103 Lockerbie deal being in that range, we were comfortable making such a demand as well.

By October, the complaint was ready to file. We had all agreed that former Ambassador Robert Pugh, whose wife Bonnie had been killed in the UTA 772 bombing on her way to her daughter's wedding in Virginia, would serve as the lead plaintiff. We already had been working with Ambassador Pugh as a witness in the Dammarell case against Iran, arising from the 1983 suicide truck bombing of the US Embassy in Beirut, Lebanon. His support for those victims of a terrorist attack— many of whom had served under him at the Embassy, where he was the second in command—had been of great value. Ironically, now he would put his name forward as the surviving spouse of a victim forever to be identified with this new case against Libya.

The caption on the federal court complaint would read "Robert Pugh v. Great Libyan Arab People's Socialist Jamahiriya" and every filing in the case from that point would begin with this recitation. But in shorthand, it would be known simply as "the Pugh case."

After I signed the written complaint, one of our paralegals took it to the clerk's office at the federal courthouse just a few blocks down from our offices on Pennsylvania Avenue. With the payment of the $150 filing fee, the Pugh case had commenced. Or perhaps, in the eyes of our new French friends, the UTA 772 case simply was being reopened after President Chirac and Colonel Qaddafi had thought it closed for good by their own diplomatic deal.

THE PROCESS FOR formally serving the complaint on the Libyan government took several months. Because the United States and Libya did not maintain formal diplomatic relations at the time, it was necessary for the summons and complaint—now translated into Arabic as well as English—to be sent by the clerk of the federal court to the Department of State. State then sent the papers by diplomatic courier to Brussels— by diplomatic agreement, the Belgian government acted for the interests of the United States in Libya. Once in Tripoli, the Belgian Embassy took the court papers to the Libyan Ministry of Foreign Affairs. After serving the Libyans, the process was put in reverse by the Belgians, and ultimately the Department of State informed the clerk of the federal court that Libya had been served.

The service of process under the Foreign Sovereign Immunities Act took almost four months. But Libya now had a deadline to respond. However, Qaddafi had other things on his mind beyond a new billion dollar civil lawsuit in Washington.

In February 2003, President George W. Bush had launched his invasion of Iraq. As US planes targeted sites and troops and marched towards Baghdad to topple another long-standing Arab dictator, Colonel Qaddafi sat in Tripoli watching the military strikes against Saddam Hussein on CNN and BBC. Qaddafi knew what it was like to be the target of American and British military attacks, having survived the April 1986 air attack by only the slightest of margins. No other Arab leader of a country had such first-hand experience. It did not take long for Qaddafi to imagine that his regime might be the next target of "Cowboy Bush" and his plan to redraw the Middle Eastern political map.

While the live reporting from Iraq played on his television, Qaddafi watched as his diplomats and lawyers quietly met with the Lockerbie lawyers in London to work out a final deal that would help him shed his pariah status and reduce the chance that President Bush might turn the American military machine against him.

IN APRIL, LIBYA submitted its first response to the new Pugh complaint. From the start, we saw its strategy emerge. Unlike Iran, it would not default on the case. As with the Lockerbie case in New York and my Kilburn case in the same Washington courthouse, it would mount a defense.

First, the local lawyer who had taken over the now-retired Bruno Ristau's "attorney for the damned" practice—Arman Dabiri—filed papers on behalf of both the Libyan government and the six individual Libyans convicted of murder in Paris. A young lawyer who had worked with Ristau on the Lockerbie case, Dabiri was an ethnic Armenian who had grown up in Brussels and then moved to the US, where he became a lawyer. He had worked as Ristau's associate and taken over the bulk of his practice when Ristau retired. A short, olive-skinned man with jet-black hair and finely tailored suits, Dabiri was an intelligent and articulate advocate. It was also clear that he took his orders from other lawyers in Europe and Libya.

Second, Libya's initial reaction to the lawsuit was to raise as many procedural and jurisdictional defenses as possible. It did not want to get into the merits of the UTA 772 attack or deal with the murder convictions from the Paris cases. It wanted to buy time and to delay the Washington case as long as possible in order to work on other more pressing matters that might well overtake any threat posed by the new litigation. Dabiri submitted a motion to dismiss, which repeated many of the legal defenses previously rejected by the federal courts in the Pan Am 103 Lockerbie case in New York. Clearly, Libya was engaged in a stall game.

Our team began to prepare our responses to this initial salvo and kept our eyes open for anything that might indicate that the Libyans wanted to resolve our new case as part of Qaddafi's effort to re-engage the civilized world. The mere fact that Libya would defend the case—as it was doing for all other terrorist cases filed against it—was itself a major reflection of Qaddafi's intentions. In contrast to Iran, he would not allow these cases to enter default mode and unnecessarily increase the pressure on his government to settle or risk attachment of Libyan funds. Indeed, the US government was holding over $1 billion in Libyan assets, which had been seized in the 1980s after it was placed on the terrorism list by the Department of State. Those frozen assets were a juicy target for our case—if we could push the case forward quickly and obtain a court judgment. With the Pan Am 103 Lockerbie case in settlement mode, our case was now one of the biggest threats to those frozen assets.

We would not have to wait long to see in which direction Libya was heading.

* * *

ON 14 AUGUST the Pan Am 103 Lockerbie settlement was formally announced by the victims' lawyers.

James Kreindler, who had taken over his father's New York law firm after the older lawyer had succumbed to cancer, issued a press release from London, where he had concluded his negotiations with the Libyans. Libya would deposit $2.7 billion in a special escrow account held by a Swiss bank—the Bank for International Settlements—and the monies would flow to the families of the Pan Am 103 Lockerbie victims under a payment schedule tied to lifting the United Nations and US sanctions. Each family could ultimately receive a total of $10 million, minus Kreindler's fees—but only if all the conditions set down by Qaddafi's government were met.

At the same time, it was reported that the US and British governments had negotiated the language of a letter Libya would submit to the United Nations Security Council in which it would acknowledge its responsibility for the Pan Am 103 Lockerbie bombing. Apparently, the diplomats had finally caught up with the private lawyers for the victims and they were now working in sync. The placement of the huge settlement in a special escrow account would be the first step, and the letter to the United Nations would then trigger a process that Qaddafi had sought for years.

But the news was not all positive. Many of the Lockerbie families had been kept in the dark about the details of the negotiations. Some were bitter that the man who had murdered their loved ones in the skies over Scotland was now being rehabilitated rather than prosecuted. The fact that the historic amount of settlement funds was a central part of the story gave many of the families a sick feeling in their stomachs. It appeared that money could buy justice for Qaddafi. Some even announced that they would insist that Libya remain a pariah state for some time.

But notwithstanding these sentiments, the settlement agreement seemed solid, especially where the US and British governments were now supporting it with their own diplomacy, albeit still making clear that decisions to lift sanctions would be made for political, not legal, reasons. Our strategy in the new Pugh case also seemed to be working as we established ourselves as the next big case to be resolved.

The next day, as orchestrated, the Libyan Ambassador to the United Nations, Ahmed A. Own, delivered a two-page, single-spaced letter to the United Nations Security Council in New York. It was in both English and Arabic and got right to the point: "I am pleased to inform you that the remaining issues relating to the fulfilment of all Security Council resolutions resulting from the Lockerbie incident have been resolved".

It then noted that Libya—"out of respect for international law"—as a sovereign state had "facilitated in bringing to justice of the two suspects charged with the bombing of Pan Am 103 and accepts responsibility for the actions of its officials." This "admission" had been at the heart of the diplomatic efforts to overcome the biggest hurdle in the process. It had taken months of painstaking diplomacy to come up with this short sentence. Libya, a sovereign state, was telling the United Nations that it was responsible for this notorious act of terrorism. Later, Libya would claim the sentence was more vague than people understood. It even later claimed that it was a "coerced statement under the duress of the UN sanctions." However, no matter what happened next, this sentence would be posted as the public *mea culpa* of Qaddafi for his earlier, and now rejected, efforts to use terrorism as a tool for his foreign policy.

The letter also noted that Libya had cooperated with the Scottish authorities and that it had "arranged for the payment of appropriate compensation." The huge settlement fund was not specifically mentioned, but assurances were made that the account would be funded "within a matter of days."

After reciting its compliance with all the United Nations sanctions and resolutions over the years, Libya formally requested that all the UN sanctions be lifted immediately. Qaddafi's effort to shed his pariah status had taken a big step forward.

With worldwide media reporting on the legal settlement and diplomatic moves in New York at the United Nations, it appeared that Libya would quickly obtain what it had been seeking for years. All the reports and stories made clear that everyone expected a quick approval of Libya's request to have the Security Council sanctions lifted. Indeed, the media stories implied that this was a done deal. The final step was only a formality. Qaddafi's long-awaited day had come and his country's isolation would be a thing of the past.

There was only one problem, at the United Nation's Security Council.

Apparently, no one had consulted the French.

Chapter 14

The Forgotten Flight

THERE WAS WORLDWIDE media attention for the announcement of the Pan Am 103 Lockerbie $2.7 billion settlement as well as the submission of Libya's "acceptance of responsibility" letter to the United Nations Security Council. But there was extraordinary silence regarding the other notorious aircraft sabotage case that had, along with Lockerbie, been the impetus for the original UN sanctions against Qaddafi's regime. At first, none of the global press coverage of the Lockerbie settlement even mentioned the UTA 772 disaster, or the fact that the DC-10 had been blown up by a suitcase bomb, just like the jumbo jet over Scotland. It was as if Lockerbie was the only terrorist attack by Libya that had taken place. At least that was the impression given by all the coverage.

But there was one place where this silence was noticed. In Paris, the victims of the UTA 772 bombing began to call each other, asking how their own case—the murder of 170 people on a commercial jet—had been so neglected. The bitter taste of the farcical criminal trial in Paris, the empty defendant chairs emphasizing the fact that not one of the suspects had been brought to justice, was made worse by the fact that at least one of the Lockerbie suspects had been handed over to a Scottish criminal tribunal and convicted of murder. The French UTA 772 victims had watched the Lockerbie proceedings at The Hague from afar, mostly through the media, shaking their heads in bewilderment at the stark reality that the perpetrators of the UTA 772 bombing lived in splendor on the Mediterranean beaches outside Tripoli, protected by the French President's agreement with Qaddafi to allow them to remain free.

Even worse was the notion that the Libyans had only paid a total of approximately $35 million to the French government to cover the court-awarded costs and damages for some of the French victims of the UTA 772 attack. After the French government had deducted a large portion of that payment to cover its own expenses for the investigation and prosecution, a handful of French victims had received checks. But the amounts—in the region of a few thousand euros—now seemed insulting in comparison with the $10 million per family that Libya had agreed to pay each and every one of the American and British Lockerbie victims. To the French and African victim families, Qaddafi had not only got away with the murder of 170 innocent persons—he had bought off their leader at a bargain-basement price.

Françoise Rudetzki, whose organization, SOS Attentats, was closely monitoring the Lockerbie settlement and diplomacy in New York, was sickened by the spectacle of Qaddafi buying his way back into respectability. When asked about the Lockerbie deal by the French press, she dryly noted that "it is is a pity that Libya has managed to buy its impunity. It is not a good way of dealing with terrorism."

Many of the UTA 772 families, particularly those in France, felt the same way. But few had any idea of how to express their disgust and anger. The practical and forward-thinking Jacques Chirac had entered into a binding and public bilateral agreement with Qaddafi. The French criminal court cases were also concluded. None of the "convicted" Libyans would ever be extradited to France, or even face their accusers in a court of law. Finally, there was no procedure in France to bring any damages claims against the Libyan government—sovereign immunity was still the law of the land. Thus, there was no legal method to replicate the court settlement in New York that had helped force Qaddafi to pay victim families of the Lockerbie bombing.

In every sense—political, legal and diplomatic—the UTA 772 matter was a closed file as far as the French government was concerned. Indeed, they had never made payment of compensation to victims part of the United Nations Security Council criteria for the UTA 772 attack, in contrast to Lockerbie. But the intensive media coverage of the Pan Am 103 settlement continued to stick in the throats of the families who had lost their loved ones in the Ténéré desert.

PRESIDENT CHIRAC ALSO read about the Lockerbie settlement with great interest. From his perspective, it only proved his point that eventually the United States and Britain would come around and do business with Qaddafi. The world was a practical place, he always said, and the expensive Lockerbie settlement was the "American way" of dealing with dictators such as Qaddafi. His way, the French way, was just as effective, since his deal with Qaddafi a few years earlier had paved the way for French firms to get into Tripoli in advance of other companies and obtain lucrative contracts worth many billions of dollars. In comparison to the Lockerbie families settlement, the Chirac deal was actually a business proposition for French companies, who would be able to create jobs and bring cash back to France.

Or so it seemed.

Chirac had not counted on one thing. The huge amounts of the Lockerbie settlement—the $10 million per family—were an insult to the French victims. Apparently, an American or British victim of Libyan terrorism was worth a lot more than a French one. His advisers were hearing rumors from their contacts in the French press that SOS Attentats and the French UTA 772 victims were very upset. There were rumblings that Chirac had sold out the French victims and that he did not value a French victim's life.

This was especially ironic since under French law and procedure it was unheard of for a victim of any wrongful death case to receive multi-million-dollar settlements or court judgments. The French legal system, like most European civil law systems, typically would award very low damages for "pain and suffering" or even "economic losses" from a death. French legal scholars had, for years, derided the American tort system as more of an unpredictable casino than a thoughtful legal adjudication device.

The biggest, and most recent, legal settlement in France was itself unprecedented, and yet grossly smaller than the Lockerbie settlement. In July 2000, an Air France Concorde supersonic flight taking off from Charles de Gaulle Airport on a flight to JFK in New York caught fire and crashed, killing all 109 persons on board, plus 4 people on the ground. Investigators learned that debris from an earlier flight had hit the Concorde's wing, quickly causing a rupture in the fuel tanks and a catastrophic failure of the aircraft's engines and navigation systems. The disaster was the death knell of the once-proud supersonic aircraft, which was taken out of service by Air France shortly before the Lockerbie settlement was announced.

Each of the 109 families who lost a loved one on the Concorde had received a single 1 million Euros payment—far greater than anything ever paid in the past—in full satisfaction of any claims for negligence. The settlement was the largest ever made under French law and was widely considered necessary because of the prestige Concorde—a symbol of French engineering and travel—had brought Air France.

Even with the Concorde settlements, Lockerbie overwhelmed the French psyche. Qaddafi was paying American and British victims almost ten times more than had ever been paid to a French victim of a notorious air disaster. The growing outcry—how could French people be worth so much less than Americans and Brits?—was being picked up by French commentators, who bridled at the insulting comparison.

Chirac was a stubborn man and convinced in his heart that his earlier deal with Qaddafi was entirely the correct way to have wrapped up the UTA 772 file. But he was also not stupid and had a finely tuned ear when it came to the indignation of the French people. He and his advisers saw that the current state of play was unacceptable as a domestic political matter. His earlier move was politically indefensible. Despite the legal and diplomatic finality of his deal with Qaddafi, bold action was necessary if he was to avoid a domestic political tsunami.

* * *

SINCE ITS CREATION after World War II, the Security Council of the United Nations has acted as the principal international organization to maintain peace and security. One of its founding principles was that the world's major powers would maintain a permanent seat on the Council while other UN members rotated on and off. The most important power these permanent member states possess is an absolute right to veto any actions of the Security Council. Over the decades the United States and the former Soviet Union (now Russia) had exercised their veto powers regarding all sorts of disputes and military ventures.

The other three permanent members—Great Britain, the People's Republic of China and France—rarely exercised their veto. Diplomacy and consensus were their hallmarks. Simply the threat of a veto could change the minds of a diplomat, and usually did just that.

The economic and legal sanctions imposed by the Security Council on Libya in the early 1990s—specifically arising from the Pan Am 103 Lockerbie and UTA 772 terrorist attacks—had been one of the few times in its history that all the permanent members took affirmative and fairly aggressive action against a UN member state. The fact that none of the permanent members vetoed the sanctions had been a remarkable act of consensus.

With Libya's August letter to the Security Council taking responsibility for the Pan Am 103 Lockerbie attack and confirming the historic financial settlement, as well as renouncing terrorism generally, it appeared that Qaddafi's regime had satisfied all of the criteria set down by the Security Council a dozen years before. There was no tension at the New York headquarters between the permanent members or anyone else participating in the discussions. Libya's representatives were assured that the Security Council vote to lift the sanctions would be a mere formality.

But in a private phone call from President Chirac to his Foreign Minister Dominique de Villepin, a sophisticated and handsome descendant of royal French blood, the leaders of the French Republic decided that they had to negotiate a new deal with Qaddafi regarding the UTA 772 attack. Significant monies would have to be paid beyond the "final" deal negotiated back in 1999. Acting quickly, de Villepin instructed his ambassador at the UN to quietly suggest to the other members of the Security Council that France was prepared to veto the lifting of the Libyan sanctions.

This set off the diplomatic equivalent of a hand grenade. The Americans and British had spent several intense years negotiating the deal and had supported the Lockerbie lawyers as they completed their

Shortly before Christmas 1988, Pan Am Flight 103 was destroyed by a suitcase bomb while en route from London to New York. It crashed into Lockerbie, Scotland, killing 270 passengers, crew and local residents at ground zero.

In September 1989, French paratroopers landed in the remote Ténéré desert of Niger to investigate the wreckage of UTA Flight 772. The murder of 170 passengers and crew on the wide-body DC-10 set off the biggest criminal investigation in French history.

Even today, most of the wreckage of UTA 772 lies half-buried in the desert sand.

A French soldier stands watch over the wreckage of UTA 772 in 1989 as medical and forensic personnel from Paris begin their investigation.

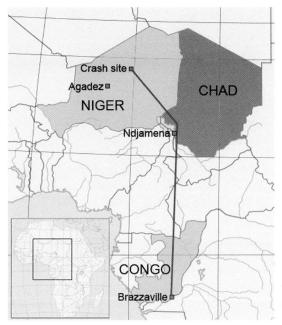

The French airline UTA flew the DC-10 on a regular round-trip route from former French colonies Brazzaville, Congo, and N'Djamena, Chad, to Charles de Gaulle Airport in Paris.

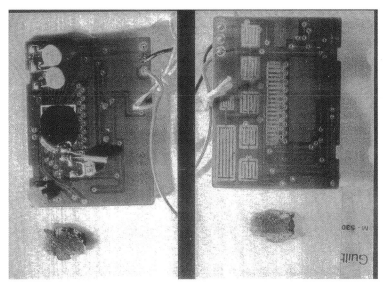

As French investigators reassembled the baggage section of UTA 772 outside Paris, they discovered a critical piece of evidence—a 5 millimeter circuit board fragment (shown here in Bruguière's Report), that was part of the timer for the suitcase bomb.

Investigating Magistrate Judge Jean-Louis Bruguière and his team proved Libya was responsible for the UTA bombing. Françoise Rudetski, herself a victim of a terrorist bombing in Paris, founded the victim organization l'association SOS Attentat Terrorisme, and provided the author with the extensive files from Bruguière's investigation.

Colonel Muammar Qaddafi and his brother-in-law Abdallah al-Senoussi, chief of Libyan Intelligence. Although Senoussi and 5 other Libyans were indicted in France for the UTA bombing, a deal between Qaddafi and French President Jacques Chirac ensured that no one ever faced murder charges.

In March 1992, the UN Security Council, backed by the Arab League, imposed a series of harsh sanctions on the Qaddafi regime on the basis of evidence pointing towards Libya's responsibility for the Lockerbie and UTA bombings.

In April 1995, a truck bomb exploded outside the Alfred P. Murrah Federal Office Building in Oklahoma City, killing 168 people. The victims' families joined with the Lockerbie victims' families to lobby Congress to enact the Anti-Terrorism and Effective Death Penalty Act of 1996, allowing suits against "state sponsors of terrorism" such as Libya.

Doug Matthews built the third-largest commercial aircraft leasing firm in the world, based in Atlanta. When one of his DC-10 aircraft went missing in the Ténéré desert in 1989, he began a tenacious quest for justice in Washington, D.C. federal court.

Career diplomat Robert Pugh was serving as Deputy Chief of Mission in Beirut, Lebanon, in April 1983 when Hezbollah set off a devastating truck bomb at the US Embassy. Six years later, while serving as US Ambassador to Chad after his appointment by President Ronald Reagan, his wife Bonnie was killed in the UTA 772 bombing.

Career State Department lawyer Jonathan Schwartz played a critical role in navigating the intricate maneuverings between the US, France, the UK, Libya and the UN, including extensive discussions with the author regarding the UTA case against Libya in Washington.

US District Court Judge Henry H. Kennedy presided over the Pugh v. Libya UTA litigation in Washington, holding the Libyan state and the 6 Libyan agents responsible for the bombing. The 2008 Bilateral Settlement Agreement between Qaddafi and President George W. Bush was a direct result of Judge Kennedy's rulings.

Part of the price for the 2008 Bilateral Settlement Agreement was that US Secretary of State Condoleezza Rice bore the unpleasant task of meeting Qaddafi in Tripoli on a well-publicized diplomatic visit designed to demonstrate to the world that Libya was no longer a pariah state.

Guillaume Denoix de Saint Marc founded the victim group Les Familles de l'Attentat du DC10 d'UTA, which built the UTA Memorial in the Ténéré desert near the crash site. When he met Qaddafi in Tripoli, his first words were "My father was on the DC-10."

Seen from a low-flying airplane, the UTA Memorial stands in stark contrast to the bleak emptiness of the Ténéré desert.

The memorial was constructed with rocks trucked in from the mountains to form a life-size silhouette of the DC-10. A wing from the wreckage was hoisted to hold a plaque listing the names of the 170 victims and broken mirrors were placed on the perimeter to honor each of them.

settlement discussions with the Libyans. When they were informed that France would stand in the way of this historic settlement, they were furious. In contrast to the United States and Britain, France had never demanded compensation as part of its position regarding UTA 772 and its inclusion in the original sanctions. Moreover, France already had informed the Security Council that its demands underlying the Libyan sanction resolutions—cooperation with Bruguière's investigation—had been fully met. The payment by Libya to France of the $35 million court penalties arising from the six criminal convictions had been accepted and honored, just as Chirac and Qaddafi had agreed.

But the French threat was serious and could undermine the entire Lockerbie agreement as well as the plan to integrate Libya back into the civilized world. The Americans and British accused France of hypocrisy given its earlier resolution of all these matters with Libya. One uniden-tified American diplomat was quoted as saying "They are trying to piggyback on our settlement and they are trying to blackmail the Libyans."

US Secretary of State Colin Powell called his French counterpart, de Villepin, on the telephone to urge him not to undermine the Lockerbie deal. Some US diplomats even threatened to "call the French bluff" and move ahead with a Security Council vote, daring Chirac to stand in the way. Arab diplomats, relieved to get the "Qaddafi problem" out of their hair, expressed concern that the Libyans would back out of the agreement.

Chirac and de Villepin stood their ground despite public and private attacks. The French Foreign Ministry issued a public statement saying that fairness required a "complementary settlement" for the French victims of UTA 772. The French might not favor large monetary settle-ments in their own legal system, but on the international stage they would make every effort to duplicate the success of the Americans in the Lockerbie matter. Chirac was serious and made clear he was not bluffing. France would veto any lifting of the sanctions at the Security Council.

Unless, that is, a new deal could be negotiated between France and Qaddafi.

FOLLOWING THIS SURPRISING development, a reporter for BBC News named Paul Reynolds wrote an online story mentioning the UTA 772 bombing—the first story not about Lockerbie to appear for some time. He described the reaction of the French to the Lockerbie settlement and the efforts of the French victims of the UTA 772 attack to reopen negotiations with the Libyans. He also referenced my law firm's website to recount the details of our federal court complaint for the seven Americans and Interlease in the Pugh case, which had never really been disclosed on a large international scale.

Summarizing the history of UTA 772 and the earlier French decision quietly to resolve the matter directly with Qaddafi, Reynolds noted how Chirac had staked out his own path to resolving things with Libya. An astute observer of French politics, the reporter could see that Chirac had made the decision to go his own way partly to distance France from the United States and its main ally, Great Britain. He also came up with the best description of UTA 772 I had yet heard. "Other than for those it directly affected," he wrote, UTA 772 was "the forgotten flight."

CHIRAC AND DE VILLEPIN had to move quickly if they were to use the threat of a French veto effectively at the UN Security Council. They needed to convince Qaddafi to reopen what he, and everyone else, had believed was a closed deal. Given this fact, and Qaddafi's well-known propensity for unpredictable behavior, a resulting tantrum could well undo all of the careful work that the French politicians had been able to accomplish since 1999.

The most important factor was that any approach to the Libyans, and any possible new deal, must be accomplished in a way that allowed all parties concerned to save face. Qaddafi had made several bold moves regarding Lockerbie, at some risk to his own domestic support. To capitulate to Chirac's Security Council blackmail might expose a weakness that any dictator could not afford. After some hushed discussions between French and Libyan diplomats, a plan was drawn up to allow the possibility of a deal that could remove the threat of a French veto but not embarrass Qaddafi.

It was secretly agreed between the French and the Libyans that there would not be any bilateral government-to-government negotiation. At least for appearance's sake. Chirac would simply request that a group representing the French victims of UTA 772 be allowed to meet with someone from the Qaddafi International Foundation for Charitable Associations, a "private" family organization run by Qaddafi's son, which performed "humanitarian work" around the world. Any discussions between these groups would avoid all issues of legal liability, governmental responsibility for the terrorist attack or linkage with Lockerbie and the UN sanctions. This was simply a humanitarian outreach by concerned private citizens.

To carry out this mission, Chirac arranged for Madame Rudetzki to be part of a delegation that would travel to Tripoli for discussions. This was especially awkward for the chief of the SOS Attentats group—her being Jewish and a woman was clearly not going to be a comfortable fit in the business environment of Qaddafi's strict Islamic and Arabic society. Also included in the delegation was the leader of a group formed by families who lost relatives in the UTA 772 bombing, Les familles du DC-10 d'UTA! He was a resident of Paris whose father had been on the flight, and who had organized the victim group to advocate for some recognition of the true losses they had suffered. His name was Guillaume Denoix de Saint Marc, a young, passionate spokesman who had been able to persuade the French press to pay attention to UTA 772 after Chirac's 1999 deal with Qaddafi appeared to have closed the file. Saint Marc, who wore light European-style glasses, simple clothes and who had the look of someone older than his late thirties would travel to Tripoli with his beautiful and stylish Parisian wife, Emmanuelle, and his cousin Valery, a well-respected Paris lawyer, along with Rudetzki.

Also included in the delegation was the Paris lawyer who had been representing SOS Attentats in the earlier criminal cases against the six Libyan murder suspects. Francis Szpiner was a short, intense French Jew who was highly regarded in legal circles for his courtroom skills and knowledge of criminal procedure. He had offered his services to Rudetzki back in 1999 pro bono, in order to assure the victims of a proper voice in the criminal trial.

But Chirac had his own reasons for selecting Szpiner for the mission to Libya. Szpiner also represented some of the most powerful political figures in France in highly sensitive and potentially embarrassing criminal investigations. He was the "man to see" if you were a French public figure caught up in a prosecutor's net. When Chirac was Mayor of Paris he was subject to many allegations and investigations of corruption, but none stuck. When he became President, official immunity protected him from the normal criminal system. But he had kept on his payroll the Paris lawyer who, so far, had kept him out of trouble. That same lawyer, his personal criminal lawyer, would travel to Tripoli on behalf of the UTA 772 victims. Francis Szpiner would make sure that the interests of his other client, the President of the French Republic, would not be implicated by the upcoming negotiations.

By the first week of September, the French delegation representing the UTA 772 victims had flown to Tripoli. Once there, they were greeted by Saleh Abdul Salam, a close confidant of Saif al-Islam Qaddafi, the Leader's son who ran the family foundation. The negotiations began in earnest and the French quickly learned how insulted the Qaddafi regime was to have heard that President Chirac had broken his word and decided to renege on their earlier settlement. There was much chest-pounding by the Libyans, who felt this was an insult to their country's honor. They had concluded the 1999 settlement in good faith and met all their legal and political obligations. That was what civilized countries were expected to do. And here was France, the apex of civilization and reason, turning its back on a solid and legally binding agreement. The French representatives were quite put off. They had not expected such a reaction. There was talk of going back to Paris empty-handed—they had deduced that Chirac had sent them in his place precisely to take the heat for his political decision to renege on the earlier settlement.

At this point the discussions were rescued by a career French diplomat in Tripoli who was observing the situation and reporting back to his boss de Villepin that the strategy was at risk of complete failure. This outcome would not only force the French government to return without a new agreement with the Libyans, but would also force Chirac to make good on his threat to veto the Lockerbie deal and continue the UN sanctions, despite intense pressure from the US, Britain and Arab world. When de Villepin heard from his man in Libya that the talks were about to collapse, he instructed the diplomat to step into the discussions and attempt to structure a deal that everyone could live with.

Ambassador Jean-Jacques Beaussou was a highly respected professional diplomat who was very familiar with the Arab world. From prior postings in Damascus and Tunisia, he had great experience resolving all sorts of problems, many so confidential they would never see the light of day. He had been sent to Tripoli as the French Ambassador— l'ambassadeur de France à Tripoli—in 2001, shortly after the full resumption of French–Libyan relations resulting from Chirac's 1999 deal with Qaddafi. He had spent many late nights in Qaddafi's Bedouin tent in the desert, listening to the Leader deliver rambling remarks that were intended to make their way back to Chirac. He knew Qaddafi's son Saif and understood the delicate tightrope that everyone needed to tread if a new deal was even possible. And he knew how to handle the work in a way that his superiors in Paris—the President and the Foreign Minister—could bear politically.

A tall, square-jawed bear of a man, more akin to a lumberjack in a suit than a mousy bureaucrat, Beaussou jumped into the process as soon as de Villepin gave him the green light. Focusing on the essential points, he suggested to both sides how to approach the stalemate created by Chirac's surprising moves and threats at the UN. Any deal must not appear to be the result of pressure, or legal threats, on the Libyans. It must be a humanitarian gesture from Libya to the French victims, who must embrace that gesture with friendship and appreciation. And there must be money. Enough to help Chirac save face in light of the huge Lockerbie amounts. But not so much that the Libyans would lose face in light of their earlier—presumably binding—agreement with Chirac in 1999.

Working around the clock, Beaussou managed to nudge the parties towards a mutual set of principles. Following his Ambassador's example, Guillaume Denoix de Saint Marc, leader of the French victim group, embraced the "spirit" of the meetings that was necessary to make progress. Szpiner, Chirac's lawyer and confidant, made sure that nothing came up to embarrass his other client.

But Rudetzki could not stomach the diplomatic niceties. These were the very same people who had murdered 170 persons in September 1989 by placing a bomb in the luggage hold of a French commercial jet. They were most likely the same people who had orchestrated the Pan Am 103 Lockerbie bombing and all the other acts of Libyan terrorism in the 1980s and 1990s. As a victim herself of a vicious attack in Paris that had left her unable to walk without a cane, and unable to accept the direction and tone of the negotiations, Rudetzki went back to France before things were resolved. Saint Marc and Beaussou were left to finish the job.

At a certain point the conversation turned to compensation. The Libyans made clear that a Lockerbie-type amount was simply not going to happen. That case had very different legal, political and diplomatic issues, all of which had contributed to the global settlement. The French understood this point, but also made clear that a number needed to be put forward that would show respect for the French victims. And they made the additional point that many Africans had been killed on the flight, and also needed the respect that would come from a revised settlement.

After a particularly grueling night of discussions and negotiations, both sides seemed to have reached a consensus. But there was not enough time to draft a comprehensive settlement document, or to finalize a financial figure. However, the Libyans made representations that, if the deal could be agreed to in principle, a detailed agreement would be banged out by the lawyers over the next few months. Some good faith would be required by both sides. But there was a looming deadline that drove the Libyans hard—the Security Council wanted to hold the sanctions vote as soon as possible, something that Qaddafi needed.

The threat of a French veto at the UN had worked. Chirac's gamble had caused great tension between him, his Western allies and the Arab world, threatening the détente he had so carefully cultivated. But he had guessed that Qaddafi wanted the sanctions lifted above all else, and, with Beaussou pulling the parties closer and closer, Qaddafi had blinked. They even had a financial agreement, one that saved face for both sides.

Although not yet prepared to make things public, Libya was ready to pay each of the victims of the UTA 772 bombing exactly €1 million—a total of €170 million. This was a per-victim number identical to the amount paid by Air France to the families of those killed in the Concorde disaster. It was nothing close to the Lockerbie deal, but it was still a lot of money, especially to the African families, and a multiple of what the French victims could imagine under French legal procedures.

Each side received something that it had sought. The French threat of a veto would be removed; the UN vote could proceed. A short memorandum was prepared to summarize the status of the discussions, an "Accord" barely two pages long, given the present lack of detail, a "humanitarian" gesture between the UTA 772 victims and the Qaddafi Foundation. A simple and private agreement between well-meaning parties.

But it also anticipated that everyone receiving this "humanitarian payment" must waive their rights to seek any other legal relief or compensation. The Libyans were not stupid. They had already done one deal with the French. They wanted this to be the definitive conclusion to the UTA 772 matter. They did not trust Chirac and were privately insulted and angry at his betrayal. But the two-page document, dated 10 September, was formal enough to provide Chirac with what he needed to remove the threat of a veto, and it made clear that France would not stand in the way of the upcoming and, for Qadaffi, all-important vote at the UN.

The short document was signed late at night by Saleh for the Qaddafi Foundation, by Saint Marc for the UTA 772 victims group, and by Szpiner for SOS Attentats, given that Rudetzki had already left in disgust. To honor their achievement, the Leader invited them to an audience at his residence. Qaddafi was thrilled that the UN vote to lift the sanctions was now cleared to proceed without the threat of Chirac's veto. The cost to reopen the UTA 772 matter was stiff, but his diplomats, and his son Saif, had trod carefully through the thicket.

As the French delegation was introduced to Qaddafi, Saint Marc approached the long-time dictator who had orchestrated so many terrorist attacks and murders. Speaking in French, with a translator making sure the Leader understood, Saint Marc shook Qaddafi's hand and said "Mon père etait dans le DC-10." "My father was on the DC-10." He would later write a book of this title in which he recounted the negotiations in Tripoli that cleared the way for Libya to rejoin the world and pay each victim €1 million, far more than anyone had ever imagined. It was the only book ever written about the UTA 772 bombing. Until now.

* * *

ON 12 SEPTEMBER 2003, only two days later, the UN Security Council in New York adopted Resolution 1506, lifting all of the international sanctions and removing Libya entirely from the Council's agenda. No country exercised its veto powers. However, the United States decided to abstain from the vote rather than provide an affirmative statement of support to the Qaddafi regime.

In its statement explaining this decision, the Administration of President George W. Bush made clear that it did not oppose the vote because it wanted to allow the Pan Am 103 Lockerbie families to receive their first $4 million installment of the settlement, but it did not want to provide Qaddafi with a stamp of rehabilitation. At the time, the Bush White House and CIA were secretly negotiating with the Libyans about a wholesale reversal of Libyan policy in the Weapons of Mass Destruction (WMD) area. The details of those discussions were so secret that the Administration could not mention them in its statement, and thought it necessary to give the appearance of lingering adversity to the Qaddafi regime.

This secret brought a dramatic change to the landscape. On 19 December, Libya, the United States and the British publicly announced that Qaddafi had agreed to abandon the nuclear weapons program that he had purchased from the infamous Pakistani scientist Dr. A. Q. Khan. He also would stop any work on long-range missiles and chemical and biological weapons, and turn over to the West everything associated with these weapons programs.

Apparently, Qaddafi had been engaged in top-secret discussions with a high-ranking CIA official named Steve Kappes, a former Marine known for his tough, no-nonsense approach to problems. The talks had been personally authorized by President Bush. The breakthrough came in October 2003, just after the UN sanctions were lifted and the first Pan Am 103 Lockerbie payments were distributed. At that time the US

Navy intercepted a ship heading from Dubai to Libya that was found to be carrying centrifuge devices necessary to build a nuclear bomb. The CIA and other intelligence agencies had finally cracked the Khan nuclear ring and their information allowed the Navy to grab the ship, and its cargo. This actually provided Qaddafi with the diplomatic excuse to "give up" his WMDs by saying he had no choice—the "evidence" proved what he had been denying for some time. With this convenient scenario, President Bush and Qaddafi could close the deal on WMDs and put the resumption of US and Libyan relations fully back on track. American and British experts subsequently went to Libya and physically verified that Qaddafi was out of the WMD business, even shipping back to the US vital components of the dictator's nuclear cabinet.

Once again, Qaddafi took a risk that enabled him to turn around his regime and make friends with the former enemies that had bombed his country and almost killed him in 1986. As a dictator, he was able to control the direction of his regime while covering his back to make sure he did not appear weak to his domestic constituencies. The former outcast, the world's most notorious supporter of terrorism, was now back in the family of nations. Paying out large amounts of cash, surrendering his WMD program and allowing a process for the conviction and imprisonment of a single Libyan agent had allowed the Leader of the great Libyan Socialist Jamahiriya to discard the scarlet letter he had earned as the world's most dangerous sponsor of terrorism.

The Pan Am 103 Lockerbie families and their lawyers now had their settlement, despite the misgivings of many of the families. As a result, their case in the federal court in New York was dismissed. The French and African victims of UTA 772 had a new and much better deal than the one extracted in 1999, with monetary sums unheard of in their own legal systems. In what some commentators characterized as a gross rationalization, President Bush bragged that his invasion of Iraq had helped convince Qaddafi to turn over his WMD program. And Chirac had overcome a potentially embarrassing domestic situation to extract what, in France, was considered a very positive and honorable result.

In January 2004, the French Foreign Minister de Villepin and his Libyan counterpart, Abdel Rahman Chalgham, signed the formal settlement between the UTA 772 victims and the Qaddafi Foundation, watched by a large group in the ornate surroundings of the Foreign Ministry building in Paris. The €1 million payment per victim had been formally announced and a French Foundation, headed by Saint Marc, would oversee the payments. Libya had deposited the funds and the UTA 772 matter was, once and for all, resolved with finality.

Or so it seemed. There were a few people in the United States who were not so sure. Doug Matthews and I had watched from afar as the new French settlement had been quickly constructed and organized. The final agreement would require anyone who desired to obtain the payment, including the seven American families I represented, to drop any and all legal claims against Libya or its agents and officials.

The time had come for my clients in the Pugh litigation to decide how all these developments would affect our own case in Washington.

Chapter 15
The Race

SHORTLY AFTER THE French and Libyan governments announced their new settlement in September and the path was cleared for the United Nations Security Council to lift the sanctions, we appeared in federal court in Washington for our first procedural skirmish in the Pugh case against Libya's counsel in Washington. At that time, it became clear that Qaddafi's principal tactic in the Pugh case was to delay the court's decision on the substantive "merits" issue—Libya's responsibility for blowing up the DC-10 and killing 170 people—for as long as possible.

Up to this point, diplomacy, unique court proceedings and secret settlement negotiations had worked well for the Libyans. The rapid deal negotiated between the French and African victims of UTA 772 and the Libyans had been accomplished behind closed doors in Tripoli, with the quiet assistance of Chirac and his diplomats. It was based simply on the promise of a large check from a "humanitarian" organization, not the Libyan government: there was no closure for the families, no accountability by the Qaddafi regime for its murderous conduct. Libya's vast oil money was buying off a political problem, and with a rather large discount.

The Pan Am 103 Lockerbie litigation in New York had settled and was now dismissed without moving the case into the merits of the victims' claims. Indeed, that was one of the reasons why so many of the Lockerbie families felt dissatisfied, despite the substantial dollar figures. In contrast to their earlier case against Pan Am—where victims had testified, experts had presented detailed evidence and the air carrier had been declared guilty of gross violations of airline safety regulations—no one connected with Libya had been held accountable for the bombing over Scotland. No court findings had been made. No families had testified in court. There had simply been a large payment, and even that in stages, dependent on how quickly the United Nations and President Bush lifted various sanctions. The families of the victims felt left out as they waited for the outcome of the secret negotiations by their lawyers and then the public announcement of the settlement.

For many of the Pan Am 103 Lockerbie families, this created an empty feeling of dissatisfaction. Money was clearly not enough to declare victory over Qaddafi and the men who had murdered their loved ones in cold blood. Very few felt they had obtained any sense of closure or justice for the tragic hole left in their lives.

After President Bush publicly announced the resolution of the WMD program in December, I could sense that there was still other quiet diplomacy going on between the US and Libya. With the New York Lockerbie case settled and dismissed, and the French portion of the new UTA agreement signed, Libya was handling these problems quietly, not in the public arena of a federal courtroom.

In contrast, our Pugh case in Washington was still a threat to the Leader's global strategy for closing all these chapters of his violent past. The Libyans could see from our detailed complaint in the Pugh case that we had somehow obtained a lot of the incriminating evidence compiled by Bruguière and his investigators—evidence they would later try to exclude on legal grounds.

Given that most of the developments in the quickly evolving state of US–Libyan relations would be accomplished in this quiet, and for the most part secret, manner, it was clear that part of my work in the Pugh case was going to extend beyond the courtroom. To represent my clients, this would require my having a close connection with the US

Department of State—the critical government agency handling the Libya diplomacy for President Bush.

I figured that I could help the Bush Administration, and in return they could help my case, as events developed, with my keeping American diplomats informed of the progress and strategy in our case, perhaps receiving some off-the-record intelligence in return. Given the frayed relationship between the Bush and Chirac governments after the threat of the French veto of the UN sanctions, I also thought I might be able to bridge some of the connections between the two countries in a way that helped the prosecution of my own civil case.

With regard to the court proceedings in the Pugh case, in October 2003 the federal judge who earlier had decided the Terry Anderson case and several other prominent terrorism cases, Thomas Penfield Jackson, held the first hearing in Pugh. Libya's lawyer, Dabiri, had made his first response to the case a request that the property damage claims brought by Interlease against the Libyan government be dismissed, since the FSIA statute did not expressly authorize "non-personal injury or death" damages. This had always been an open legal question for our case, and our written briefs to Judge Jackson had made what I thought were good arguments why such claims should be included. But Libya was going to mount an aggressive defense, leaving no issue off the table. Dabiri and I engaged in a spirited legal argument in the ornate courtroom at the federal courthouse, the same courtroom where I had previously argued many other cases.

Judge Jackson was fully engaged and enjoyed the Socratic give-and-take of the arguments. With Doug Matthews watching from the front row, and my team at the counsel table in support, we left the hearing with the feeling that Judge Jackson was struggling with the issue. Of course, the wrongful death claims of the seven families would not be dismissed, a point Dabiri had conceded. But we were jockeying for position in the case, trying to strengthen our hand for a possible settlement negotiation down the road. Such procedural issues directly affect the value of many cases. With millions of dollars of a destroyed DC-10 at stake, we would have to fight for every inch of ground.

As for the Department of State, I had reviewed some of the briefs filed several years earlier by the US government in the Pan Am 103

Lockerbie litigation up in New York. I had recognized one of the names of the lawyers who had drafted the government's papers as a long-time member of the Legal Advisor's Office: Jonathan Schwartz. Earlier efforts to reach out to the State Department's Legal Advisor to seek assistance in the Kilburn case had pointed us to Schwartz as the person working on the Libya file. After the October hearing in Pugh, I decided to give him a call.

Schwartz was one of the senior lawyers working for the Department of State and had served as one of the advisers on all things relating to Libya. He had been working closely with Kreindler's law firm throughout the Lockerbie negotiations. He also was helping the Bush Administration shape American policy towards Qaddafi in the rapidly changing relationship with the dictator who had formerly been Public Enemy Number One, at least in the terrorism universe.

After serving as an editor of the *Stanford Law Review*, Schwartz, a native Californian, had come to Washington to clerk for Judge David Bazelon of the US Court of Appeals for the DC Circuit, one of the most prestigious clerkships in the country. He had immediately joined the Legal Advisor's Office at the Department of State, where he had risen up the ranks by working on some of the most challenging and interesting foreign policy issues in the world. In an office known for hiring the best and brightest young lawyers in the country, Schwartz was long considered one of the very top legal minds. He had a special interest in the problems arising in the Middle East, and regularly accompanied Secretaries of State and even Presidents on important diplomatic missions.

I had first met Schwartz, a native of California, when we were both young law clerks at the federal courthouse back in 1979. My judge, Harold H. Greene, was a prominent trial judge who sometimes was asked to sit on the Court of Appeals because of the respect he had throughout the bench. Judge Greene's own mentor was the same Judge Bazelon, who had helped guide Greene's career when he had clerked on the Court of Appeals a generation earlier. Through that connection, I had some contacts with Schwartz as law clerks assisting the judges in their work. When I later served in the US Attorney's Office, the Department of State was one of my client agencies and I had some further, albeit minor, interactions with Schwartz on a few cases.

Although not close friends at that point, I felt comfortable calling him on the phone to renew the connection, and to explore how we might be able to cooperate regarding the fast-moving Libya matters that were now on both of our desks.

Schwartz and I touched base a few times, just sharing some initial thoughts and gingerly feeling out how much we might be able to co-operate together. Confidentiality was a hallmark of the Legal Advisor's office, and Schwartz was extremely careful about what he told me, or what the Bush Administration might be thinking. But we agreed to keep each other posted on developments. The bitter taste in his mouth regarding Chirac's midnight-hour threats to veto lifting the Libya sanctions at the UN—after all the effort and achievement accomplished by the US in its diplomacy with Libya—was still quite strong.

Based on the fact that we had known each other most of our careers, and my earlier work as the State Department's advocate in court when I had been in the government, a solid line of communication was opened. But despite our relationship, I knew that Schwartz would only share with me information that assisted the Bush Administration in its own agenda. He would provide me assistance because it was good for American foreign policy. That policy favored the support of American victims of Libyan terrorism, under US law. This was no gift to me by the Department of State's top lawyer on the Libya file. It was part of his job.

In February 2004, Schwartz shared with me the first pieces of information that would provide a sense of the direction of US policy towards Qaddafi's regime. At that time, he gave me a heads up that President Bush was about to lift the long-standing ban on Americans traveling to Libya on US passports. This was not a measure designed to enhance the local Libyan tourism industry. Instead, it was specifically intended to allow US oil companies with "historical holdings" in Libya dating back before the Colonel's regime to return to those oil fields and aging equipment in order to inspect the state of things on the ground. Knowing the strong connection the Bush Administration had with the oil industry, I was not surprised. It also demonstrated the clear desire of Qaddafi to open up his energy sector to US technology and markets. Chirac's desire to get a leg up on the Americans had only provided a small advantage to the French oil companies, which were not yet fully engaged in Libya. As usual, Qaddafi was playing off the French against the Americans and British.

A short time later, Schwartz informed me that the US would reopen its diplomatic mission in Libya by June, after working through the Belgians for so many years. Technically, formal relations between the US and Libya had never been broken, in contrast to our diplomatic relations with the Islamic Republic of Iran. To take this progress in stages, President Bush would only characterize the new diplomatic post as a "Liaison Office" and not an Embassy. Such a title would have to await improvements in the relationship.

Around that time Schwartz also told me that the President would lift certain sanctions that related to the United Nations agenda being resolved, another step in the carefully calibrated give-and-take that each country was employing in the wranglings of international diplomacy. President Bush was required to certify to Congress Libya's compliance with certain measures, and by June he had done just that. With that certification, several of the legal barriers that had prevented US businesses from returning to Libya were eliminated. Again, the US oil industry was driving this process, and their friends in the Bush Administration were opening the necessary doors.

Schwartz and I got into a rhythm. Before any significant measures were introduced, he would provide a brief note to me, right before they became public. I did not consider this process to be a special favor between former colleagues or friends. We were both lawyers doing our jobs, for our respective clients, whose interests overlapped.

With these developments on the diplomatic front throughout the spring of 2004, we had to evaluate how best to position our Pugh case in court to be ready for what we hoped were the inevitable settlement discussions with the Libyans. Judge Jackson had ruled on Libya's motion to dismiss the property claims of Interlease, and sided with Dabiri on this legal issue. He also ruled at the same time that Interlease could still move ahead with its property damage claim against the six Libyans we had sued on an "individual" basis, although the chances of collecting from the six convicted murderers living comfortably in Tripoli was remote, to say the least. While not a shock, given our concern that the law might be vague on this subject, it was still disappointing since it provided Libya with some leverage in the case. Lawyers spend years on a case trying to wind up in a position where they have the best poker hand to employ in a negotiation. What surprised us more was that, despite winning this issue, Libya decided to take an immediate appeal of Judge Jackson's ruling! Their strategy of delay was being played out on a frivolous level.

In a normal case, the parties cannot appeal a trial judge's legal rulings until the completion of the case, either after trial or when all the claims are dismissed. This rule prevents cases from bouncing up and down in the court system, and allows a federal trial judge to keep a tight rein on managing the proceedings. It is also a way to force the parties to settle, as they may not have the time, patience or energy to wait for an appeal to be resolved.

This rule has a small but important exception. When it comes to countries being sued in court under the Foreign Sovereign Immunities Act, that country can take an immediate appeal of any issue resolved against it by the trial judge that relates to a defense of "jurisdiction" or "sovereignty." Such non-final, or "interlocutory," appeals have been imbedded in our legal system for decades, and reflect the basic notion that sovereign immunity is not just a defense against losing a case it is an absolute defense from even being sued in the first place. If a trial judge denies a country's assertion of sovereign immunity, that ruling can be appealed immediately to the Court of Appeals, and the entire case in the trial court must be brought to a standstill until the appeal is resolved.

This would be Libya's standard delaying tactic in our case. Even though Judge Jackson had agreed with its immunity defense on the Interlease issue—ruling that only the families, not commercial entities, could move forward with their claims against Libya as a sovereign state—Dabiri filed an appeal. Clearly, he was being instructed to employ any conceivable procedural measure to delay the case, however frivolous. This brought our efforts to a full stop in the trial court, as we turned our attention to convincing the DC Circuit that the appeal was frivolous and should be dismissed. This would take time, of course. Which was exactly Libya's plan.

With this dynamic in play, in the summer of 2004 I received a call from Dabiri asking if my seven client families in Pugh would be willing to accept the €1 million payment per family from the French Foundation that had been set up to administer the recent Libya–France UTA 772 settlement. Of course, this would require us to dismiss the entire Pugh litigation and bring our efforts to a conclusion. He also indicated that there "might be some money" for Interlease for the loss of the DC-10 if we accepted this proposal, a hint that the Libyans understood the importance of honoring commercial contracts and property rights in the newly emerging world of Libya as a good place to conduct business.

This became the moment of truth for Matthews and the families. Our plan to push the litigation aggressively against Libya had been stalled through Dabiri's frivolous appeal of the first ruling by Judge Jackson. Even if we won the appeal, which I fully expected would occur, it would take many months and temporarily relieve the pressure against Libya. The French settlement money was tempting to some of the families, who figured that over $1 million was still a good outcome given how long they had waited for justice and the fact that it was not taxable as income under US law. Interlease might be able to negotiate an additional payment if the families were ready to accept this amount, and all the recovery would be put into the pot created by Matthews and the families under their Joint Prosecution Agreement. It was tempting. Even my law firm took a hard look at the proposal, since we would completely recover our investment in the case to date and even show a small positive return. But such a deal also would not succeed in accomplishing our initial goal of holding Libya accountable for mass murder in a court of law.

Upon reflection, and from a financial viewpoint, I thought we could do much better than the deal Dabiri was proposing, even with some extra money for the loss of the DC-10. The Lockerbie families were eligible to receive up to $10 million if all the conditions of their settle-ment were met. They already had received the first $4 million payment when the UN sanctions had been lifted, so we knew the Libyans were probably good for the money if we negotiated a settlement. We also believed the DC-10 was worth up to $40 million, and I also had heard through some sources that Libya might be willing to pay Pan Am and its London-based insurers for the value of the 747 blown up over Scotland. Thus, from a strictly financial perspective, Dabiri's offer was a start, but was simply too low to accept. We also had other factors to consider, which pushed us away from a quick and inequitable resolution.

One of the things that had motivated many of my clients in other terrorism cases was the opportunity for a federal judge in Washington to conduct a trial and actually make specific findings about a country's responsibility for carrying out a terrorist attack. The notion of holding the country responsible—what I characterize as "accountability"—in a court of law was a central part of every case we were pursuing.

Qaddafi had managed to settle the French portion of the UTA 772 case without any accountability against his regime. He could easily characterize those settlements as political or humanitarian gestures wholly unrelated to any judicial determination of his country's responsibility for mass murder. Notwithstanding Bruguière's extensive and detailed investigation, the murder trial in Paris had been something of a farce, with the six suspects not appearing at all to put on a defense or face their accusers, with the complete blessing of the French government and President Chirac. Qaddafi could brag that he and the Libyan agents had never been properly convicted of any crime whatsoever. And of course, the Libyan government could not even be sued in a French court.

In the case of Lockerbie, the letter provided to the United Nations Security Council in September 2003 fell far short of a federal judge making specific findings about Libya's responsibility for that act of mass murder over Scotland. That case was settled without any judicial findings—something the Libyans had made a part of their strategy in the New York case. The UN letter could be explained away as a politically expedient gesture, a realpolitik approach to settling diplomatic disputes. It was hardly a confession. And it could be excused as a note derived under economic duress by the sanctions. The United Nations letter simply lacked the level of finality and detail that a court judgment could provide.

In talking to several persons familiar with the Lockerbie case, it was even suggested that the lawyers handling that case might have been hesitant to go to trial exactly because they were afraid the evidence gathered by the FBI and Scotland Yard might not carry their burden of proof. After all, one of the two Libyans charged with the Scotland bombing had been acquitted outright, and the other was convicted on circumstantial evidence that might not be strong enough to find a government liable under the FSIA. A settlement made such measures unnecessary and avoided the risk—to both sides—of an uncertain outcome.

The Pugh families had another factor to consider that also played into the equation. Receiving a large check might allow a family to purchase a home, pay off a mortgage or finance a child's college education. But it did not bring closure to the personal loss and grief that they had suffered when the DC-10 went down in the desert. Many of the spouses who lost loved ones would never really overcome that loss, and even getting remarried did not heal the wounds. Those who had lost a child were even more unfulfilled in their grief, despite the passage of fifteen years, as they pondered what path their children and possible grandchildren might have taken. Children who lost parents had drifted, suffering from depression, some even to the point of despair.

In short, the promise of a trial in a Washington federal courtroom where they could unburden their grief after all these years and confront the party that had killed their loved ones—even if only through their lawyer, Dabiri—was an important element to consider. If closure for the families was part of the plan, a quick and unsatisfying financial settlement would just not do the trick.

Another important factor was that the US government was still holding over $1 billion in frozen Libyan assets. Those funds would be our target to satisfy any court judgment in the case, since under US law they had to be turned over to us upon entry of a final federal court judgment against Libya under the terrorism exception to the FSIA. This was a significant safety net for our strategy.

With that in mind, and the other factors clearly presented as favoring a continuation of the case, I called Dabiri and told him we would not participate in the French UTA settlement. The Pugh plaintiffs were prosecuting their case under US law, in a US courtroom, and Dabiri's effort to encourage us to drop the case and accept the French Foundation payment was rejected.

We decided to push ahead.

* * *

PART OF OUR strategy in pursuing Libya was to handle all of our Libya-related cases in a manner that created the best overall environment to force Libya to settle. To accomplish this goal, we had been pushing hard on another terrorism case against Libya, which was now also in the Court of Appeals for the DC Circuit.

Peter Kilburn, the Librarian at the American University of Beirut, who was kidnapped by Hezbollah terrorists working at the direction of Iran and held as one of the many hostages seized in Lebanon in the mid-1980s, had been "purchased" from his captors by Qaddafi's agents in April 1986. They then tortured and eventually shot him to death in reprisal for President Reagan's bombing of Tripoli, which itself was in reprisal for the La Belle bombing in West Berlin. The never-ending cycle of violence in the Middle East had not resulted in anything positive or constructive.

Kilburn's brother had retained my law firm to represent his brother's estate in a wrongful death claim against Libya. The trial judge had rejected all of Dabiri's jurisdictional defenses and immunity objections, and, following its strategy of delay, Libya had taken an immediate interlocutory appeal. The case was one of the very first against Libya to be argued in the Court of Appeals and in May 2004 we found ourselves in the historic courtroom on the fifth floor of the federal courthouse on Constitution Avenue. The portraits of famous jurists lining the walls reminded the lawyers of the court's significance as the "second most important court in the land," after the Supreme Court.

I was going to argue the case for the Kilburn family, and two of my colleagues who had helped draft the briefs, Mike Martinez and Cliff Elgarten, sat at the counsel table across from Dabiri to get ready for the oral argument. Both of them were quite involved in the Libya cases, with Mike having served with me in the US Attorney's Office before joining our firm, and Cliff having clerked for Justice William Brennan of the US Supreme Court earlier in his career. Unlike most cases, however, the United States government had decided to participate in the argument as a "friend of the court," or *amicus curiae*.

This was partly the result of my conversations with Schwartz, and partly because the Bush Administration did not need me to educate them as to the importance of "setting the rules" in these cases at an early stage. Important issues affecting the country's foreign policy interests could be implicated by the Court of Appeals' decision, and every issue, big and small, was carefully evaluated by the lawyers at the Departments of State and Justice, as well as at the White House. The results of the Kilburn case would have a direct bearing on all the terrorism cases pending against Libya, including the Pugh case, which was stuck in neutral in the same Court of Appeals as part of Dabiri's strategy to delay as long as possible.

The oral argument in the Court of Appeals was before what I would call a Supreme Court panel. In the center seat was Chief Judge Douglas Ginsburg, who had been nominated to the US Supreme Court by President Reagan only to withdraw his name when it became public that he had smoked marijuana while teaching at Harvard Law School. A brilliant and dedicated legal scholar and judge, his personal history with recreational drugs was just a bit ahead of the curve considering that several Presidents thereafter—Clinton, George W. Bush and Obama—had "experimented" with drugs.

To his left was Judge John Roberts, the top appellate lawyer in town until nominated to the Court of Appeals. A few years later, he would become Chief Justice of the United States. Roberts was universally considered one of the most capable lawyers ever to practice in Washington, both in and out of government.

To the other side of Ginsburg, on his right, was Judge Merrick Garland, a Clinton appointee who was no stranger to terrorism cases— he had previously served as one of the lead federal prosecutors of the Oklahoma City bombing defendants. He and Roberts had even attended Harvard Law School together, where they both shone. At the time of my writing, he had been nominated to the US Supreme Court by President Obama, but was denied the post when Donald Trump was elected President.

With this best-and-brightest appellate bench, the Kilburn case would receive the finest judicial scrutiny in the land. Dabiri faced a series of tough technical questions, and the government lawyer from the Department of Justice, Douglas Hallward-Driemeier, was forced to dance carefully around many questions on which the Bush Administration clearly did not want to take a position. I got my own share of tough questions from the panel, and Roberts and Garland were especially sharp in probing the legal angles raised under the arcane Foreign Sovereign Immunities Act. They were seriously engaged in the importance of a federal court resolving issues that directly affected American foreign policy and mindful that even victims of terrorism could only receive as much justice in the federal court system as Congress had been willing to dole out. This area of the law was complicated and untested, and three of the best legal minds in the United States were working hard to make sure they got it right.

After over an hour, it was difficult to determine where the panel was headed. Dabiri then rose to present a rebuttal argument to many of the questions I had fended off during my time at the podium. This was something I had done many times in this court. But still, it never failed to be exciting as an advocate, and as an intellectual matter. Jousting with brilliant legal minds was what it was all about in my world of lawyering.

As Dabiri attempted to explain to the panel why it was so difficult to determine which substantive law to apply to Libya—a foreign sovereign state—he made a serious mistake. He reached out and employed the example of the Pugh case to argue that it was unfair, and thus improper, to subject Libya to the laws of many different states where a number of victims were from all over the country. Leaning over the bench, Judge Garland looked over his glasses and, in the gravest tone I had ever heard from the bench, revealed to us all in the courtroom his inner thinking: "Well counsel," he began. "Don't blow up airplanes if you don't want to be subject to the laws of fifty different states."

Both Ginsburg and Roberts jumped in, noting their agreement with Garland. The packed courtroom became stone silent. Dabiri did not know how to respond. The court had made clear that, even with the

Pugh case not before them that day, Libya was not going to get any slack. I turned to my two partners sitting at counsel table with me, Elgarten and Martinez, and whispered under my breath: "Oh boy. That was nice to hear."

Dabiri managed to recover after what seemed like a full minute of stunned silence. He finished up his argument and the panel retired from the bench.

Our strategy seemed to be working.

* * *

A FEW MONTHS later, in June, I got a call that indicated the Court of Appeals might be more with the program than I had even imagined.

Jill Sayenga, the Circuit Executive for the Court of Appeals, asked if my clients in Pugh might be willing to submit their case to a court-appointed mediator in an effort to resolve the case. Libya's appeal in Pugh was still pending in the appellate court, and, with the Kilburn argument still fresh in their minds, perhaps the judges believed that the Lockerbie–Libya settlement model widely reported in the press might present an opportunity for a settlement of this other airplane disaster case. Of course, I jumped at the idea, but cautioned it would take two to tango. Mediation was strictly voluntary, and Libya could not be compelled to participate.

I also suggested that the best way to make this happen was for the court to engage the US government in the process, perhaps as a "facilitator." Sayenga agreed, and asked whom she should contact. I told her to call Schwartz, the key man at State on the Libya file who had been involved in the Lockerbie case. She agreed. I made a quick call to Schwartz to give him a heads up, and to suggest that having the Bush Administration sit in on the mediation could help resolve the case and thus further US and Libyan diplomacy.

Only a few days later, I received a letter from the Court of Appeals scheduling a mediation at the courthouse between my law firm and Libya's lawyers. I called Matthews and told him to book a flight. We might get the settlement process moving a lot faster than we had anticipated. The letter also noted that lawyers from the Departments of State and Justice would attend, not as parties, but to facilitate the discussions. Schwartz had agreed with my suggestion. The United States government would extend its diplomatic efforts into our Pugh litigation.

THE COURT OF APPEALS had reached out to a respected lawyer in private practice to act as the mediator. This was an accepted procedure in court-ordered dispute resolution proceedings, since the judges still had to decide the case if the mediation did not succeed.

John Nolan was a senior partner at the respected Steptoe & Johnson law firm, one of the city's older litigation powerhouse shops. A short and compact man with a firm handshake and probing eyes, Nolan was a former US Marine and had worked for Attorney General Robert "Bobby" Kennedy in the early 1960s as a young government lawyer. He had spent decades handling complex cases around the country. This request by the Court of Appeals was a great honor for him, despite the fact that he would act pro bono and not receive any fee for his efforts. Public service is not limited to full-time government employees. Washington had a long history of lawyers with private firms performing acts of public service. The Pugh mediation in the DC Circuit fit that tradition like a glove.

After submitting confidential proposals to Nolan that would not be reviewed by the other side, we agreed to conduct our first meeting for the mediation in the Court of Appeals conference room on the fifth floor of the federal courthouse. Libya's appeal in Pugh was not scheduled to be argued until November, and thus the mediation would be the only game in town to move the Pugh case forward. Nolan wanted both sides to bring "principals" with authority to settle the case on the spot. This is a common practice in mediations, and Nolan's years of experience had taught him that anything less would just degenerate into a room of verbose lawyers unable to close a deal.

From our side, Doug Matthews would represent all the families as well as Interlease. His Florida corporate lawyer John Metzger also would attend. From my firm, I would bring my partners Laurel Malson and Mike Martinez, who had been working on the case for some time, and Beth Nolan, another partner who had joined my firm after serving as

President Clinton's White House Counsel. Beth also had run the Department of Justice Office of Legal Counsel, the central nervous system that advised the entire United States government on every aspect of policy. Beth's extraordinary experience in government and her focused energy were a welcome addition to our team. We needed all the skills we could muster given the combined legal–political forces that would determine the course of our efforts.

On Libya's side, Dabiri would attend as its litigation counsel, as we expected. But we would not see a Libyan government official sit in on our efforts. The progress in building up US–Libyan diplomatic efforts had not yet reached a point where Libyan officials could travel to Washington for settlement discussions. Instead, Libya would authorize one of its Paris-based lawyers to speak on its behalf, and carry a settlement proposal to present in our meetings.

On a hot, humid day in late August, the summer sun and haze forcing all Washingtonians to flee the City or hide inside air-conditioned rooms, the parties gathered in the conference room used by the Court of Appeals judges to conduct court business and decide cases of national significance. Fortunately, the air conditioning was in good working order, and our team arrived a few minutes early to get settled. John Nolan (no relation to my partner Beth Nolan) was already present, having met with the Circuit Executive Sayenga to finalize the arrangements for the mediation.

Schwartz arrived a few minutes later. A thin, slightly pale figure in a gray pin-striped suit, the Department of State's principal lawyer for all things relating to Libya was no stranger to the fifth floor. He had clerked there twenty-five years earlier and was comfortable in the judicial surroundings. He spoke separately with John Nolan to clarify his role, and to make sure the Bush Administration was not viewed as a party to the mediation, merely a helpful observer. Diplomacy required as much. And Schwartz was the lawyer for all the diplomats working to improve the country's evolving relationship with the Qaddafi regime. The fact that he was even present in a dispute such as this was itself significant. We were quite pleased, of course, because it provided the process, and the Libyans, with some political cover.

At precisely 10:00 a.m. Dabiri arrived at the conference room, dressed as always in a beautiful European-style suit. With him was a short, slightly stocky man in much more modest attire, his head mostly bald and his skin slightly dark, a combination of sun and Mediterranean heritage.

Professor Abdurazek Ballow, Avocat au Bureau de Paris, or member of the Paris bar, was a dual French and Libyan national who had spent many years living and working in France. The government of Libya was a major client. His Paris law firm, known as Cabinet Sefrioui, special-ized in handling French–Arab matters. The firm had negotiated the Lockerbie settlement and Dabiri clearly received his instructions from the Paris-based lawyers.

Ballow spoke English with a strong dose of French and Arabic accent and grammar. A very polite and civilized demeanor reflected his French training and Libyan background. He treated the mediation with full respect and John Nolan as if he were a federal judge. He was especially polite and formal with Schwartz. Despite the judicial process that gave rise to the meeting, the bigger diplomatic game was very much in the room.

After John Nolan made introductions and indicated he had reviewed each side's confidential submissions, we got down to business. He thought a settlement was possible based on our respective positions, and he made note that the Lockerbie settlement had been widely reported around the world, so that there was some precedent for our work. Each side summarized where they were, and how they viewed the situation. Jockeying for position was expected.

From our side, we noted that our case had stronger evidence of Libya's responsibility for blowing up the DC-10 than had existed in the case of Lockerbie and that we were prepared to take the case to trial if a settlement could not be negotiated. That's what a plaintiff's lawyer must present if he or she is to be credible in a negotiation. We also noted that President Bush was still holding over $1 billion in frozen Libyan government assets which, if necessary, would be used to satisfy any court judgment we obtained down the road. I made sure to look at Schwartz on that point, as if to emphasize to Ballow that we and the US government held a card that could leverage a settlement.

Ballow spoke in a slow, halting style, very formalistic and vague about

Libya's intentions. He noted repeatedly that while a settlement of the Pugh case was desirable, his client was constrained by many political and emotional factors that would limit their ability to provide what we were seeking. He also made clear that his client denied any responsibility for the UTA 772 bombing, and that Libya's letter to the United Nations was limited to the Pan Am 103 Lockerbie attack, and nothing more. Any settlement must accept that situation, he made clear. This was about negotiating the size of a check and nothing more. No accountability. No apologies. As with its other efforts, Libya was dangling some of its oil money to pay off the political and legal problems that this same money had created since the 1980s.

From his perspective, he had come with a proposal. The Libyans were prepared to settle Pugh for amounts greater than the French settlement of €1 million per family. So Dabiri's earlier offer to me was already being raised. But any settlement could not reach the $10 million amount in the Lockerbie case, since that matter had much greater visibility and the "extra" value to Libya of removing the long-despised United Nations sanctions that had made Qaddafi a worldwide pariah. Ballow also noted that money could be allocated for Interlease's loss of the DC-10, despite the fact that Judge Jackson had already ruled that Interlease could not seek damages directly from the Libyan government.

Our team discussed the proposal over the lunch break. Sitting in the cramped government-run cafeteria in the courthouse basement, we all felt that Libya was making some progress towards a resolution, but that this would be a long and tough negotiation. We came up with a counter-offer and put it forward to Ballow and Dabiri at the afternoon session. We still felt that the threat of a trial and the safety net of the frozen assets held by the Bush Administration would provide enough leverage to push the settlement closer to resolution.

We requested an amount greater than the Lockerbie figures, and a large amount to reflect the full value of the DC-10. Plus lost interest. Plus some letter of acknowledgment or acceptance by Libya regarding the UTA 772 bombing. We were prepared to negotiate these figures and demands, of course, but understood that this was part of the negotiation process. John Nolan summarized our position and then met separately with Ballow and Dabiri to gauge their reaction. During all these discussions, Schwartz did not take sides or comment on the parties' proposals. But he did make clear that the Bush Administration believed a settlement of this case was in the interest of all concerned, and would be supported by the President and his diplomats.

After a long break to allow John Nolan to work his skills on the Libyan lawyers, we resumed late in the day to hear Ballow's position. He made clear, again using the most flowery and formal language, that there was "some room to negotiate," but that he was constrained by the greater political forces and would need to consult with the senior Libyan officials before he could advance his offer.

We left the mediation feeling that progress had been made, but that we were still far apart. Schwartz noted that he would inform all the relevant US officials of where things stood. Since the Pugh case was stalled in the Court of Appeals we could not push the leverage of a trial for some time. Because the Pugh appeal was scheduled to be argued for November, we knew the case would not get back to the trial court, and on course for a trial, for almost another year.

Unfortunately, the Libyans also understood this dynamic. They were still playing for time. Despite the slight progress in the mediation, and the hope we could close the gap with further discussions, we braced ourselves for further fights in court rather than a quick settlement. It would not take long for us to discover that the fight was nowhere near close to being over.

* * *

A FEW WEEKS after the August mediation, Dabiri informed me and John Nolan that Ballow was going to meet with Libyan officials in Tripoli to discuss the status of our negotiation. This would take time, Dabiri noted, and things moved slowly in that part of the world.

When I informed Schwartz, he noted that his diplomats now working at the almost-Embassy in Libya were engaged in extensive contacts with their Libyan counterparts. He also gave me a hint that his boss, President Bush, might soon announce further developments in the diplomatic arena that might influence our negotiations. Government secrecy precluded his sharing this information with me, he made clear. I understood the limits of his ability to pass along privy information. We had an unspoken agreement not to push each other too hard. It was important we keep the lines of communication open, but he had his own obligations to the US government, and I had my ethical obligations to Interlease and the seven families. We knew there was common ground between those interests. Just how much would soon be tested.

ON 20 SEPTEMBER 2004, less than a month after our mediation in Washington at the federal courthouse and before Ballow got back to us, the White House issued a formal statement. It had a direct impact on our entire strategy.

On behalf of President Bush, the Office of the Press Secretary announced "another milestone" in his efforts to control the spread of weapons of mass destruction. Of course, that had been the stated reason for the President's earlier decision to invade Iraq and depose Saddam Hussein. The spin doctors had to earn their pay.

With regard to the Qaddafi regime, the President noted that Libya had been cooperating to eliminate its own nuclear and WMD program as part of the "path to better relations with the United States and other free nations." Those efforts also had provided substantial intelligence regarding the infamous black market for atomic secrets being sold by Pakistani scientist Dr. Khan. As a reward for Qaddafi's cooperation, President Bush revoked a series of long-standing executive orders that had prevented American companies from obtaining valuable trading licenses to do business in Libya. He also lifted air charter and air service restrictions so that such flights could resume to Tripoli. In short, he was removing the US economic sanctions on Libya that had remained in place even after the United Nations had lifted its own sanctions.

The President's press release noted that lifting these American sanctions would result in the second major instalment payment to the Lockerbie families. This would constitute the second $4 million per family release from the escrow account in Switzerland that had been set forth in the historic settlement, totaling over $1 billion more in payments for that case. The Lockerbie families would now have received $8 million per family, or over $2 billion in total.

Despite the wide publicity that the $1 billion payment to the Lockerbie families was given by the press, we were stunned by a very different aspect of the President's announcement. As part of lifting the sanctions against Libya, President Bush was releasing the separate $1 billion in frozen assets that had long been held by the US government as a diplomatic weapon. This money was being released notwithstanding the fact that the President was going to continue to list Libya as a "state sponsor of terrorism" until further progress was made in the evolving diplomatic relationship.

Our safety net of frozen assets to employ in the Pugh case when we obtained a court judgment was now gone. The threat we had raised with Professor Ballow in the mediation was now empty, the bullets removed from the litigation gun we had pointed at Libya to leverage a quick settlement. The President would hand that money back to Qaddafi, even though his regime was still considered by the US government to be a sponsor of terrorism. This was all part of the grand design to persuade Qaddafi to move closer to the West, and all in a press release. Apparently, Bush did not desire to announce this dramatic change in US policy himself, standing at the podium in the Rose Garden, broadcast on the evening news. That was too much even for the President to swallow.

But all was not lost, at least for the moment. Also contained in the President's press release was a small bone that had been placed in the announcement to reflect the fact that Schwartz had participated in our mediation, and that the Administration desired to send Qaddafi, and the seven American families suing him for murder, a message of support:

> In conjunction with U.S. action to unblock frozen assets, with respect to the remaining cases brought against it by U.S. victims of terrorism, Libya has reaffirmed to us that it has a policy and practice of carrying out agreed settlements and responding in good faith to legal cases brought against it, including court judgments and arbitral awards. We expect Libya to honor this commitment.

HAVING HANDED QADDAFI back our safety net, President Bush was making it a matter of national policy that we could still count on Libya to respond "in good faith" to our Pugh litigation at the federal courthouse. How the President of the United States expected the leader of a terrorist state and "mad dog of the Middle East" to demonstrate such "good faith" was not explained.

My subsequent telephone conversation with Schwartz failed to make this any clearer, since even the Department of State did not quite know what that phrase would mean if and when we obtained a court judgment. Schwartz told me that diplomatic efforts were still in flux and that Qaddafi had insisted that the frozen assets be returned as part of the evolving relationship, both as a matter of national honor and to deprive litigants like my Pugh clients of a weapon. But he noted that the Libyans appeared to be moving down a one-way street that would result in better political ties, as well as a dramatic increase in commerce between the two countries. As an experienced lawyer, Schwartz had to understand that if I had a federal court judgment in hand, it could pose a serious threat to the growing flow of trade. Another form of safety net, if you will. We both certainly understood that dynamic.

Not surprisingly, shortly after the President's decision to lift the US sanctions was announced, I received a call from Dabiri. Ballow had met with his folks in Tripoli. A settlement in Pugh along the lines of our mediation efforts was not possible in the "current political climate." Perhaps in the future as the case moved along, he suggested.

Knowing that the $1 billion in frozen assets would now be wired back to Libya as a result of the President's announcement had removed an important arrow in my litigation quiver. The pressure had been taken off the Libyans, for now, and their policy of delay was put back into gear.

It was time to press on in the courts.

Chapter 16

Accountability

SHORTLY AFTER THE President announced that he was lifting the economic sanctions against Libya—and returning the frozen $1 billion in assets we had long coveted—the Court of Appeals issued an order canceling the oral argument on Libya's appeal in Pugh. Instead, the Court announced it would resolve the matter "on the papers" without the lawyers making oral presentations. Such a procedure typically was followed in frivolous appeals, since the DC Circuit had a tradition of hearing almost all appeals with live lawyer arguments. In early January 2005, we received a one-page Order, simply announcing that it lacked appellate jurisdiction to even hear the appeal because Libya—the appellant, or appealing party—had not even lost the issue it had tried to bring to the Court of Appeal's attention.

With this, we were finally headed back to the trial court to resume our march towards trial. But many months had been lost, and the mediation process conducted in the interim had only served to delay the case. The loss of the frozen assets as a target and leverage tool had also made our job tougher, since the threat of a court judgment would no longer result in an automatic payment from those funds. At the same time, the increase of oil trade between Libya and large American oil companies was quickly building a secondary target to satisfy any judgment we received. So we plowed ahead.

OUR BIGGEST CHALLENGE was to find a way to present the strongest case to prove Libya's responsibility for the bombing of UTA 772, but as quickly as possible. If we could implement this strategy—strongly, and fast—it might create a better environment to leverage a settlement that was closer to our view of the case. Libya's frivolous appeals, the fruitless mediation and its overall strategy of delay had served it well. We were well into 2005 and, despite overcoming many hurdles, not even close to the goal line.

* * *

WITH THE CASE now back in the trial court, we had to recalibrate part of our strategy. Judge Thomas Penfield Jackson had retired after a long career on the bench. Under the federal court rules, all his cases were reassigned to the other active judges in the US District Court. An electronic notice from the court informed us of the new judge. Judge Henry H. Kennedy was a product of the Washington African American professional elite that had blazed historic paths in and out of government for most of the twentieth century. His father had been a highly respected physician, and Henry had attended the best private schools, Princeton and Harvard Law (where his brother Randall later became a famous professor). He returned to his hometown to launch a career in government that eventually led to President Clinton nominating him to the federal bench. His distinguished demeanor was enhanced by a well-trimmed gray beard, bespoke suits and physically fit form. He had long made up for his short height with a vicious tennis game, and was considered one of the best players in his league.

As a jurist, Kennedy was known as a thorough and thoughtful man on the bench who took great pride in running a tight ship in his courtroom. Efficient, fair and very hard working, the soft-spoken and polite judge could be very tough on lawyers and parties who were not honest or prepared. My team was pleased with his taking on the Pugh case, mostly because he would cut through any nonsense Dabiri raised as part of Libya's strategy to delay.

We put together our plan to move the case forward. Our principal goal from the outset had been to obtain a federal court judgment that detailed Libya's responsibility for blowing up the DC-10 over the Ténéré desert. The French criminal cases against the six absent Libyan agents had not reached as far as the Libyan government itself. Just as importantly, the evidence assembled by Judge Bruguière and his team was not available to the French public at large, given French procedural rules. The United Nations sanctions had never amounted to any type of judicial findings, and of course had been withdrawn regarding UTA 772 as a result of President Chirac's second deal with Qaddafi. Holding Libya publicly accountable in a court of law was our goal, since it had been able to avoid that very result at every turn and in every venue. If we could accomplish this decisively and quickly, we might be able to leverage a satisfactory settlement.

In the federal courts, judges were conducting fewer civil trials, both in front of juries as well as "bench" or judge trials. The reason for this was simple. In the 1970s, the US Supreme Court had encouraged the trial courts to employ the "summary judgment" procedure as a central tool to quickly decide, and quite often dispose of, cases. In short, the parties would be forced to present all their evidence and witnesses in advance of any trial to allow the judge to determine if there were "genuine issues" of any "material facts." If the facts were not really contested, the court could decide the case on the papers without the need for a trial or the attendance of witnesses and experts. Only if there was a "genuine dispute" would a trial be necessary. Under this procedure, strongly encouraged by several Supreme Court decisions, the federal trial bench embraced a dispute resolution mechanism that was essentially a paper exercise. With appellate courts blessing this process in many cases, summary judgment was the key to running an efficient and faster docket. Thus, the judges conducted a lot fewer civil trials.

The record we had obtained from the criminal case in Paris contained a rich and diverse body of evidence from which we believed Libya's responsibility for blowing up the DC-10 was clear. After discussing this with my team, we decided to ask Judge Kennedy for summary judgment.

We would focus solely on Libya's liability for the bombing, but not the amount of damages our clients might obtain. A damages assessment by Judge Kennedy would require that he hear their testimony and allow Dabiri to cross-examine them on the record.

Accordingly, we decided to prepare a "partial summary judgment" motion that would put forward all the evidence from Bruguière's investigation. Even if Judge Kennedy rejected such a summary procedure, this strategy would also have the benefit of forcing Libya to come forward with its own evidence to counter the French record. Given the one-sided nature of the Paris criminal proceedings, Libya and its agents had never presented "their case" in rebuttal to Bruguière's voluminous findings. This would help us educate Judge Kennedy if the case did have to go to trial, and flesh out any surprises that Libya might have in mind to rebut the record we had collected from Paris.

But there was a potential legal problem with this strategy. Technically, the government of Libya had not been a party to the French criminal case—only the six Libyan agents had been parties, albeit in absentia. It was possible under US law that Judge Kennedy might rule that the French evidence, compelling as it was, would not be admissible because it had been entered into those proceedings without the benefit of the adversarial process that ensures that evidence is properly subject to legal challenge before it is accepted by a court. Our legal research demonstrated that we had good arguments to admit the French evidence, but we did not want to provide Libya with a strong legal issue they could raise with the judge, or on appeal, that could overturn or undermine our liability case.

To compensate for this legal challenge, we decided to put forward the French evidence and add another independent element to balance out any risks of a "French-only" case. For our second pillar of proof, we would seek the support of President Bush and the weight the US government could bring to bear in the federal court if it sided with our case. This had never been done in any of the terrorism cases. Thus, our biggest challenge was to convince our own government to help us prove Libya's liability in court. With all the emerging and fast-moving diplomatic progress in US–Libya relations, we might hit a brick wall on this approach. Luckily, we already had a few cards in our hand.

One of the first things I did when we took on the Iran and Libya terrorism cases was consult with retired senior US government officials to determine if they could provide some background guidance in this complex and murky world. As noted, in the Iran cases we had handled, I relied on the former Director of the Department of State's Bureau of Counterterrorism, Ambassador Robert Oakley. Ambassador Oakley had spent years working in and then overseeing the US government's efforts to combat state-sponsored terrorism, and had played a critical role in the Reagan Administration after the Iran–Contra scandal to restore professionalism to the White House and National Security Council. Having served as US Ambassador to Congo, Pakistan and Somalia, he was well acquainted with the subject. After his retirement from the Foreign Service he taught at the National War College and did some consulting. I was a regular customer of his consulting services, which were invaluable in understanding the intricacies of Iranian terrorism in the Middle East.

When the Libya matters came in to my law firm, I asked Ambassador Oakley whether he could perform the same consulting role for that file. Although familiar with the background of Qaddafi's terrorist profile, he recommended another recently retired official who had led the efforts at the United Nations to isolate Libya and obtain the Security Council sanctions. According to Oakley, this was the best man for the job. That was good enough for me.

Ambassador Thomas "Ted" McNamara had been a protégé of Oakley, and had followed him in the job of Director of the Bureau of Counterterrorism at State. A tough-talking New Yorker who also was a fluent Spanish speaker, McNamara had served as US Ambassador to Colombia at a time when narco-terrorists were trying to take over the country. His work at the United Nations had been instrumental in obtaining the very sanctions Qaddafi had spent so many years trying to get lifted, and only recently succeeded in doing. Oakley gave him a call at George Washington University where he was teaching and writing. Within a few days he was sitting in a conference room at my law firm.

It became clear after a few minutes of discussion that Ted McNamara knew every nuance of the US–Libya dynamic. He could recite chapter and verse the entire history of how and when Qaddafi's regime had carried out certain terrorist activities, and the underlying political events that had triggered these attacks. He also was familiar with the details of the UTA 772 bombing and had spent many hours with Judge Bruguière when the French and US governments were cooperating on the Lockerbie–UTA front. Clearly, he knew his stuff.

Oakley had done us a big favor by referring us to McNamara. As a retired government official, he could comfortably provide us with background and counseling to help shape and guide our litigation efforts. But it also became clear when the Pugh case came back from the Court of Appeals that McNamara might be our key to getting the US government to assist our effort to hold Libya accountable for the UTA 772 bombing.

For all of his assistance as a consultant, McNamara was in the same boat as other former government officials when it came to the subject of testifying in court about his prior duties. Under the law, former government officials were generally prohibited from appearing as fact witnesses in any case—except, of course, if a case involved the US government and they were testifying for their prior employer, Uncle Sam. In Pugh, private American citizens were suing the government of Libya. The United States might be closely following the case and had even participated in the mediation. But it was not a party, and thus McNamara could not testify as a fact witness before Judge Kennedy about his extensive knowledge of Libya's responsibility for the UTA 772 bombing—unless we could convince the State Department otherwise.

Working with my partner Beth Nolan, who had run the White House Legal Office under President Clinton and was an expert on government ethics, we drafted a request to the Department of State under what are called the "Touhy regulations." These laws and rules govern the strict circumstances that apply to former government officials who are asked, or compelled by subpoena, to testify in court about their prior positions. Of course, without such rules, anyone could drag a former official into a court case and obtain access to information that is otherwise secret or confidential. Beth and I had to weave our way through this thicket.

Of course, this was no ordinary request. The Bush Administration, principally through the Department of State, was seriously involved in the process of attempting to bring Qaddafi back into the fold. Diplomats at the highest level of the US government, including President Bush himself, were committed to making further progress in the US–Libya relationship, especially now that the sanctions had been lifted by both the United Nations and the United States. Qaddafi had turned over his entire WMD and nuclear program and was providing extensive intelligence to assist efforts against the common foe of Al Qaeda. We were asking President Bush to allow one of his former senior advisers to come into a federal court and testify in detail about Qaddafi's responsibility for a notorious terrorist attack. This was not the sort of outreach most diplomats had in mind in the midst of a significant political effort with a former adversary.

Fortunately, the diplomatic dance in which President Bush and Colonel Qaddafi were engaged was not a simple affair. Libya was still on the list of state sponsors of terror, and despite the major progress on a host of fronts the US government was still holding back certain benefits to ensure that Qaddafi did not get cold feet and return to his evil and unpredictable ways. The Pugh case, and our strategy to obtain a liability judgment for the first time in any Libya case, presented the Bush Administration with a tempting opportunity to apply more pressure to Libya without much political cost. After all, the US had repeatedly declared that Libya had been responsible for the UTA 772 bombing and—after Lockerbie—the destruction of the DC-10 over the Ténéré desert was one of the most notorious acts of aircraft sabotage in history.

Our request to allow McNamara to testify in the case triggered much debate within the Administration. At the end of that internal process, we got what we wanted. As usual, the US government was not doing us any favors. The decision to allow McNamara to testify in support of our case was a calculated political decision that, on balance, was viewed by the diplomats and government lawyers as providing leverage to the President in the emerging bilateral relationship. But we did not care about the President's reasons. Only the results.

With a formal letter from the Legal Advisor of the Department of State authorizing McNamara to testify, the team got to work helping him draft a lengthy and detailed affidavit that we would put forward as part of the summary judgment motion. We now had the makings of the right "optics" to convince Judge Kennedy that he should rule that Libya was responsible for the UTA 772 attack without the need to even conduct a trial. We would present the case with the support of two governments—France and the United States. As far as I knew, no one had ever done anything like this in the federal courts.

* * *

OUR NEXT MOVE was to visit Bruguière again and determine if he also would testify in our Washington case. As the man who oversaw the French investigation that was at the heart of our evidence, it was critical that he come forward with an affidavit to explain the background of his work uncovering the Libyan role in the UTA bombing. My partner Laurel Malson and I drafted what we thought would be an appropriate outline of what Bruguière might testify about and then flew over to Paris. As with my earlier meetings with the most powerful investigating magistrate in France, we had to get through some very heavy security at the Palais de Justice, and then wind through the maze of hallways and offices to reach his secluded—and locked—sanctuary.

Sitting in his haphazard office, Judge Bruguière puffed on his pipe as Laurel and I described how we would envision his written testimony in support of the summary judgment motion. We had prepared the draft outline in both English and French to make it easier for him to review. Listening to our outline and absorbing our strategy, Bruguière was seriously interested in helping us achieve this uniquely American form of justice. The entire process was foreign to him, as the French civil courts did not follow such summary procedures. But we had a bigger hurdle to jump.

"I would like to help you, Mister Newberger," he said. "I will look this paper over, but I also must show it to the French prosecutor and the other lawyers. You are a lawyer so you understand." He smiled and puffed on his pipe. Clearly, he liked what we were trying to accomplish and would continue to help us in any way he could. Getting a US court to hold Libya responsible for his greatest investigative achievement after his own government dropped the prosecution of the Libyan defendants was music to his ears. We left his offices hopeful that we could present both Bruguière and McNamara as our star witnesses.

Sadly, French law and bureaucracy would stand in the way. Under French law, there is no such thing as an affidavit or the presentation of factual testimony in a court case by written affidavit. The French prosecutor's office informed us in a letter just a few days later that they could not authorize Judge Bruguière to sign such a document since it would not be accepted in a French court. But I suspected there was another more nefarious reason.

Checking back with some sources in Paris, I discovered that our request to Bruguière—and his recommendation that it be accepted— had been rejected by the French Foreign Ministry. Apparently, word had spread that we were trying to rope the French government into our case in a formal sense, and that this would be used to prove Libya's responsibility for the UTA 772 bombing. Incredibly, the French government did not want to assist our efforts to obtain, finally, a court judgment regarding the most notorious terrorist attack in French history. Chirac's deal with Qaddafi, or, more correctly, his second deal on the eve of the United Nations vote to lift the sanctions, was not to be disturbed in any manner. If the crazy Americans wanted to offend Qaddafi and pursue such legal avenues, that was their business. But the French government would not approve any measure that might possibly come back to haunt them and disrupt French–Libyan relations.

Thus, we would not have Bruguière testify as a witness, despite his desire to assist our efforts. We would press on, but Le Sheriff would have to watch from the sidelines. However, at least we had his entire file, and his detailed report, to put before Judge Kennedy.

SHORTLY AFTER OUR unsuccessful efforts to obtain a witness statement from Judge Bruguière, State's Schwartz told me that the US government was moving even closer to normalizing relations with Libya. Although it was not publicly announced, Ambassador David Welch, a senior career diplomat and Assistant Secretary of State for Middle East Affairs, was taking a trip to Libya to meet Qaddafi. He would be the highest-ranking US official to visit Libya formally in almost thirty years.

Clearly, the State Department's decision to allow Ted McNamara to testify in our case had been taken with the full knowledge that senior-level meetings were about to move forward as the US–Libya relationship picked up speed. On 17 June 2005 the State Department issued a press release revealing that the trip had already taken place a few days before. The Bush Administration characterized it as a "historic" visit given the decades of isolation, noting that this "high-level dialog" included serious discussions across the political, financial and international spectrum. But Libya still remained on the list of terrorist states, a card President Bush had decided to keep in his pocket so that Ambassador Welch had some negotiating room with his host. Notably, the press release also made clear that Ambassador Welch had not forgotten about the legal cases brought by American victims of Libyan terrorism. He "reiterated the importance of Libya's policy and practice of carrying out agreed-upon settlements and responding in good faith to legal cases brought against it."

Schwartz later provided me some details about the visit and made clear that he and his colleagues had ensured that Lockerbie, Pugh and the other terrorism cases were on the table alongside other important issues.

APPARENTLY THE LIBYANS got the message. Just a few days after Welch and Schwartz returned from their historic trip, I received a call from Dabiri. He asked if I would fly to Paris and meet with Professor Ballow about trying to settle the Kilburn case. We had obtained a terrific ruling in Kilburn from the Court of Appeals, setting the leading precedent for how all such cases should be managed by the trial judges. That had been our goal from the outset, and now there was at least an opening to settle two active cases. I immediately accepted and the following week my partner Mike Martinez and I were in Paris.

The offices of Cabinet Sefrioui, the Paris law firm, were located in a beautiful old building in the 17th Arrondissement, across from a park lined with large trees and manicured lawns. The late June weather was perfect, with blue skies and sunny days blending into warm nights, and all of Paris seemed to be outside enjoying the warm temperatures. The sidewalk cafes were jammed at lunch and dinner, and we had already enjoyed a wonderful brasserie meal when our taxi pulled up to the law offices.

Welcoming us was Dabiri, dressed as always in an impeccable suit, his thick dark hair and cufflinks both shining bright. He led us through a series of ante-rooms filled with ancient books, prints and artifacts, many with Arabic themes. This was not a surprise, since the firm had been founded by a French–Moroccan lawyer and his French wife and represented many Middle East interests. Professor Ballow came out to meet us and, in a combination of Arab hospitality and French formalism, greeted us as if we were long-lost brothers. We then met Madame Anne Sefrioui, whose husband had founded the law firm and left it to her when he had died. "Madame," as she was called—the emphasis on the second syllable in French style, Madame—was an elegant French lady in her fifties with perfectly coiffed hair, a very expensive and stylish suit, and a cigarette in a golden holder. She oozed charm and sophistication. I was immediately on my guard.

Mike and I had expected a bit of theater as part of the negotiation process, but we were simply not prepared for the water-torture methods the Libyan lawyers put in play as soon as we sat down in the firm's grand conference room. After several hours of background and explanations, most prominently repeated exhortations that they had limited instructions and this whole affair required sensitive handling in Tripoli, it became clear that we were not going to reach any settlement in Kilburn in the first day of talks. Apparently, it would have been bad form to make any constructive progress in a single day. Stuck far apart on the number, by several millions of dollars, we adjourned for the night and were Madame's guests at a Moroccan restaurant that her husband also had left to her.

My daughter Elana had flown to Paris to join us as she had a break from college and her summer job. Fluent in French and having spent a semester at the Sorbonne just one year earlier, she sat next to Madame at dinner and spent the evening speaking to her in Parisian French. I had hoped this might provide Elana a nice addition to her education. I also hoped it might loosen up Madame and help us advance the settlement discussions. I was only successful on the first point.

The next day, we resumed our meeting at the opulent offices. After several hours, we were still millions apart, and it was now clear that the only way we might settle Kilburn was simply to surrender and take a very low number. We had not worked this hard or come this far to throw up our hands in a case we had just won in the DC Circuit, and so we were at an impasse.

As we were leaving to go back to our hotel, Dabiri jumped up and blurted out of nowhere, "What about Pugh?" We had not expected the case even to be on the table for this meeting, especially given the tough time the French lawyers had given us for a "simple" case like Kilburn. However, I was not one to miss an opportunity, formalities aside, and told him we had thought that the mediation in the Court of Appeals the prior summer had reached a dead end.

He noted that Ambassador Welch had just paid a visit to Tripoli and that trying to resolve this "big" case should be a priority. I told him we agreed, but that we needed to receive a serious settlement offer from their side if any progress was to be made. After consulting with Madame and the Professor, they asked if they could have a few weeks to consult with the political people in Tripoli and get back to us for a discussion of UTA 772. We agreed and then flew home.

* * *

AT THE END of July we were back in Paris, along with our Brussels partner Emmanuel Gybels, whose command of French might come in handy since neither Madame nor Professor Ballow was completely comfortable discussing matters in English. It had been very difficult to get a plane ticket or a hotel room in Paris. I only found out the reason when we were lucky enough to book accommodation. Apparently, we had decided to conduct our negotiations during the last stage of the Tour de France, when the world's greatest cyclists complete their marathon rides throughout the country and finish their pedaling on the Champs-Élysées. American Lance Armstrong was set to win his seventh Tour and the city was jammed with what seemed like a million racing fans.

We reconvened at Cabinet Sefrioui and launched into another tedious discussion with the Libyan lawyers, the sum of which was that any settlement of Pugh must be "sensitive" to the parameters of the Lockerbie settlement. We continued to insist that we had a better and stronger case, and that our mission was to prove that Libya had blown up the plane, not simply collect a pot of money.

To prove our seriousness, we explained that we were almost ready to file our summary judgment motion, which could ruin Libya's political image, not to mention its legal position in the case, by having the court make specific findings about Libya's responsibility for the UTA 772 attack. This made the Professor and Madame quite agitated, as they had not considered the possibility that we might get an early decision even before the court conducted a trial. They repeatedly asked us to delay filing the summary judgment, as this would "ruin" any chance for a settlement in Pugh or Kilburn. We kept asking them to put forward solid settlement offers for us to take back to our clients. They continued to refuse, and only spoke in general terms about the "parameters" of the Lockerbie settlement.

After most of a full day, it became clear that they did not have a concrete proposal to present. They were playing for time, or so it seemed to us. We packed up our papers, thanked them for their time and left the offices. After a quick call to Doug Matthews back in the United States, Mike Martinez and I both agreed that the only language the Libyans understood was a direct threat of action. Talk would only produce more talk, no matter how nice their Paris offices might be.

WE SPENT THE rest of our time standing on the streets of Paris as the Tour de France sped through the town in a blur. We saw Lance Armstrong—who won his seventh race and retired, his fall from grace many years away—for a fleeting moment, the peloton of riders a blur. We then flew back to Washington to file our summary judgment motion. Another long battle lay ahead.

* * *

THE SUMMARY JUDGMENT filing was a major effort. Consistent with the court rules, our team had prepared a detailed narrative of all of the evidence of Libya's plot to blow up the UTA 772 flight. Although we did not have a witness statement from Judge Bruguière, we attached his entire original report, in French and translated into English, along with several volumes of exhibits we had translated from the Paris criminal trial proceedings. Of course, we featured Ambassador McNamara's detailed written testimony, which the State Department Legal Advisor's Office had carefully reviewed and edited before it was ready to file with our court papers. In short, our factual case reflected the considered views and investigations of both the French and American governments, in the most formal and official manner possible. It was quite impressive and unique. It also got Libya's attention.

One week after we filed and served the summary judgment papers on Dabiri, he called me to ask if Mike and I would come back over to Paris for one more meeting with Professor Ballow and Madame Sefrioui in an effort to bridge the gap in our Kilburn and Pugh discussions. I expressed great pessimism to Dabiri given the circular and non-productive discussions over the summer. He assured me that the summary judgment filing had raised our profile even more, despite the warnings in Paris that it would scuttle any negotiations. Reluctant as I was to waste another trip, we booked a flight, and by Labor Day weekend we were back in France. At least the food was worthwhile.

Mike and I again met with the Libyan lawyers at the Sefrioui offices. Both Ballow and Madame seemed more mellow than at our last meetings, and the fact that we had filed the summary judgment motion did not seem to have created the problems they had raised before. By all appearances, they were almost relieved we had filed, perhaps because it provided an opportunity to their masters in Tripoli to appreciate directly the threat our case posed to Qaddafi's plans for a new era in his relations with the United States. Sometimes a gun to the head is the most effective form of diplomacy when dealing with a ruthless dictator.

Despite the improved tone of our talks, the numbers did not move in any material manner. Their idea of a settlement of Pugh began and ended with the notion that it could not be as much as the Lockerbie deal, given how much more "visible and important" the Pam Am 103 Lockerbie case had been for so many years. They emphasized how Lockerbie had set the agenda for almost all of the diplomatic and legal wrangling that had taken place between Qaddafi and the West. No matter how strong our case in Pugh, the "political situation" would simply not allow the Libyan government to pay more to our clients than they had to the Lockerbie families.

They also emphasized that even the Lockerbie families were not likely to receive more than the $8 million per family already paid from the escrow, since the condition for the final $2 million payment—removing Libya from the State Department list of state sponsors of terrorism by a certain date—was about to expire. Thus, from a practical viewpoint, $8 million was the ceiling for the Lockerbie families, and we could not expect to receive even that amount given the "political reality" that Lockerbie was a special case.

After two days of such talks, we knew there was not going to be much progress. The Paris lawyers were on a very short leash and, once again, appeared to be more interested in stalling the negotiations through endless chatter and apologies than substantive exchanges. We had reached the point where we were talking past each other. I had a strong feeling that any progress could only be made if we opened a different, and more direct, channel to the decision makers in Tripoli.

Mike and I had brought our wives along for this Labor Day trip to Paris. While we sat in the Sefrioui offices listening to all the reasons why our clients should expect to receive less money than the Lockerbie families, they enjoyed the pleasures of the City of Light. But halfway through the weekend, and as our talks with the lawyers reached an impasse, the pleasures of Paris faded away as we sat glued to our hotel television sets watching CNN. A city was under water, its citizens standing on rooftops as helicopters plucked them to safety.

We watched in shock as New Orleans took on the appearance of a developing nation inundated with plagues of biblical proportions. We could not believe that such a scene could unfold in our own advanced country. I had been to New Orleans many times over the years for business and pleasure. I had friends there who clearly had evacuated and could not know when they would be able to return. The streets, restaurants, bars, music halls and homes that had stroked the soul of so many visitors appeared to be falling into the sea. It was like a bad dream.

We flew back to Washington sobered by the lack of progress in our talks with the Libyans and by the disaster we had watched unfold on our television sets.

* * *

BY THIS POINT it was clear that the Paris lawyers could not deliver a deal at a level that I could sell to our clients. We needed a different approach—once again, something outside the normal legal channels.

During a trip to Paris I had befriended one of the people who had been directly involved with the French aspect of UTA 772—Guillaume Denoix de Saint Marc, the soft-spoken, serious Frenchman whose father had died on the flight and who had taken a prominent role in negotiating the second French deal in 2003. That resulted in the €170 million payment and allowed the United Nations sanctions to be lifted. Except for the money marked for the Pugh plaintiffs, since we had forsaken that settlement in order to continue with our case in Washington.

Guillaume understood the reasons that our seven Pugh families had refused to accept the Libyan money now sitting in the French Foundation that he managed. He was very supportive of our efforts, and shared Bruguière's view that President Chirac had allowed Qaddafi to escape any genuine accountability for blowing up the French airplane in 1989. He used his newsletter, website and contacts to publicize our efforts in Washington, and to keep the French victims informed of the American side of the DC-10 case. Like many French people I encountered, he was impressed and thankful that our legal system provided a mechanism under the rule of law to bring a terrorist state to justice.

During one of our meetings in Paris that summer of 2005, he mentioned that a former French diplomat now in retirement might be willing to share with me some of his experience in dealing with the Libyans in general, and Qaddafi in particular, regarding UTA 772. With our frustrating communications with Libyan lawyers not producing tangible results, I was quite willing to explore any other avenues that might shed light on a way to close the wide gap.

In November I made time in my schedule to visit my law firm's offices in Brussels, where I had some other business. As the dual capital of Belgium and the European Union, Brussels is an interesting hybrid of charming continental culture, but on a smaller scale compared to Paris or Rome or Vienna. The placement of the European Union's offices in this northern city famous for steamed mussels and "French fries" (actually originating in Belgium, not France) and dreary North Sea weather had brought to it a wave of lawyers, technocrats and lobbyists more fitting for Washington. Our law firm's offices were in a lovely part of the historic city center and had the added attraction of being right next door to the city's best chocolate shop, which featured photographs of presidents Clinton and George W. Bush as they sampled the confections hanging on its walls.

Meeting me in the office one gray, rainy day was a large, burly man with a thick head of gray hair, huge hands and a business suit that clearly had seen much travel. At over six feet tall and powerfully built, Jean Jacques Beaussou did not reflect my mental picture of a distinguished diplomat and Arabist. After a long and intense career in the French Ministry of Foreign Affairs, his last posting was to Tripoli as the French Ambassador, and he had managed the critical negotiations between the French victims of UTA 772 and Qaddafi's government. He knew all the players, and all the background of the case. He had retired from service and was now providing consulting services to clients able to pay a retainer. We hit it off immediately.

Ambassador Beaussou was intrigued by the legal avenue our case in Washington had kept open even after the French, and the Libyans, had long considered the DC-10 file closed. He shared with me his extensive knowledge of how Qaddafi and his sons ran the government and ruled the country, employing the secret police and military infrastructure to oversee the oil-rich economy. His observations of Qaddafi opened my eyes to a new view of the dictator, as it became clear that Qaddafi actually sat atop a diverse collection of tribes, alliances and allegiances more complex than a simple one-man-rule kingdom. He also provided stories of Qaddafi's idiosyncrasies, observed first hand from many late-night meetings and lectures in the dictator's desert tent.

Most importantly, Beaussou knew, and was well known by, all the senior officials and family members who ran the country. While it was certainly the case that Qaddafi ran the system with an iron hand, there were many complexities and nuances that he could guide me through if the "political avenue" was employed in parallel to the legal avenue.

It did not take long for us to agree that Beaussou would act as my law firm's private emissary to Libya. He would provide strategic advice about the political system, make enquiries in Tripoli to facilitate any negotiations of our cases, and keep both the US and French governments informed of his activities. This last role had a dual purpose—to make sure we did not trip over any secret diplomacy that might conflict with our legal efforts, and to stay current with vital intelligence so that our own efforts could attempt to stay ahead of political surprises. Beaussou and I shook hands as he left to return to Paris on the afternoon train. We had opened a new diplomatic front in our dealings with Libya.

WHILE BEAUSSOU AND I mapped out a plan to approach the Libyan government as a back channel to the litigation, we devoted a lot of energy to the briefing and responses regarding the summary judgment proceedings. Dabiri had asked for an extension of time to respond given the lengthy and detailed record we had presented to Judge Kennedy in our initial filing. It would take several months to complete that briefing by both sides. During this time, which extended into early 2006, State's Schwartz and I stayed in touch to coordinate information, and I kept him up to date about Beaussou's new diplomatic role in our efforts.

Schwartz was intrigued by the newest member of our Pugh team. His contacts in the diplomatic corps knew of Beaussou as a professional who had played a significant role in bringing order and rational behavior to the overall evolution of French–Libyan relations. Schwartz made a point of inviting Beaussou to visit the new US diplomatic mission in Tripoli on any visits, and to allow the local diplomats on the ground to exchange information informally. The business of diplomacy, especially in the fast-moving dynamic of opening up Qaddafi's Libya to the West, extended beyond the parameters of our case. Business was business. And the US government would welcome any insights Beaussou could offer.

One of the young American diplomats working at the new mission in Tripoli was an Arabist named Chris Stevens. He would play an important role in Beaussou's efforts to navigate the Libyan labyrinth. His skills were so obvious that several years later Stevens would be appointed as Ambassador to Libya by President Barack Obama, only to be killed in a terrorist attack in Benghazi, along with several of his security guards, a tragic loss of an outstanding professional diplomat.

* * *

BY EARLY APRIL Judge Kennedy was ready to hear the lawyers argue the summary judgment motion. Dabiri's written responses had been very thin on substance, and carefully avoided taking a firm position on Libya's role in the UTA 772 bombing. Most of his arguments raised technical and legal defenses, trying to chip away at our evidence. One of his biggest attacks was the one we had anticipated from the outset— he asserted that the entire pile of French evidence, including Bruguière's report, was inadmissible because no one had challenged it in the French criminal proceedings. It was not reliable evidence because it had been a one-sided affair, one in which Libya itself had never participated.

As we stood in front of Judge Kennedy on a warm April day in Washington, Dabiri and I jousted around all these legal issues. Judge Kennedy was clearly prepared and had become familiar with the entire record, asking precise questions of both lawyers and not showing his hand or the direction in which he might be leaning. Asking a federal judge to declare a foreign government responsible for a notorious terrorist attack was unique enough. Having the terrorist state appear in the federal courthouse and defend itself against the charges was even more unique, as none of the other cases against Libya had progressed to this stage. Even Lockerbie, the big case that had dominated the news and political agenda, never got past the initial jurisdictional phases of that case. It had famously been settled long before any substantive evidence was placed on the record to hold Libya accountable for that bombing. Asking a judge to rule that a trial was not even necessary to decide the issue of liability—and that he should "summarily" make such a determination—was pushing the limits of federal law.

We were all on virgin ground, judge and lawyers alike, and Judge Kennedy was not a jurist known for taking unnecessary risks or untested positions. I had to temper my usual aggressive posture in court against the natural caution and skepticism Judge Kennedy expressed at the hearing.

When we were done, it was clear that Judge Kennedy was struggling to come up with the right balance of evidence, procedure, fairness and justice. Federal judges wield enormous power in our legal system. The life tenure they enjoy under Article III of the US Constitution allows them to decide disputes without the influence of the political process that constantly affects the President and Congress. And in the federal court in the nation's capital, the judges are especially sensitive to their role in our three-way system of checks and balances of federal power. Judge Kennedy had spent his entire life in that environment, except for his years studying in Princeton and Harvard. He would not make any decisions that he thought exceeded his powers or that caused tension between the two political branches of government. This case would be by the book. Since the book for this type of case had not yet been written, we were all at a bit of a disadvantage.

Four weeks later, in early May, we received Judge Kennedy's written ruling on our summary judgment motion. He had carefully reviewed every piece of evidence and all the relevant legal authorities. In his view, all the French criminal court evidence was properly in his record and was admissible despite the lack of a "defense" in the French criminal proceedings. The fact that Libya itself had not even been a defendant in Paris was of no concern.

Relying on "principles of comity," Judge Kennedy ruled that the French foreign judgments in the criminal cases "should be given weight as prima facie evidence" of Libya's responsibility for the UTA 772 attack, and that it was Libya's burden to come forward with competent evidence of its own and "impeach the judgment" from Paris. With the Libyans having failed to produce any such evidence, Judge Kennedy ruled that he would rely on Bruguière's report and the volumes of evidence from the French court case. On top of that, he added, we had come forward with Ambassador McNamara's written testimony detailing Libya's responsibility for the attack from the perspective of the US government. This additional evidence, Kennedy ruled, corroborated the French evidence and made even more clear Libya's responsibility for the bombing.

Taking all this evidence into account, Judge Kennedy held that our evidence "stands undisputed and overwhelmingly establishes Libya's culpability and involvement in the bombing of UTA Flight 772." He would enter partial summary judgment on the issue of Libya's responsibility for this notorious act of terrorism that resulted in the murder of 170 people, including the 7 Americans on board. This was an extraordinary accomplishment. A court of law had finally found Qaddafi's government guilty of a terrorist act that constituted mass murder. The government of Libya itself was now judicially accountable. Qaddafi's earlier success in having the United Nations sanctions lifted, his global deals with President Chirac that closed the French file, his diplomatic victories with President Bush in lifting the US sanctions and restoring diplomatic relations had all moved him far ahead in his effort to remake his image in the West. But we had now obtained something that he could not escape or unwind through diplomatic moves and piles of oil money. Libya had been held accountable. The evidence had proven it, and in such a convincing way that the judge did not even need to conduct a trial.

IT WAS NOW time to move to the last phase of the case and calculate the damages our clients had suffered as a result of the 1989 bombing. All paths were now clear to finishing this saga and delivering to my clients what they had hired us to do five years earlier. I even hoped that we might accomplish a quick settlement now that the liability issue had been so decisively resolved. Once again, though, my optimism was overtaken by events outside the courtroom.

* * *

ONLY FOUR WEEKS after we obtained the summary judgment ruling from Judge Kennedy, President Bush made another political announcement that would tilt the dynamics of our legal effort against Libya. On 6 June 2006 he determined that Libya had made enough progress in its efforts to cooperate with the US on a wide range of issues that his Administration would remove Libya from the list of states that sponsored terrorism.

This was the final piece in Qaddafi's political strategy to regain a place at the diplomatic table. It was also the first time a terrorist state had been able to get off the list through bilateral negotiations and political exchanges. President Bush made much of this progress, and ascribed it to his tough diplomatic stand as well as his military efforts in Iraq. This was not a universally accepted view.

One of the consequences of this action was that, according to the Pan Am 103 Lockerbie families, it had taken too long. Their settlement with Qaddafi made clear that the last $2 million payment—over $500 million—from the settlement escrow would not be paid if Libya was not removed from the terrorism list by a certain date. That date had been extended a few times, but eventually it had expired, and the decision in June 2006 by President Bush was outside the time allowed by the terms of the written settlement agreement. Qaddafi had won his last and most symbolic victory, and the Lockerbie families had lost over $500 million in the settlement escrow, which would now revert to the Libyan treasury—a double victory for Qaddafi, whose diplomats made clear they were honoring the Lockerbie settlement to the letter.

The other consequence arrived in my office mail in early July. Despite Judge Kennedy's momentous ruling that Libya was responsible for the UTA 772 bombing, Dabiri had filed a brand-new request with the court. Because Libya was now officially off the Department of State's terrorism list, Dabiri asserted that our clients could no longer sue Libya in court under the Foreign Sovereign Immunities Act. President Bush, he declared in a lengthy brief, had exercised his constitutional powers and under the law Libya was now immediately immune to our lawsuit. The case should be dismissed forthwith, Dabiri argued. The law was clear, and any other result would violate the constitution and create a terrible tension between the federal court and the President of the United States.

Qaddafi was playing every card in the deck and had pulled out a few new hands from under the table. The battle continued.

Chapter 17

The Last Mission

OUR TEAM QUICKLY concluded that while Libya's effort to obtain an immediate dismissal of the case was not likely to succeed, this most recent move certainly threw another wrench into our efforts.

The language of the Foreign Sovereign Immunities Act made clear that American victims of terrorism killed or injured by a "listed" country such as Libya could bring their case because the country was listed as a "sponsor of terrorism" at the time of the terrorist attack. Libya certainly had been listed by the Department of State as a terrorist state in September 1989 when the DC-10 blew up. The fact that President Bush had now, many years later, decided to remove Libya from the list, a remarkable step for sure, would not deprive Judge Kennedy of his authority to continue with the case until we obtained a final damages award.

We drafted our responsive papers and put forward what we believed was a very compelling argument for Judge Kennedy to deny Dabiri's motion to dismiss. The Judge certainly agreed, since he issued a written ruling denying the motion to dismiss right after Labor Day, in early September. Apparently, Judge Kennedy had no trouble reading the plain language of the law the same way we did. The fact that he had worked so hard and spent so much time hearing the case and issuing the summary judgment ruling was another factor in our favor. He had held Libya accountable for a notorious terrorist act and was not going to let Qaddafi off the hook on some frivolous legal argument.

As with his past efforts to delay the case, Dabiri also knew that he could buy more time simply by appealing Judge Kennedy's ruling rejecting the "off the terrorism list" argument. It was a jurisdictional/immunity defense that a sovereign nation like Libya could appeal as a matter of right. Within days of Judge Kennedy's Order, Dabiri noticed an appeal. Our march towards a final judgment was, once again, pushed into the slow lane of appellate procedure.

Of course, we had our own procedural weapons to expedite the process. And we used them. In November, as soon as allowed by the appellate rules, our firm asked that the Court of Appeals "summarily affirm" Judge Kennedy's ruling and return the case to the trial court for the hearing on our client's damages. Between briefing schedules and holiday breaks, the Court of Appeals did not address our request for a summary ruling for several months. The wait only frustrated our clients even more, as it was difficult for them to understand how a case they seemingly had already won on the critical question of liability could be delayed. It is not always easy explaining to clients why the judicial system, even the best parts of it, sometimes drag things out in a manner that is frustrating to both the lawyers and affected clients.

In May 2007, after what seemed like an interminable wait, the Court of Appeals issued a two-page order granting our request and summarily affirmed Judge Kennedy's rejection of Libya's last-ditch effort to have the case dismissed. Libya had been on the terrorism list when it blew up the DC-10, the Court of Appeals ruled, and so it could still be sued for damages in the Washington federal court, notwithstanding the decision of the President of the United States later to remove it from that list for political reasons.

The path to a damages trial and final judgment was now, finally, clear of any remaining hurdles or political delays. Judge Kennedy quickly issued a scheduling order and we were set to have our clients testify in the damages phase so that a final judgment could issue. We would appear in Judge Kennedy's courtroom in early August. Our clients would finally have the opportunity to tell their story to a federal judge, with Libya's lawyer sitting right in front of them, and with the court already having decided that Libya had carried out the bombing that killed their loved ones.

This had never happened before in American legal history. A diverse group of family members who had waited eighteen years for this day would now have a chance to achieve some closure after all their years of pain and suffering.

WHILE MY TEAM prepared for the damages trial in Washington, Ambassador Beaussou and I were pressing ahead with our private diplomacy in Tripoli. He had made several exploratory trips to Libya to meet with important government ministers and diplomats. He made clear to the Libyans that he was working with my law firm and was attempting to help bring us closer to a settlement that could avoid the risk and uncertainty of a large damages verdict. In a detailed aide memoire that Beaussou and I drafted—and which he then had translated into French and Arabic to hand to his Libyan counterparts—the former French Ambassador to Libya presented a range of political and financial arguments. He was trying to convince Libya that it made sense to settle with our firm, just as they had with the Lockerbie families.

With each visit to Tripoli, Beaussou would also brief the French and American diplomats on the ground, partly to make sure he could learn of any other political developments. I would get his reports by telephone after he left the country, since we assumed his calls were intercepted by the Libyan secret police while within their borders. I would then brief Schwartz at State so that our own government was aware of Beaussou's efforts, and to see if Schwartz could share any information with me.

After several efforts, it was made clear to Beaussou that although the Libyans believed a settlement was in everyone's mutual interest it would not be possible to come to terms acceptable to the Pugh families and Interlease until the court issued some sort of baseline award against which serious negotiations could commence. The Libyans explained to Beaussou that it would only be possible to pay the Pugh plaintiffs more than the Lockerbie victims if there were a final judgment. In short, someone else had to take the blame for paying them more money, and Judge Kennedy's "anti-Libya bias" would allow the Libyans to save face if they paid more. Ambassador Beaussou left his communication lines with his Libyan contacts open and promised to visit Tripoli after Judge Kennedy issued an award.

* * *

AUGUST IN WASHINGTON is notorious for the heat and humidity that hangs over the city like a wet blanket. Judge Kennedy had set aside three days for the damages trial and instructed us to come up with a procedure that would allow him to complete the case in the allotted time. Those three summer days turned out to be some of the hottest and most oppressive the city had seen in years.

To meet Judge Kennedy's deadline and schedule, we knew that not all the family members could travel to Washington to attend the trial and testify in person. So, working with Matthews, we set up a process that would allow every single family member to testify and have their own story heard by Judge Kennedy. To do so, many of them would have their testimony taken in the weeks before the trial, in a video deposition conducted in their home town. Dabiri would participate and ask whatever cross-examination questions he desired. The DVD of the deposition, called *de bene esse* or "preservation of testimony", would be introduced at the hearing so that Judge Kennedy could watch it at his leisure. To carry this out, my team scattered to Texas, Montana, California and New York. These witnesses would have their day in court even if they did not sit in Judge Kennedy's room.

With these video depositions in hand, we focused on presenting in the courtroom representatives of each of the families who could explain to the judge what the loss of each victim on the DC-10 meant to them. We would also present Doug Matthews, of course, and several experts to explain how and why the estates of the seven victims were entitled to damages, as well as the economic loss of the aircraft. Although the Libyan state was no longer on the hook for the Interlease economic damages, we still had the six Libyan individuals in the case, and an award against them could be useful in a subsequent negotiation. Dabiri had listed several experts of his own to counter ours, and so we expected his defense to focus on chipping away at the damages figures and thereby reduce Libya's overall financial responsibility for the bombing.

The night before the trial was to begin, a huge thunderstorm raced through the city as the families, Doug Matthews and my team gathered in our offices for a light supper and preparation session. Our large conference room's air conditioning and food was a welcome relief from the oppressive heat, humidity and storm raging outside on the streets. Despite our plans and logistics, there was one thing we had not anticipated. None of the families had ever met or been in touch with each other before that evening's session at 1001 Pennsylvania Avenue. Matthews had been the only conduit between them, the driving force that had gathered them together to be part of this historic trial.

As our guests introduced themselves to each other, Matthews gently inserted the name and background of the family's victim so that each person would understand whom they represented. The seven Americans who had died together in the Ténéré desert had not known each other, but had been brought to their final journey by the forces of fate. Now their families had come together under the guidance of a former aviator on whose plane their relatives had died. Eighteen years had passed since the DC-10 had crashed in the desert. Five years had passed since we filed the case against Libya and began this journey. We all felt a special aura that evening as we sat around the table and listened to each family and team member describe their background and history, and their connection to the case.

When the conversation eventually turned to me, I rose and thanked each person for their efforts and commitment. It had been a long road for them, and for my law firm. We were all traveling together on this journey. I explained that, in my experience handling other terrorism cases over the years, the very process of appearing in a federal courtroom in Washington and telling their story to a federal judge would itself be an act of closure, as well as a victory over the September 1989 perpetrators. Without exception, they all noted that the grief and loss carried inside them for eighteen years had never really disappeared, and for many it remained almost as strong in August 2007 as it had been in

September 1989. Many had never discussed the bombing or its effect with other family members or professional counsellors. This would be the first time many of them had bared their souls—in public and on the record, no less, with a court reporter taking down every word and a room of strangers listening, and the lawyer for the government that had killed their loved ones sitting across from them, able to ask probing questions about their unspeakable losses.

As the storm outside dropped its last buckets of rain and the final flashes of lightning lit up the sky behind the US Capitol Building down the street, the group broke up and returned to their hotel to get a good night's rest. We would all need it.

THE NEXT MORNING we all gathered outside the E. Barrett Prettyman United States Courthouse that sits on Constitution Avenue across from architect I. M. Pei's modernist East Wing of the National Gallery of Art. The evening's thunderstorm had only increased the level of humidity. Even at 8:30 a.m. we had worked up a sweat walking from our offices just six short blocks down the street.

The air conditioning of the courthouse gave us all a chill. Judge Kennedy's courtroom was located in a recently opened building, a grand edifice named for Judge William Bryant, the first African American judge to serve on the federal court in the nation's capital. The spanking new annex had courtrooms that many lawyers called the "Ritz Carlton," given their beautiful design and decoration. I led our large group of Matthews, members of the families, team members and experts up the elevator and into the hushed courtroom where they would testify.

In my many years of trying cases, many in the older section of this same courthouse, I have always enjoyed the stillness of the courtroom in the early morning. There is a sense of quiet before the storm before the judge comes on the bench with his law clerks and the court reporter and courtroom clerk set up at their desks below. We were the only case on the judge's schedule that day, at least according to the docket sheet posted outside the courtroom. The families sat, taking in the high ceilings and ornate surroundings, the plush carpeting and polished wood benches in the audience section. The room still had its new car smell and feel. The American flag stood on one side of the bench; the red and white District of Columbia flag stood on the other. A large seal of the United States hung on the wall behind the judge's bench, its engraving announcing that we were all before the United States District Court for the District of Columbia. It was in this grand room, in the heart of Washington, that the rule of law finally would be applied to Qaddafi and his government. What had started in 1989 in Brazzaville with the placement of a suitcase bomb in the cargo hold of a DC-10 would end in a distinguished courtroom on the corner of Constitution Avenue and Third Street, Northwest Washington. The case had wound its way from the Ténéré in Niger to the streets and palaces of Paris to the electronics manufacturing center of Taiwan to technical companies in Germany to the halls of the United Nations in New York, and even to a tent in the Libyan desert, but would come to rest in this quiet room.

AT PRECISELY 10:00 a.m., the United States Marshal banged on the thick wooden door leading to the judge's chambers, announced "All rise" and everyone in the courtroom stood to attention. My colleagues and I were at the counsel table on one side; Dabiri sat across from us at another table, by himself. The audience section was pretty well filled by the families, Matthews, his corporate lawyer John Metzger and some spectators, including some other folks from my firm. Judge Kennedy sat soberly on the bench, his black robes complemented by his well-trimmed gray beard. He nodded at the deputy clerk sitting in front of the bench, who picked up her docket sheet and announced the case.

"Civil Action Number 02-2026, Robert Pugh, et al. versus the Socialist People's Libyan Arab Jamahiriya, et al."

She turned to look back up to the judge and nodded.

"Are you ready to proceed, Mr. Newberger?" Judge Kennedy asked as a formality.

* * *

THE ELDERLY MAN walked hesitantly up to the witness stand next to Judge Kennedy. He was frail, had trouble moving his feet and was focused on reaching the chair. Dressed in a light suit, white shirt and striped tie, his pale blue eyes acknowledged the judge as he stood to take the oath. The clerk looked on with respect as she made sure the man was comfortable.

"Would you please state your name for the record?" she asked.

"Robert Pugh," he answered, his voice a bit weak but clear.

I stood at the attorney podium and began the process of helping the witness and lead plaintiff tell his story to the court.

"Mr. Ambassador, where were you living on 19 September 1989?"

"N'Djamena, Chad."

"And at that time, what was your job in Chad?"

"I was serving as Ambassador," he replied.

With this introduction, Ambassador Pugh brought Judge Kennedy and those in the courtroom back to the events that had led us all to this trial.

Speaking slowly, and at times with emphasis, Pugh explained to the courtroom his career in the US Marines as an officer and then his long hitch as a foreign service officer. This was a career that had taken him around the world, from Turkey to Iran, from Greece to London, and finally to Beirut, Lebanon, in 1983 as the number two at the Embassy, the Deputy Chief of Mission, DCM. With him throughout his career was his life-long companion and partner, his wife, Bonnie. She had been an integral part of his public and private life, even when they had their first serious encounter with international terrorism.

Describing that sunny day in April 1983 when an Iranian-sponsored suicide bomber drove his truck directly into the Beirut Embassy's front door, Pugh recalled the horror of being a target of a major terrorist attack.

"There was a terrific explosion. I was in my office in the highest floor that was occupied by people. The windows came in, and, were it not for the fact that the windows had been covered with Mylar, we would—"we" I say that because my administrative officer was with me at the time talking over efficiency reports … Had it not been for the Mylar, we both would have been pretty badly cut up by the window, the glass. But the Mylar kept it in one sheet and it came in at us and just fell on the corner of my desk. I didn't get a scratch.

"We went to the next door office ... The Ambassador's secretary was standing in a frozen posture unable to comprehend what had just happened. We went into the Ambassador's office to see how he had fared. He was trapped under a heavy blanket of rubble from one of the walls that had come in, but he was conscious ... I grabbed ahold of the American flagpole that had fallen on him and pulled and lifted and got this slab off him ... And as it was, he turned out not to have any serious injury."

Having escaped with their lives, he then described how he and Ambassador Robert Dillon had dealt with the most serious attack on a US Embassy in history. Scores of American and Lebanese workers had been killed and many more injured, and through it all his wife Bonnie had defied the risks of another attack and worked tirelessly, side by side with Pugh, to help the survivors, and bury the dead.

Bonnie then went with him to his next assignment, this time as the Ambassador to Mauritania in Africa—his first ambassadorial post, and the top rank for a career foreign service officer. Three years with his own flag and seal. His service there was exemplary and their next assignment was to N'Djamena, Chad, also as the US Ambassador. Bonnie also traveled with him to the Central African country, still recovering from the long civil war that had found Qaddafi and his Libyan troops on the losing side, a loss the French government surmised gave rise to Qaddafi's desire to attack a French airliner in retaliation.

Looking out at his daughter, Ann, in the audience, Pugh smiled weakly as he got to the most painful part of the story. We had discussed this before, and he knew what was coming.

"On 19 September 1989 while you and your wife, Bonnie, were living in Chad, did your wife have occasion to leave the country and return to the United States?"

He looked directly at Ann, who sat transfixed in the front row of the audience. She was obviously worried about her frail father's health and his ability to describe the forthcoming events.

"Not until our daughter, Ann, became engaged and a wedding date was set, and she arranged to go back two weeks before Ann's marriage and help her prepare for the marriage. That was flight UTA 772."

"When was the last time you saw your wife, Bonnie?"

"I was able to accompany her out on the tarmac and to the foot of the stairs going up to the forward part of the aircraft, and we exchanged the kind of remarks you make when you're going to be separated from a mate. And she went up the steps, and that's the last I saw of her."

I paused as Pugh appeared to be lost in thought, or in memory. I could see that Judge Kennedy, who had heard a lot of tragedies in all his years on the bench, was quite moved. The courtroom clerk was moist eyed. You could hear a pin drop in the room.

We were walked through the horror of his hearing about the crash from a Marine security officer later that day, and the French investigation and identification of bodies. Bonnie's remains had been found mostly intact, still strapped in her seat. We then relived the long wait of several months for her remains to be examined in Paris as part of Bruguière's enquiry and their tragic return to Dulles Airport outside Washington several months later. Based on her husband's service record and her own devotion to the US Marines who were stationed at the embassies, she was buried at Arlington National Cemetery, with US Marine honors.

Following through with what he believed would have been Bonnie's final wishes, Ann went ahead with her wedding shortly after the burial. It was not a happy occasion, as he made clear to the courtroom.

But the family tragedy did not end there. Pugh described how his career as a diplomat had also come to an end with the death of his lifelong partner. Having experienced two notorious terrorist attacks, he agreed to the request of his two children, Ann and her younger brother, Malcolm, that he leave Chad and stay out of harm's way with a position in Washington. He resigned as Ambassador and returned to Foggy Bottom and a post at the headquarters of the Department of State. However, Malcolm had experienced severe depression as an adolescent and in college, and his symptoms became worse when he lost his mother, with whom he was very close. Three years after the DC-10 crashed in the desert, Malcolm committed suicide. This final family tragedy was too much for Pugh to bear, and he resigned from the Foreign Service shortly after he buried his son. He considered Malcolm another victim of the DC-10 bombing.

Asked why he had decided to participate in the lawsuit and sue Libya,

Pugh looked straight at Judge Kennedy and sat up proudly, his years of Marine and diplomatic training coming to the fore.

"I never thought that there would be any chance of actual punishment of the perpetrators, but I hoped that at least they would be identified and pilloried in public opinion."

He turned and looked at Dabiri.

Pugh had been on the witness stand for two long hours. After Dabiri asked him some perfunctory questions, I helped him walk back to the front row so he could sit next to Ann and watch the remainder of the trial. He was visibly tired and drained, both physically and emotionally.

The Ambassador had completed his last mission.

IOANA ALIMANESTIANU WAS a small, slim woman dressed in conservative clothes and smart shoes. She sat in the witness chair and described how she and her late husband, Mihai, had escaped the Communist regime in Romania in the 1950s and made their way to the United States. They had become US citizens, raised a family and enjoyed life in their adopted country. Mihai had spent many years working as a gas pipeline engineer based in Texas and New York—where Ioana had become a translator at Radio Free Europe—and then in Chad for the US Agency for International Development on a special contract to rebuild the country after the end of the civil war.

Mihai had been on his way home after a work session in Chad and was going to visit his new twin grandchildren in Belgium before heading back to his home in New York. He was seventy years old when he went down with the DC-10.

Ioana described for Judge Kennedy how her late husband had intended to work for a few more years, despite his advanced age, so that they could afford a large piece of land just north of New York City for their retirement. He had dreamed of putting up a house and leaving the other thirty-five acres as a park.

"The view is incredible," she explained to the judge. "On a clear day you can see all the way to Manhattan. And you see the Tappan Zee Bridge and all the Hudson River going by and the other side, and it's beautiful."

Mihai's remains were returned from Africa and the Paris autopsy several months after the plane crashed. The family was told firmly by the State Department that they should not examine the inside of his coffin because it was "horrible." The only personal effect Ioana recovered from the crash site was her husband's briefcase.

To fulfill Mihai's dream, they buried him on the lot he had hoped to use as their retirement home. The property was then transferred to a public trust so that the entire thirty-five acres would remain a pristine and contemplative oasis. The family had put a bench near Mihai's grave with his name on it so anyone who later sat there and enjoyed the view would remember and honor him.

Dabiri did not ask her a single question.

MARY KATHRYN HASSETT had driven up to Washington from her home in Charlottesville, Virginia. She described how her daughter Margaret Schutzius, the baby of her family, had majored in French at the University of Chicago, one of the country's best colleges, and postponed her senior year to join the Peace Corps. She had been attracted to a job of teaching English to French-speaking villagers in a small town in Chad called Mondou and was among the first group of Peace Corps volunteers to return to Chad after the dangerous civil war had ended.

Looking at Ambassador Pugh and his daughter sitting in the front row, whom she had never met before the trial, she described how her daughter had written long and eloquent letters from Chad to keep her mother informed of her African adventure. In one letter, she had written how wonderful Bonnie Pugh, the Ambassador's wife, had been to the Peace Corps volunteers, and how she was a "mother" to the young Americans living in harsh conditions in the destitute country. She specifically noted this for Pugh's benefit from the witness stand, having listened intently to his own testimony and memories.

In her letters, Margaret had made clear her intention of finishing her studies at Chicago, then pursuing a degree in International Studies. The fact that she had come down with a tropical disease at one point and been flown back to Washington for treatment at the National Institutes of Health had not dissuaded her from her career choice. She had insisted on returning to Chad to finish her tour and extend her stay to train the new teams that would replace her in the village. It was only because she had stayed beyond her tour date that she was on the doomed UTA 772 flight.

When Mary Kathryn heard about the French plane going down, her first thoughts were about the Lockerbie crash. Losing her youngest child in the bombing had devastated her and her other children. Margaret was only twenty-four years old when she was killed.

Pulling out a letter Margaret had written shortly before she died, Mary Kathryn asked the judge if she could read a part of it into the record, since she also had done so at her daughter's memorial service back in 1989. Judge Kennedy agreed to her request, and she put on her reading glasses and paused for several moments to collect herself.

"For all of its many problems," the letter began,

I like Chad and Chadians. I can't tell you why, maybe I like going to market instead of to Safeway. Maybe because time here moves slowly and not quickly. Life seems to be a continuous flow, not a series of career moves or not just on a demographic chart: Child, teenager, young adult, young married adult, parent, middle-aged, retirement-age, senior citizen, older senior citizen, extremely old senior citizen, burden to society, dead. The other side of this coin, the closeness of life and death, is the confusing simplicity of it all. Having been taught that life is more than just surviving—it's ideas and beauty and good works. I am learning that a lot of life is surviving. How can I reconcile these opposing and equally powerful viewpoints? Every day I see children who are undernourished and may be dying. For them, life is today and tomorrow seems far away if you have to beg for food and go hungry. I see this world where the importance of a strong fiscal policy is unknown and irrelevant. The importance of Descartes' establishment of the scientific method in philosophy, whatever its flaws, might be as far away as Andromache. I think growing up in a place where teenagers die a little if they can't afford to buy the latest fashion and young children clamor for electronic toys makes me appreciate the closeness of these people and their closeness to nature.

Mary Kathryn stopped for a moment, looked up at the ceiling to reflect, and, taking a deep breath, continued to read. The courtroom was so silent I could hear my own breathing.

> Despite their ignorance of the beauty of Mozart's great Mass, Chadians are amazing. They can work a full day with no food, they can build a house with nothing. Mechanical difficulties are like games for them. They can build fires, plow fields, repair anything, and carry huge bundles on their head. They know plants and animals the way I know the Chicago public transit system. I am, of course, hopelessly tied to my culture. The sound of tom-toms is stirring, but American jazz is what I love, and a night at the symphony is more comfortable than a traditional funeral procession. I prefer a night discussing politics and the philosophy of development of the US role in Central America to pounding millet.

This caused her to look up and explain to Judge Kennedy that millet was the Chadians' chief grain. She then continued.

> I think coming here and experiencing this world has made me realize that despite the many things I dislike about the US, I also love it. I am hopelessly and gratefully Western. I can love Chad, but only as an outsider. Being born in a country binds you inextricably to it; like being born into a family binds you forever and inextricably to every member of it.

Stopping at that point in her reading, Mary Kathryn looked up, took off her reading glasses and through moist eyes and tightly pursed lips turned to Judge Kennedy and said, "And then the letter says stop worrying, my health is fine."

Waiting a moment for the sad memory of her daughter to receive the respect it deserved from the people in the courtroom, she answered the same question each of the family members was prepared to share with Judge Kennedy.

"For me," she started, "it's having the opportunity to be here in this courtroom. I mean, I went to the French trial, and I was so grateful to the French for inviting us, and particularly to Madame Rudetzki for making that possible, but it wasn't the same as being here in this court-room speaking for her voice, speaking on behalf of all the voices that were silenced."

Smiling for a moment, she caught herself and nodded that she had something else to add.

"A year after she died, in 1990, an infirmary was dedicated to her in the town where she taught, in the high school where she taught. It was sort of a student infirmary that they hadn't had before. And it was a very nice ceremony there. They had a choir that sang health songs about washing your hands and things like that, and several people spoke. And John, her brother, and I went over for that ceremony. And the dispen-sary is named after her, Dispensaire of Margaret. They couldn't—I think they couldn't pronounce Schutzius, so they just did Margaret."

She turned to the audience and looked directly at Matthews.

"I just thought it would be overwhelming. But having read her letters just a couple of nights ago, they sort of brought her back whole, as a picture of a whole person who had—who was doing what she wanted to do. And that was somehow comforting. And a chance to speak for that voice that was silenced here today is a great comfort, and I appre-ciate having that chance and getting that call many years ago from Doug Matthews to give us this chance."

She and Matthews looked at each other for a moment.

"Stuart Newberger told us last night that this trial is really about the victims. That's why I really wanted to be here. I mean, I think I might be dead before we ever see any money from this, so that was— it's been five years to get to this point. So it's more of a chance to speak in the hope that—I mean, all of us are—have to rejoice that Libya has decided to rejoin the community of nations. But all of us have to say as well that they cannot ignore the past, they have to face up to the consequences of what they did, as well as the promise not to do it again."

OVER THE NEXT two days the witnesses continued to unburden their grief and loss to the judge and the other families sitting in the courtroom.

Eighteen years was not a very long time for people who had suffered such a sudden and devastating loss.

Ermine Hailey had traveled to Washington from a small town in Texas where she taught English to college students. Her husband Pat Wayne Huff had finished a twenty-eight-day rotation as the drilling foreman of an oil rig in Chad operated by Parker Drilling when he boarded the UTA 772 flight on his way back home to Texas. After getting out of the Air Force, he had spent his entire working life in the oil fields around the world, starting as a roustabout, a laborer, and rising through the ranks to become a foreman.

Pat had essentially adopted his wife's two kids from a failed first marriage. They called him "Pat Daddy." Ermine and her kids had relied heavily on the Texan for support and strength. She described him as a "John Wayne"-type of person, tall and broad, who stood out in the crowd and always looked out for his own. He was not supposed to have been on the UTA flight, but schedules had got mixed up and fate had intervened.

Her son could not attend the trial because he was serving in Iraq, but Ermine's daughter sat in the front row of the courtroom as her mother described how devastating his death had been for her, causing a bad run with alcohol until she worked her way out of the depression and loss. Despite having recently remarried, she told Judge Kennedy that she still wore Pat's wedding band on her finger as a memory. He was thirty-eight years old when he died in the crash. She turned to Judge Kennedy and began to explain how she had struggled to know what to do when Matthews had called.

"I'm here for Pat and my children and me, but mostly for Pat, because he was an innocent person. And no matter what he did or didn't do in his life—and there's so many people that I've heard testimony of that were wonderful people," she began, looking at Mary Kathryn Hassett in the audience. "And Pat was one too, trying to make a difference in the world to where people could help each other instead of blow each other up. And the people that were killed don't have a voice, and they didn't get a jury trial. We don't have the six people, the perpetrators, as well as the government and the head of that government over here answering, but at least we can say what we would say to them.

And I appreciate the opportunity to say what these people meant to us and what a travesty it is that people with such potential and love and wanting to make the world a better place are the victims in a situation where senseless killing of innocent people is done, and I would like justice for that."

CARLA MALKIEWICZ ALSO came from Texas. She told Judge Kennedy about her husband Mark Corder, a geologist who "looked at rocks for Exxon" all around the world in a never-ending quest to discover more oil. He also had been coming off a long shift in Chad when he boarded the UTA flight and was heading back to London where the couple had made a home. They had grown up down the street from each other and were married after she had experienced two other unsuccessful relationships.

Her words came very slowly as she tried to describe the pain she felt when she heard about the crash. She had waited several months for the French autopsy to be concluded and attended two memorial services.

"I decided that I wanted to go meet the plane that had his body on there, and went to the gate. I knew the gate he was coming in, I knew the flight number and the gate. And there's a little cafe there that had glass, and I stood there and watched his body come off that plane, and it looked so little. He was such a big man. It looked so little. And I thought—we spent a lot of our life in airports. And I thought, this is the last time I'm going to meet you at an airport. And the hearse took him away. And Mark's dad went to the cemetery and had a graveside ceremony. And I just couldn't do it."

Taking a breath, she pointed to her heart.

Judge Kennedy asked, "You're pointing to your heart?"

"I lost my soulmate."

She stopped for a moment.

"I really didn't want to be a part of this." She pointed around the courtroom. "I had—I didn't participate in the French thing, and I didn't want to prosper from Mark's death. But Doug"—she pointed at Matthews in the front row—"was very persistent, and he told me if I didn't want the money I could give it to charity. And, you know, now

I think that it's the right thing to do, because Mark's life was taken without his—without his permission, without his knowledge, and by people who don't value life. And maybe if it cost them money, they'll think before they do it and someone else has to go through what I've had to go through."

OTHER FAMILY MEMBERS described how their father, another oil man, had survived a kidnapping in Chad a few years before, only to be killed on the flight. Several described how the news of the UTA crash caused their minds to "go right to Pan Am."

Dabiri trod carefully around most of the family members who testified, only asking questions about their economic history or career plans. He obviously would steer away from issues of pain and suffering and focus on how to chip away at the amount of economic damages the judge might award each estate. This was simply proper lawyering on his behalf: create as good a record as you can and attempt to keep the damages lower.

IT CAME TIME for Matthews to testify. The families had spent almost two days describing their emotional and personal loss. For Matthews, of course, his loss was economic, since his company had lost a $41 million wide-body jet, only part of which was insured. Dressed in a tailored gray suit, monogrammed shirt and a London silk tie, the former Delta pilot and Vietnam veteran airman seemed humbled by all the accolades he had received from the family members who had come to the witness stand before him.

What had started out as a commercial venture for Matthews had evolved into something quite different. He had become intertwined with the lives of the families of the seven diverse Americans who had perished on his DC-10. He had never met these families before approaching me and my law firm five years earlier. Until the seven, along with many others, died in the Ténéré desert, thousands of people had flown on his company's jets all around the world. Thousands more had been passengers on Delta flights he had piloted. They were all just statistics in a complicated and expensive business. I stood at the attorney lectern as Matthews took the oath and got comfortable in his seat next to Judge Kennedy. He walked the judge through his career as a Navy aviator, flying combat missions over North Vietnam, and his years as a pilot flying jumbo jets for Delta. The judge seemed quite captivated by Matthews' tale of how he stumbled into the aircraft leasing business almost by accident and built Interlease into a major lessor of aircraft for the world's leading airlines. He had owned a number of DC-10s that were leased to UTA and others and had never lost a single plane until 19 September 1989.

The main point of his testimony was to support the claim for over $40 million as part of the damages phase, although an aircraft valuation expert would follow him to the stand and provide the details and "Blue Book" (the report filed by insurers in the USA) support for the property loss claim. Eventually, he described how he had learned of the crash from someone at Lloyd's Insurance in London while he was in a meeting with British Airways, negotiating a new aircraft deal, and how he had followed the French investigation and trial before approaching my law firm to pursue a US case. Had spent almost a year tracking down the seven American families to inform them of his intention to bring a case, offering them an opportunity to join him in the fight.

Looking out at the families in the courtroom, Matthews saw that he had done much more than put a lawsuit together for the opportunity to collect money. As he explained to the Judge, he wanted "to give everybody a chance at, at bringing justice, mainly to, to have Libya identified, you know, as the guilty—not the guilty parties, it's not a criminal proceeding, but the party that was responsible, and to—and for the families to have a chance."

Judging by their faces in the audience, he had more than succeeded.

THE REST OF the trial was comprised of our experts, who presented evidence on a range of topics to Judge Kennedy to round out our damages case. The labor economist calculated the expected income of each of the seven victims with technically complicated and tedious descriptions of formulas and discounted cash-flow summaries. An aircraft valuation expert supported Matthews' calculation that the DC-10 was worth at least $40 million when it crashed. Most of this expert testimony was dry, and the audience lost interest as the Judge asked technical questions that seemed very unimportant after their emotional stories.

But then we called Donald Sommer, an expert in the world of reconstructing aircraft accidents and disasters. We had retained Sommer to bring to life for Judge Kennedy the events of 19 September 1989 when the Libyan suitcase bomb exploded in the baggage compartment. He had prepared a report that was sitting on Judge Kennedy's bench. After describing his world-class credentials to the Judge, and his obvious qualification as an expert, he brought everyone in the courtroom back to the terror event that had triggered this case.

My partner Mike Martinez handled this expert's testimony, and he focused Sommer on the report he had prepared for Judge Kennedy. Except for Matthews, none of our clients sitting in the courtroom had heard his evidence before the trial. We had thought it might upset them too much. They leaned forward in their seats to hear his reconstruction of the disaster that had taken their loved ones in September 1989. He began with the routine.

"The flight was approximately 2,300 miles. And the aircraft climbed without any notable discrepancies ... up to 35,000 feet. The communications were normal at 35,000. The aircraft continued for approximately 45 minutes into the flight, when according to the flight data recorder, the aircraft met its demise."

The polite word "demise" could not cushion what he next described.

"It essentially broke up into four major pieces. The break-up was a result of a suitcase bomb that was planted in the right forward lower baggage hold. That suitcase bomb caused a violation of the structure of the airplane in the area essentially behind the cockpit in the middle of the first-class section, caused the airplane to become fragmented and break-up ... However, it also broke into essentially into many, many little pieces and was, in fact, scattered over an 80-kilometer piece of the Ténéré."

After describing the DC-10's weight and load—close to 380,000 pounds of airplane, fuel and passengers—Sommer walked through the consequences of what happens when a wide-body jet breaks into pieces at 35,000 feet.

"One of the first things that happened was 'instant compression,' or what's called explosive compression, which means it happens that quickly ... This means that the atmosphere inside the airplane fills instantly with the atmosphere outside the airplane ... and it takes less than a second to equalize the internal and external pressure.

"Section A, the nose section of the airplane, remained essentially intact. It came down by itself and hit the ground more or less as one piece and essentially stayed at one piece. Section A is shaped like a bullet. Obviously, a very big one. But what happens is when it falls, it tends to stabilize. That is, it tends to be more like a dart or an arrow or something that's aerodynamically stable. And rather than tumble and flutter and fall in a confusing and random manner ... it won't tumble, like Sections B and C.

"Section B essentially disintegrated. And once the bomb went off and the structure was lost, that is the backbone of the fuselage is lost, the wind hit it, and it just essentially tore it to shreds. It was found scattered over many, many miles of desert, and the pieces were relatively small.

"Section C, of course, was the wings and back portion of the airplane, and contained the fuel, and fuel caught fire, as it often does, during an in-flight break-up. The section itself was very non-aerodynamic ... and we found that, based on its shape, that it actually tumbled as it fell to the earth. That tumbling, of course, would help promote the fire from the standpoint that the wind is hitting that section in all different directions. And because it tumbles, it also takes it a longer period of time to fall to the earth than say Section A. So there was actually a period of several minutes from 35,000 feet before Section C came to the earth."

At this point, Mike asked Sommer the question we needed Judge Kennedy to hear if we were going to convince him to award substantial damages against Libya.

"Did you reach any conclusion as to whether any of the passengers on board survived the explosion and were alive as they fell to the ground?"

"Well, based on the French authorities' report on the condition of the bodies after analysis, after they fell to the ground, as well as what we know about the explosion and the break-up of the airplane, there were certainly a number of people alive after the explosion."

The courtroom was completely quiet. Despite the number of people in the audience, and lawyers around the courtroom, it seemed to me like no one was breathing. No papers were being shuffled. No one shifted in their seats. No one seemed to move. Especially the families, who had never really been told about the details of how their loved ones had died. And now, Sommer was telling them that many of the 170 people on board had survived the initial explosion forty-five minutes into the flight, only to face the inevitable truth that, having survived the blast that blew the airplane into four sections and a lot of smaller pieces, there was still 35,000 feet between them and the earth. The calm forensic expert continued his horror story.

"You have a huge amount of wind that becomes entangled with the passengers that are both within the portions of the airplane still intact and without the portions of the airplane. A number of these passengers … fall free, either sometimes still attached to their seats or sometimes not attached to their seats. So some of the passengers would have been ejected from the airplane, some of them would be riding down with the structures of the airplane, especially those sitting in the area of the center fuselage.

"From there you have the normal environment; you're instantly producing 300 miles-per-hour wind, which is a tornadic wind … The discomfort and sound level of that would be absolutely terrifying.

"The explosive decompression has a physiological effect on the body where if there are any entrapped gasses, which typically there are in your body at any given time, it doesn't give those gasses time to equalize—your inner ears, your intestinal tract, your lungs. And what happens is all of a sudden the gasses that are in your body quickly expand and present extreme discomfort. You literally can't equalize quick enough to overcome that problem."

Mike then asked if it was possible that some of the passengers were awake or if they had blacked out after the explosion and before the fall from 35,000 feet.

"Well," Sommer continued, "you've got two things going on. When I say you black out, the time of useful consciousness … you are going to remain conscious for a period of seconds, possibly even thirty, forty seconds, but in the meantime you're falling. So as you're falling the pressure is getting higher. As the pressure is getting higher, it's fighting the effects of hypoxia, hypoxia being the lack of oxygen in your blood, so that you have a little contest going on as to whether the pressure is being raised high enough to overcome the lack of oxygen caused by the high altitude and low pressure from the initial explosion."

Sommer paused for a second and looked at Judge Kennedy.

"And it's my understanding," he said calmly, "that there's a pretty good chance, as a matter of fact, probably better than even, that a lot of passengers were conscious until they hit the ground."

Looking back to the audience, I noticed that the facial expressions of several of the family members had changed from intense attention to horror. They had never known that the passengers would have had a chance of understanding what had happened to them after the bomb went off. What Sommer was describing made them aware that for many the explosion was only the start of their terror.

"There are those passengers that got the direct effect of the explosion, that is, were injured by shrapnel. These were documented by the French, and basically it's … you have an explosion going off inside a metal structure, there are shards of metal which are shot out from the center of the explosion, and those shards of metal, of course, embed themselves and may or may not result in enough energy to kill somebody, but certainly caused a lot of damage to the people.

"In addition, you had the fuel fire, the fuel-fed fire. Some of the occupants, according to the coroner's inquest or the post-mortem analysis by the French, did succumb to the in-flight fire due to burns. Some others were burned but did not necessarily succumb until they came to the ground."

Mike then turned Sommer to the part of his science that would form the basis of our request for "pain and suffering" damages. He asked him if it was possible to calculate how long it took for each section of the airplane to fall to the earth. With passengers conscious, a tornado of wind blasting in their faces, jet fuel searing their lungs, shrapnel piercing their skin, the decompression in the atmosphere setting off gas explosions inside their bodies. Perhaps 170 human beings were all aware of and terrorized by their imminent death.

But for how long? Mike asked.

"We found that Section A took 91 seconds to fall to the ground, about a minute and a half ... It impacted the ground at 185 knots, which is about 220 miles per hour."

They went the fastest.

"Section B, as I mentioned, disintegrated in the air. So for that section I just calculated the time and velocity of a free-falling body ... The terminal velocity was about 113 knots or 140 miles an hour. It would have taken them 178 seconds .... Almost three minutes."

Three minutes of freefall from the sky. Probably awake the entire time.

"Last the wings and tail, Sections C and D ... We calculated it took around 130 seconds. It hit the ground doing 123 knots or 150 to 160 miles per hour."

Several family members were quietly crying. The judge looked stunned. The members of my team were overwrought. Even Dabiri sat silently, not wanting to disturb the silence.

After Mike indicated that he had concluded with Sommer, Dabiri sat for a long minute, obviously trying to figure out what to ask, if anything. He asked a few perfunctory questions to determine that Sommer had not been involved in the original French investigation and autopsies, and that he could not determine exactly which passengers were in what part of the dismembered airplane or how long it took for them to die. After a few minutes, he said he was done as well.

OUR LAST EXPERT was Dr. Richard Levy, a retired Air Force and NASA flight surgeon, who testified about the effects of the trauma on the human body. After Sommer's dramatic testimony, Levy's medical opinion seemed almost dry. Dabiri did not ask him a single question on cross.

With the evidence concluded, the lawyers discussed with Judge Kennedy a schedule to submit post-trial briefs so that the judge could prepare his findings and issue a judgment. Dabiri clearly was trying to find a way to lower the temperature we had set through the trial, tamping down the emotional wave that had sucked the air out of the courtroom.

The judge would give both sides plenty of time to brief the case and the damages issues. He thanked us and stepped off the bench.

Our trial was over. The families could go home. They would take with them the renewed pain and grief from the confines of the court-room, but also the relief that everything had all been put forward in a court of law so many years later.

Chapter 18

Unanimous Consent

SEVERAL MONTHS AFTER we finished the trial in Washington, I was in London working on another matter. It was late in January 2008, and the English winter night came early, the northern latitude bringing the sun's descent by 5:00 p.m. After a long day, several of my partners who were also working in London that week invited me out to a pub for the obligatory pint, after which we moved on to a restaurant for food and French wine. With the five-hour time difference, it was late in the afternoon in Washington when we started to cut into our Scottish Angus steaks.

Of course, the differences in time zones had no effect on our most constant companion—the obligatory BlackBerry. All through the meal, almost like a nervous tic, each lawyer would glance at his or her hand-held machine, the e-mails and messages buzzing non-stop around the table. It was as though each had brought an electronic date to dinner, with whom they had regular conversation. So much for the benefits of technology.

Just as we were pouring the last drop of a very nice Saint Emilion, I took a glance at my BlackBerry to check on some filings in a case my team was handling back in DC. At that moment, the soft-lit screen signaled a new notice from the federal court's electronic docketing system. Having waited several months for Judge Kennedy to complete his work on the Pugh case, I saw instantly that we had received his judgment.

In the modern world of law, we do not often get an opportunity to sit "live" in a federal courtroom and listen to a judge announce his or her verdict in a case. Gone also are the snail-mail envelopes containing a court opinion or award sent via the US Postal Service. Instead, we live in the virtual world of electronic filings—paper is banned as too cumbersome and bulky to store at the clerk's office—and the judge's rulings arrive as a flashing electronic message on your computer screen. Or BlackBerry.

Stepping away from the noisy table and toasted lawyers, I squeezed into a small alcove to try to read the message and attachment. It was clearly an award in the Pugh case, accompanied by an over-100-page memorandum opinion and a separate order listing each of the awards to the family members, estates and Interlease. But I could not read the letters and numbers on the tiny BlackBerry screen no matter how hard I squinted or how much I attempted to enlarge the font. Technology has its limits, and I had reached mine in the overheated, crowded restaurant in London's financial center.

I went back to the table and told my colleagues that we had received an award in the Pugh case after all this time. The stakes in the case, and our multi-million-dollar investment in it, was no secret around the law firm. As anxious as I was to share the news with them, I could not get the details off the screen. After a round of applause simply for the fact that we had received the ruling, I made a quick exit and walked back to my hotel through the cold, dark London night in order to access my laptop and review the court's judgment properly.

As I sat in my room waiting for the laptop to boot up, my thoughts raced back over the five-year ordeal, which had culminated in this point of decision. The trips to Paris to investigate and assemble the case. The tragic lives and shattered dreams of not only the seven Americans who had died in the crash, but the other victims who had perished. The tortured politics that had allowed Qaddafi and his regime to re-emerge as a "civilized" player on the world stage, despite the documented mass

murder that they had carried out around the globe. The drama of the
only contested trial ever to have taken place against a terrorist state.
The painful wait for Judge Kennedy's ruling, now only seconds away
as my laptop came to life and I worked my way into the law firm's
coded website, and eventually my e-mail message from the court.

I pressed a button on the keyboard, more nervous than usual as the
court's memorandum opened. I hurriedly, and with a trained eye,
scanned the pages to determine what exactly Judge Kennedy had decided
as the proper damages figures for this extraordinary case. As the judge's
ruling scrolled, the laptop screen images flashing quickly as I scanned
pages for figures and calculations, I was relieved that I had not had too
much wine with dinner. It was late in the evening in London, it had
been a long day, and I was trying to review over 120 pages of detailed
and technical findings. After a few minutes, I sat back in the chair and
looked up at the ceiling in disbelief. I had to catch my breath.

Judge Kennedy had been convinced by all of our various damages
legal theories and expert opinions. He recited each, chapter and verse,
detailing the testimony of each witness and family member as he
recounted their pain, anguish and loss from the testimony. He would
award lost economic damages to each of the seven estates, some in the
millions of dollars, all against the Libyan state. And he would award
Interlease $41 million for the value of the DC-10, albeit against the six
individual Libyan defendants and not the Libyan state. And then I got
to the numbers. It was staggering.

For the "pain and suffering" of the seven American victims, Judge
Kennedy agreed with our experts that it was likely that they had survived
the initial explosion of the suitcase bomb in the luggage compartment
at 35,000 feet, and that they had experienced almost three unimaginable
minutes of terror as the sections of the DC-10 plummeted towards
earth. He described the passengers strapped in their seats as tornado-like
winds, burning jet fuel and metal debris forewarned them of the certain
death that awaited them when their 200-mile-an-hour descents were
broken by the desert sands. Acknowledging that "there is no set formula
for quantifying the pain and suffering plaintiffs experienced as a result
of Libya's intentional and malicious acts of murder," Judge Kennedy
noted that "the excruciating physical and emotional pain endured by

the seven American passengers aboard UTA Flight 772 before they died and the grief and anguish endured by their immediate family members over the past 18 years cannot be precisely quantified in monetary terms. Nevertheless, courts regularly have considered similar circumstances—including, specifically in the context of terrorist attacks—and have awarded damages to compensate the victims for their pain and suffering."

Remarkably, for each second of unimaginable terror on the descending aircraft, Judge Kennedy awarded $100,000. And there were three minutes of this terror. One hundred and eighty seconds—$18 million dollars for each of the seven victims' pain and suffering caused by Qaddafi and his regime's act of mass murder.

But Judge Kennedy did not stop there.

Each immediate family member was awarded millions of dollars for their own loss, some reaching $10 million for the loss of a spouse or parent or child.

There was more. He had also decided that all the plaintiffs' monetary awards were entitled to "pre-judgment interest," dating back to September 1989 when the DC-10 blew up. This was because he ruled, as a matter of law, that such interest calculations were "an element of complete compensation."

I sat at the hotel room desk jotting down figures and details from my fast read of the ruling. My quick calculations were that the Judge had ordered Libya to pay the families collectively approximately $500 million in compensatory damages, and over $1 billion in pre-judgment interest on top of that—a total of over $1.5 billion against the Libyan state for one of the most cold-blooded acts of terrorism in modern times.

Separate from the judgment against the Libyan government was the judgment against the six Libyan defendants who had remained safely in their comfortable surrounds by the Mediterranean. Having been convicted of murder by the courts of France, they now were found to be liable to the American families and Interlease for a separate amount of $500 million, plus another $1 billion in pre-judgment interest. But unlike the amount against Libya, the separate federal law allowing the families and Interlease to sue the six individuals required that the Judge "treble" all of these damages, thereby bringing that portion of the judgment against the six men up to approximately $5 billion.

When the two judgments—one against Libya, the other against the six individuals—were tallied together on my hotel notepad, I could not believe it. Judge Kennedy had issued the first serious judgment against the Libyan government and the men responsible for the UTA 772 bombing in a total amount of almost $7 billion.

It was beyond the imagination. It was unprecedented. And it would be impossible for the Libyans to ignore, especially after our long-running and frustrating efforts to settle the case through court mediation, Paris negotiations, Ambassador Beaussou's diplomacy in Tripoli and general arm-twisting by the United States government.

I called Doug Matthews at his Atlanta home to give him the news, and he then contacted all the families so they would hear about the judgment directly from him and not on television or in the newspapers. The cool-headed pilot was quite excited at the size of the award, but kept his composure, as always, as we outlined how to describe the ruling and respond to the inevitable calls from reporters. After eighteen years of waiting and struggle, it looked like the saga of the "forgotten flight" might be drawing to a successful conclusion.

Sitting back down at the laptop, I drafted a short press release for my law firm's marketing department to issue in the morning so that the news of Judge Kennedy's ruling could get out on the wires. We needed to shape the public story quickly. Judge Kennedy already had posted the ruling on the federal court's website for all the world to read.

* * *

THE NEWS FOR Libya and Qaddafi over the next week only got worse.

In Washington, Congress had been busy for the past few months debating legislation that would tighten the noose around terrorist states that refused to pay court judgments obtained by victims. While mostly focused on Iran, Congress had considered in 2007 a bill that would change the rules for enforcing such judgments against all terrorist states, making it easier for victims who had gone through the court process to collect on assets located in the United States.

Those efforts had failed in 2007 because President Bush had objected to including Iraq in the legislation, a country he had invaded, taken over and "reformed" to the point that enforcing court judgments against Iraq—even by American victims under Saddam Hussein's regime's—would run counter to his foreign policy. Indeed, he had vetoed such legislation and made clear that Iraq's assets were simply off-limits to any Americans who had successfully sued the country.

Congress got the message and by the last week of January 2008 was voting on a new legislative package that would expressly allow President Bush to exempt anything related to Iraq from the new law. With President Bush satisfied that the huge and costly effort in Iraq would not be compromised by pesky US court judgments, Congress enacted the bill into law.

This major piece of legislation was passed only five days after Judge Kennedy issued his historic multi-billion-dollar judgment against Libya in the Pugh case. In Tripoli, it appeared to Qaddafi that Congress, the federal courts and President Bush were working in unison to tighten the noose around his neck. After all, in his country there was no such thing as separation of powers—all the branches of government answered to the whims of the Great Leader.

The technical title for the new legislation was the National Defense Authorization Act—Terrorism Exception to Immunity. But everyone knew it by another name—the Lautenberg Amendment.

Senator Frank Lautenberg, Democrat of New Jersey, was a handsome Jewish man with distinguished white hair and a Palm Beach tan. He had made a fortune in the business world before running for the US Senate and enjoyed the double perk of a personal fortune and a safe Senate seat. A smart, sophisticated player in the world's most exclusive club, he knew how to pull the levers of Congressional power to satisfy the needs of his constituents. He had been the leading sponsor of legislation in the Congress when it came to the rights of US victims of state-sponsored terrorism and was most proud of his role as a principal sponsor of the original 1996 "terrorism" amendments to the Foreign Sovereign Immunities Act that had allowed the Lockerbie families, and other victims of Iranian terrorism, to sue Iran and Libya in federal court. He had kept close contact with the lawyers, families and lobbyists who pressed for continuing pressure on such countries to be held accountable. But his newest law, now signed by President Bush, was a major addition to the legal weapons victims could employ to hold terrorist states accountable.

Of particular significance to the Pugh case was a technical section of the new law that changed the landscape for victims who had obtained judgments and were attempting to enforce them. In essence, the new law lowered the bar for determining whether assets located in the United States were even indirectly owned or controlled by a country such as Libya or Iran, and allowed for seizure of such assets even if they had no connection to any terrorist activities. This was a poison pill for countries that refused to honor court judgments and might have assets in the United States. Iran had long since removed most of its assets from the United States for that very reason, and repeated efforts by victims with Iranian judgments to seize assets in the US and apply them to their judgments had failed mostly because those assets could not be tied directly to Iran. No one, other than my law firm, had obtained a judgment against Libya, so that circumstance had never arisen. But the recent giant award in Pugh, combined with this new law, was a game-changer.

The reason was simple. With President Bush removing Libya from the terrorism list and lifting economic sanctions, many US companies were quickly rushing into Tripoli in search of contracts and energy deals. And with its huge oil reserves and pent-up desire to expand trade with the United States, Qaddafi and his regime were signing contracts and buying assets in the United States as part of that dynamic. In other words, Libya was building up a huge target of commercial assets inside the United States for us to pursue in order to satisfy the Pugh judgment—once it became final. When President Bush had released the $1 billion in Libyan frozen assets a few years earlier, we had lost a powerful leverage tool. With the recent Pugh judgment and the new legislation, we had Libyan assets in our sights once again. Within days, the stakes for Qaddafi and Libya had increased dramatically.

The system established by Congress in 1996 and enhanced by the 2008 law was exactly what the United States had intended—holding terrorist states accountable in a court of law for killing and harming

Americans. The seven UTA 772 families had pursued their rights just as Congress and two Presidents had allowed, and the federal court had done the adjudication job—determining liability and damages—that the political branches of our constitutional system had assigned to it back in 1996.

With this one-two punch in late January 2008, we finally felt that the American portion of the UTA case had reached its nadir. Thus, I was not surprised to receive a call from Dabiri inviting me to attend a meeting at the newly opened Libyan Embassy in Washington just days after President Bush signed the Lautenberg Amendment. Excited at the prospect of finally reaching a point where a settlement could be within reach, I did not fully appreciate at the time that the fast-spinning forces of diplomacy and justice were about to collide.

* * *

ON 30 JANUARY, my partner Laurel Malson and I got into a taxi in front of our offices at Tenth and Pennsylvania and headed across town to the Watergate Office Building, located in Foggy Bottom near the Kennedy Center for the Performing Arts. The newly opened Embassy of Libya was renting space in the landmark Watergate Office Building, made famous by the 1972 break-in and burglary that ultimately led to the first and only resignation of a United States President, Richard Nixon.

Heading up in the elevator, we felt more like we were attending a meeting at another law office than entering a diplomatic post—one of a country that only recently had been an archenemy of the Free World and a sponsor of terrorist attacks on Americans. After minimal security checks, we were invited into a reception area whose walls were draped with tourist posters of Roman ruins on the Libyan Mediterranean shoreline, an inviting picture that certainly did not delve into the violent and deadly culture that had brought us here in the first place.

After a few moments, Dabiri came out and in his most polite and friendly manner invited us back to a conference room. Rising to greet us were two Libyan gentlemen and an American. With the formality and friendliness that characterize business dealings in the Arab world, we finally were meeting actual "principals" from Tripoli who had authority to speak for their government and negotiate a settlement.

The first to come forward was Ahmed Elmssallati, a lawyer who chaired the Litigation Department of the Libyan Ministry of Foreign Affairs. Dressed in a well-tailored European suit, white shirt and dark tie, Elmssallatti was the picture of calm, professional management. According to Schwartz at State, who had worked closely with him for some time, he was the principal adviser to Qaddafi on all international claims. Next to him was Azzan Eddeb, a judge on the Libyan Supreme Court who also served as a senior adviser to Gaddafi on these highly sensitive legal disputes. He also was the epitome of a cool-handed professional adviser, and he took a few extra moments to seize my hand and look me in the eye. He was clearly sizing me up as an adversary, digesting whatever details Dabiri had previously provided. Also at the table was Thomas Whalen, an American lawyer at the Eckert Seamans law firm who had apparently served as a legal adviser to the Libyans for the past few months, especially given the double-barreled threat posed by the Pugh judgment and the Lautenberg Amendment.

Elmssallati explained that he and Eddeb had traveled to Washington to meet with senior officials at the State Department to discuss a wide range of issues at the center of the emerging US–Libya relationship. They wanted to meet me in person, given the serious nature of our legal claims and the fact that we also had other cases pending against Libya that might also result in large damages awards. Despite the friendly banter and polite greetings, I could sense these men were all business, and viewed me and Laurel as enemies they must vanquish.

After the usual small talk, Elmssallatti made clear that the current situation presented by the double whammy of the huge Pugh judgment and the recent legislation was unacceptable and would only serve to poison the emerging relationship between these former adversaries. He wanted to know, first-hand, whether our clients would be willing to compromise and settle the case, just as he had been able to do with the Lockerbie lawyers and their clients.

I made clear we were very interested in a settlement and briefly recounted the repeated efforts we had made for several years—both in Washington and in Paris and through Ambassador Beaussou's efforts on our behalf in Tripoli—to reach an accommodation before the case went to trial. He acknowledged there had been some history, but did not want to dwell on the past. He also made clear that we would only be dealing with him, Eddeb and other senior Libyan officials. Professor Ballow and Madame Sefrioui of the Paris Bar were out of the picture. From what I could observe from body language, it looked like Dabiri might not be long for the party either.

Getting down to brass tacks, Elmssallatti asked me to provide a written settlement demand for the Pugh case within twenty-four hours so that he could evaluate the situation and seek instructions "from the top" in Tripoli. There was nothing vague in his message—Qaddafi had sent this team to Washington to cut deals and move things along. We agreed to send a demand and thanked them for the meeting. After a few more formalities and handshakes, we were in a taxi and heading back to the office.

After a quick call with Matthews, we typed up a demand letter and by the next morning had it delivered by hand to the Embassy. In short, we told the Libyans that we would start the negotiations by dropping all the claims and judgments against the six individuals—thus dropping almost $6 billion in judgments that probably could never be enforced in any event—and focus on the claims directly against the Libyan State. These totaled over $1.5 billion when the huge pre-judgment interest was included. We knew this was a first step in what could be a long negotiation, but we clearly signaled to the Libyans that we were prepared to move forward and compromise if a settlement was within reach.

AS USUAL, I kept Schwartz informed of my discussions with the Libyans and after a few phone conversations it was clear to me that the Bush Administration was engaged in its own serious discussions with these same senior Libyan officials on a broad range of subjects. What Schwartz kept emphasizing was that the Libyans wanted a global settlement that could wrap up all the outstanding claims and cases arising from their terrorist past. This included the still-outstanding demands of the Lockerbie families for the remaining $2 million payments on their settlement as well as the families in the La Belle Disco cases, who had reached a tentative settlement but had not been able to close the deal.

The State Department and White House were struggling with how to juggle all these balls at once. The Lautenberg Amendment also was a serious factor, as this recent legislation had raised the temperature so high for the Libyans that progress in the overall rapprochement could not be achieved until and unless Congress somehow took Libya off the hook. And in the middle of it was the Pugh judgment, whose huge dollars and unprecedented findings had only served to complicate the discussions even more. This was where the DC Circuit's ruling before the damages trial helped us the most—by making clear that Libya was still properly a defendant in our case notwithstanding that President Bush had removed it from the terrorist list.

All these developments in early 2008 had caught the Libyans off guard, despite Beaussou's visits to Tripoli and warnings to Qaddafi's regime. Frantic and daily diplomatic notes were coming to Washington from the new US diplomatic mission in Tripoli, as the Libyans sought guidance from the Bush Administration on how to relieve the combined pressure of a multi-billion-dollar court award in Pugh and the recent Lautenberg legislation. The Libyans simply could not believe that a court had issued a judgment for seven Americans and an aircraft owner that was three times bigger than the entire Lockerbie settlement for over two hundred and fifty people. Overnight, Congress had made it much easier for us to attach some of the huge flows of money that were now being sent between US oil companies and the Libyan National Oil Company.

Based on my discussions with Schwartz, we drafted a proposal for the Libyans that went beyond Pugh and our other cases. In the second week of February I sent a highly confidential four-page proposal to the Libyan Embassy and its lawyers that outlined several options for the United States, Libya and all the victims with pending cases. It would establish a claims and payment process that would take the cases out of federal court in return for Libya putting a very large amount of money into a pot that all the victims could share regardless of their personal situation, nationality or financial circumstances. After informing Schwartz of my proposal, we waited for the Libyans to respond.

* * *

WITHIN A FEW weeks, the lay of the land began to take shape. The messages between us and the Libyans jockeyed for position in the negotiations. After all the years of Libya seemingly taking an indifferent attitude towards the legal claims—pursuing a strategy of delay and avoidance of responsibility—it appeared we were finally making progress towards a resolution.

Like the giant oil companies with whom they now were doing business, the Libyans "lawyered up" in the Pugh case and went on the attack in the judicial arena. In response, we launched our own counter-attack in court. To anyone familiar with the US legal system, this was a natural and normal course to follow, even as we pushed forward with a proposed settlement track outside the litigation process. Of course, lawyers dueling in court are a lot more civilized than suitcase bombs on commercial aircraft and Navy fighter jets dropping bombs.

THE FIRST MOVE by Libya demonstrated that the people in Tripoli who were calling the shots understood that the stakes were high and required the proper professional support. By the middle of February, Libya had put two new law firms on the field in the Pugh case, both serious players who had instructions to achieve results. The first was the Blank Rome law firm, whose team was headed by Stephen Orlofsky, a retired federal judge from New Jersey who specialized in mediation and settlement structures. The second was White & Case, one of the largest law firms in the world, which prided itself on handling international disputes of the highest order.

Another source of pride for White & Case was that it regularly represented sovereign nations in disputes, including many resource-rich nations headed by dictators and generals. I was actually in the middle of handling a separate case against the brutal ruling family of Uzbekistan, and White & Case was the lead counsel on the other side representing the dictator's family and the government, so I was quite familiar with their international team, and their style. Our old friend Dabiri was still listed on Libya's papers, but clearly his days were numbered.

One morning I received a call from Chris Curran, a senior partner at White & Case in Washington who was taking on the role of coordinating all the cases against Libya as well as the diplomatic angles raised by my recent proposal for a global settlement. In the world of large law firms, the senior partners who appear on opposing sides quite often know each other or have teams that have worked against each other in the past.

Curran was well aware of my role in the Uzbekistan cases that his firm was handling against me, and had quickly come up to speed on the Libya docket. His call was simply to touch base and make clear to me that from now on all my communications were to go through him. I was glad for that, and told him so, since our long history with Libya and its various lawyers in Washington, Paris and even Tripoli had always lacked focus. We agreed to keep open a quiet channel of telephone and e-mail contacts. He also made clear that whatever the speed or direction of our settlement discussions, he had also been hired by Libya to do everything possible to get the Pugh judgment overturned on appeal. I respected that as a professional and braced myself for the blitzkrieg his team was capable of launching.

I was confident that Judge Kennedy had done an excellent job of structuring his rulings in Pugh, both the summary judgment on liability as well as the massive damages verdict, and that the record we had constructed over the years would stand up well on appeal. We also had taken several interlocutory trips to the DC Circuit Court of Appeals so I had some comfort that the judges on the fifth floor of the US Courthouse would continue to view our position in a favorable light. But I was also sensitive to the fact that the federal judges would cast aside their prior support for my positions if the diplomatic and political winds shifted. In short, the White House and Department of State were focused on doing a major deal with Qaddafi and his regime, and the court cases might have to be swept into any such deal. There was a terrific tension between our rights in court and the power of the President to manage foreign policy. The challenge for the Bush Administration, and for me, was to strike the right balance between these competing forces. We would soon discover just how difficult that challenge could be for all parties concerned.

The first move by Libya's new lawyers was to notice an appeal of Judge Kennedy's huge judgment. This would buy them time to sort out the legal and political landscape. And as Curran made clear in one of our calls, this time Libya would mount a serious defense on every conceivable issue. The case would finally get the "big firm treatment" on the Libyan side that Dabiri's small shop had been lacking. Lawyers tend to throw such challenges at their opponents in the manner of legal trash talk. It is part of the game. And I returned the favor at every opportunity.

Our own counter-move was in front of Judge Kennedy. Even though the case was now before the appellate court, Judge Kennedy still had authority to supervise any disputes regarding attempted enforcement of his judgment while it was on appeal. With the new legislation enacted by Congress that made enforcement of the Pugh judgment a much more serious threat to its growing commercial assets in the United States, Libya had to fight a two-front war. It had to push its appeal in the DC Circuit while resisting our efforts in the trial court to seize its assets.

One of our first moves was immediately to ask Judge Kennedy to issue orders allowing us to go to other federal districts around the country where we believed Libyan assets were sprouting like mushrooms and attempt to freeze those assets as a potential source for payment of the judgment if it were upheld on appeal. Another was to ask him to require Libya to disclose through a formal written discovery request the identity and location of all its commercial assets within the United States. We hoped to stay one step ahead of Libya and its new, aggressive lawyers through this strategy, and thus keep up the pressure for a global settlement.

Meanwhile, there was much activity going on at the US oil firms that were now sending hundreds of millions of dollars a month to Libya as part of their new contracts. The firms that were jointly developing oil fields with the Libyan government were most at risk, since the new law would allow us to attach those payments to satisfy the judgment. This threat would, if made real, be viewed by the Libyans as a breach of their contracts, lead to termination and cost them hundreds of millions, if not billions, in losses. The firms that were simply exploring for oil were less at risk, since there was not, yet, a flow of money.

At the same time, the Libyans were taking their own steps to protect themselves from the Pugh asset attachment process. To make our task more difficult, the Libyan National Oil Company decided that all of its transactions with US oil firms would be shifted from dollars to euros. The reason was simple—all dollar transactions had to be run through the US banking system, and thus were subject to court attachment. Running payments through the Euro system would lessen that risk, at least for the time being. The Libyans were in a panic, some even telling their American diplomatic contacts that the new combination of the Pugh judgment and the Lautenberg Amendment was worse than a return to the economic sanctions of years past.

As all these litigation and diplomatic efforts played out in the spring of 2008, Schwartz and I kept in touch on almost a daily basis to make sure the Bush Administration knew how I was playing my cards, and, on my part, to get whatever information Schwartz was allowed to share with me regarding the diplomatic front.

Apparently, during this frantic period, the Libyans had carefully reviewed my proposal for a global resolution of all outstanding claims in the courts. The Leader himself had gone ballistic, complaining that he had already paid enough and was not being rewarded for all of his cooperation with the West. He sent a personal letter to President Bush complaining of the insulting treatment of his regime by these recent acts of the Congress and the courts and repeated his insistence that the President work with him to find a solution. Absent of such assistance from the White House, the Leader raised the threat of expelling the US oil firms that had only recently returned to his country. The dictator did not appreciate being pushed into a tight corner after all his years of successfully avoiding this very trap.

By April, the Libyans wanted a more formal sit-down to explore our global proposal, even while we battled on the litigation front in the Court of Appeals and before Judge Kennedy. With Schwartz urging me to reach out to Curran and his clients at every opportunity, we scheduled a meeting at my law firm to explore the current state of play.

Mindful of the diplomatic aspects of these discussions, I asked Ambassador Beaussou to fly to Washington from Paris so that he could join us for the meeting. Our French emissary had remained in contact with the principals in Tripoli, who were well aware of his role as my law firm's "private diplomat." I also made sure to keep Schwartz informed of these developments, as well as Beaussou's ongoing role.

Filling one of my law firm's large conference rooms, a particularly nice one we called the Boardroom, a host of lawyers from White & Case, Blank Rome, Dabiri himself (in a very diminished role) as well as my team sat down to explore the landscape together. Doug Matthews had flown up and sat next to me and Beaussou. As a veteran of many big-dollar negotiations around the globe, Matthews felt quite at home in this environment, notwithstanding his general distaste for lawyers, who usually "got in the way" of a business deal. As the client and the manager of the entire case for the families, Matthews believed in projecting a position of strength, patience and confidence. The man who had spent a career flying fighter jets off aircraft carriers and jumbo jets across the Atlantic had waited eighteen years for this meeting. He had a lot of cards in his hand, and was prepared to play them all.

After a round of introductions and pleasantries, we got down to basics. Curran spoke for the Libyans and made clear that they could not accept the Pugh judgment as the basis for any negotiations—it was simply too much money and, importantly, was grossly excessive when compared to the Lockerbie settlement and its $10 million per-family payment. They vowed to get it overturned on appeal and to resist our efforts to seize assets in the meantime. He even hinted that the American companies whose assets would be tied up in such matters—mostly oil and construction firms—would side with Libya in such fights as it could "cost Americans jobs" and disrupt serious diplomatic efforts to improve American–Libyan relations.

Libya, of course, was paying his firm large amounts of money to do exactly what Curran described, so I hardly took things personally. This was his job, and his firm was very good at it. From our perspective, we projected the same level of confidence that the judgment would stand, and that the large amounts of assets now piling up around the country were a delicious target for our efforts to freeze them through court orders while the appeal was pending.

At a certain point in the meeting it became clear that no serious business or negotiations would commence at this stage. The landscape at the courthouse was still taking shape and the diplomatic front was still digesting my proposal for a global resolution of all things Libyan. Having Beaussou and Matthews at the table demonstrated our resolve to continue the court fight while respecting the diplomatic front. The chess pieces were in place. Time would determine how they were played.

* * *

WITH OUR MEETINGS and strategies, it was critical for me to stay close to the diplomatic front. Given the prominent role our case was playing, and Beaussou's role as our own emissary to Tripoli, Schwartz thought we should come over to State and brief his principal, Ambassador David Welch, the Assistant Secretary of State for Near Eastern Affairs. Welch was President Bush's point man on the entire Libyan file. Bush had entrusted him with the task of working out the details so that the two countries could complete the complicated transition from being mortal enemies to something else—less than allies, but at least commercial and political entities that could do business with each other.

Welch was one of the State Department's finest Arabists, a special branch of career diplomats trained in the language, customs and nuances of the Arab world to the point where they developed close relationships with the most important leaders and rulers. Having served throughout the Middle East as a diplomat and ambassador, his appointment as Assistant Secretary was the highest position a career Arabist could attain in the Foreign Service. Welch was widely respected inside and outside the United States. On a very warm and humid day in May we were ushered into his plush offices on the fifth floor of "the Building," as people at State refer to the massive State Department headquarters on Constitution Avenue and 22nd Street. His grand workplace had a panoramic view of the Lincoln Memorial and beyond the famous shrine across the Potomac River and up to Arlington National Cemetery.

The point of our meeting was to brief Welch and make sure he was in tune with our own strategy. All of my discussions over the past few years had been with Schwartz, who acted as Welch's senior legal adviser and had accompanied him to Libya and other locations to conduct serious discussions with the Libyans. As Schwartz led the way into the offices for the meeting, Welch came forward to shake our hands. The career diplomat was slim, fit and appeared much younger than his actual age. As he and I exchanged greetings, we looked at each other longer than might be appropriate. After a few seconds, we both realized that we had met before, but neither of us could place where at first. Welch asked, "Do you live in McLean?"

I responded, "Yes, but I can't recall where we met."

He smiled. "At the local gym. You were showing me some weight-lifting exercises and a few other things just last month. Remember?"

Of course. He and I both belonged to the same gym, and indeed we had chatted several times in our sweats and sneakers, a couple of middle-aged men trying to stay in shape despite our hectic work lives, schedules and lifestyles. This was Washington life. Here we were, both working intently on the same issues—Welch in government as President Bush's senior emissary to Qaddafi and Libya, me a private lawyer on a parallel path—but neither of us was aware of the other's work when we had met previously. After a few minutes of banter, the others in the room confused by our abandonment of protocol and formalities, we sat down and got to business. Life is funny, we both agreed.

But, notwithstanding our shared experience at the gym, Welch was first and foremost a diplomat who was trained to keep his own counsel and not spill important intelligence, especially to a lawyer like me, who was inserting himself into international diplomacy at the highest and most sensitive levels. I gave him a briefing on our various legal and political efforts, especially our meetings with the Libyans and their new lawyers, and Welch shared a few titbits about his own discussions with Qaddafi and his government.

What he made clear was that the Pugh judgment, combined with the new legislation, had made a very serious impact on Qaddafi and his advisers. Without question, Welch acknowledged, our success in court had pushed Qaddafi forward, convincing him that after years of delay and coy maneuvers it was time for him to reach a global agreement with the United States and "turn a new page." He thanked us for that, since this had made his life easier by providing significant leverage to President Bush's policy of engagement with the Libyans.

Welch also noted that he and Schwartz were soon to meet with the Libyans to move their discussions forward, and he hoped my proposal for a global resolution of all the pending Libya claims in court could be addressed in those discussions. He also noted that my law firm's efforts to seek some sort of freeze of Libyan commercial assets in the United States was quite a sore point for his Libyan counterparts. He smiled at this, and did not suggest that we let up on these efforts. Obviously, this was providing the United States government with extra leverage in its own diplomatic discussions.

After a generous amount of time, we stood to shake hands, and I wished him well on his upcoming meetings. We also made a point of looking for each other at the gym when he returned.

WITH THE KNOWLEDGE that Welch and Schwartz were about to meet the Libyans for what might well be critical discussions about how to settle all pending issues, including Pugh, I called Beaussou in Paris. We discussed how he might position us with the Libyans to keep our hand in the mix and ensure that all of our law firm's clients with Libya claims, including Pugh, would be beneficiaries of any global deal between the two governments. After a few long discussions on the phone and some e-mailed outlines of talking points and positions, I instructed him to catch a plane to Tripoli and arrange meetings with the most senior Libyan officials. The time was quickly upon us to make sure our clients' interests were covered when the deals were struck.

BY THE FIRST week of June, Beaussou was in Tripoli making the rounds with all the senior Libyan officials, as well as stopping in to brief the American diplomats at the new US Embassy that had reopened after almost thirty years in a black hole of diplomacy. After spending two days in various offices, coffee houses and hotels, he sent me a detailed e-mail reporting on the landscape.

The former French Ambassador to Libya had spent several hours with Mr. Elmssallati, the chair of the Foreign Ministry's legal claims bureau and the man I had sat across from at the Libyan Embassy at the Watergate in Washington. According to Beaussou, Elmssallati was so far along in his work with the United States government that he was planning to move to Washington for some time to coordinate a range of issues. The Libyan official who was Qaddafi's point man told Beaussou that his Leader and Bush were positive and optimistic about the evolving relationship and had instructed their diplomats to come up with a global settlement that each could sell to their domestic constituencies. A major hurdle was the January enactment of what the Libyan characterized as that "terrible" law—the Lautenberg Amendment—which I was employing to put pressure on Libya to settle. Elmssallati insisted that the Libyans could not conclude a global settlement unless and until Congress took some action to lift the draconian burden the law was placing on Libya—in other words, the very foundation of my litigation strategy to pressure them into a settlement.

As for any case settlements, they would be wrapped into a global deal, including Pugh and my other cases. The Libyan noted that the amount of payments and where the money would come from were still a point of contention. When Beaussou raised the specifics of the Pugh judgment, Elmssallati referred to our court award as "unfortunate" and "unrealistic." He made clear to my private French emissary that the Libyans could not swallow anything close to our historic damages award, especially given that the more publicized and sensitive case—Pan Am 103 Lockerbie—had settled for a much lower per-capita figure, as the entire world knew. The politics of Lockerbie, the politics of Congress, the "unfair" leverage I was asserting on Libya, the annoying interference with US oil firms that were doing business there—all of these had to be considered in the total package.

But Elmssallatti assured Beaussou that he would make time to meet with me when he next came to Washington, perhaps in July. One thing the Libyans had their eye on was the calendar. August would be the holy Islamic month of Ramadan, and thus none of the Libyans would spend time in the West during that period. They also were sensitive to the reality that the Americans were electing a new President in November—a major distraction under any circumstances. But, more importantly, they understood the diminishing ability of President Bush to conclude a settlement with Qaddafi before November and also obtain some sort of sign-off by Congress.

The Libyans knew that President Bush wanted to wrap up the Libya file so that he could point to it as an achievement of his Administration— the taming of a former terrorist state while things were not going smoothly in Iraq and Afghanistan. Bush had been closely handling the Libyan negotiations and was very hands-on. If a global deal could not be arranged by Bush and his team by the autumn, they doubted anything could happen until the following year. And if a Democrat was put into the White House—one not beholden to the oil firms and energy businesses like the Republican incumbent—the Libyans might lose whatever momentum they had to reach a deal. And hanging over this political and diplomatic environment was the constant threat that the Pugh case might attach large money transfers before they reached Tripoli.

Beaussou's lengthy e-mail to me concluded with the obvious advice that I should stay as close as possible to the State Department.

As if I needed that reminder.

AFTER READING MY French diplomat's note, I tried to reach Schwartz to give him a report, but his e-mail account reported that he was overseas and would not return for several days. I left a message and waited for his call back.

One week later, Schwartz called. He and Welch had been in Berlin meeting with the Libyans as they tried to hash out a host of issues that might get wrapped up in a global settlement. Many of the issues had nothing to do with lawsuits, judgments and assets, but instead focused on security, nuclear power, terrorism and intelligence cooperation matters. But the lawsuits were always on the agenda, including my annoying efforts to enforce the Pugh judgment while Libya pursued its appeal.

Schwartz reported that they had made some progress and that my earlier global proposal had elements that could assist both governments as they cobbled together a possible deal. As he had noted before, the Pugh judgment was *sui generis* because it was so large and posed such an immediate threat to the otherwise smooth maturation of bilateral relations. But it was there to deal with, as Schwartz said he reminded the Libyans, and he emphasized that he would continue to suggest to the Libyans that they attempt to negotiate a resolution of Pugh so that it could be folded into a bigger, more comprehensive deal.

Apparently, the Libyans considered three of the pending US cases—Lockerbie, La Belle and UTA—as the "Big Three" and had focused on how to get these resolved so that the rest of the cases could be swept into a deal. It was at least gratifying to know that our case had risen to this level of attention.

By early July, Schwartz's suggestions to the Libyans had borne fruit. I received a call from Chris Curran at White & Case, who asked if I could meet him for lunch at a nice quiet place between our offices. The next day we were eating crabcakes and comparing work and travel schedules as he guided the conversation to the real business. After explaining at least twice that the Libyans wanted to settle but were constrained by the politics of what they had paid for Lockerbie, he got to the point.

"Would your clients consider a settlement two or three times Lockerbie?" Curran asked, leaning forwards. This meant something in the range of $140–200 million would make the Pugh case disappear. I did not have authority from Matthews even to consider such a low number and guessed that my clients would balk at Libya's effort to wipe from the slate most of what Judge Kennedy had given them after so many years of turmoil, tension, delay and hard work. I told Curran I would speak to Matthews and get back to him. At the time, I assumed this was an opening bid in what had been a dragged-out negotiation. If they were suggesting something in this range, there might be a way to split the difference and reach a compromise. We parted after a pleasant lunch and I was on the phone to Matthews immediately.

Matthews saw it as I did—this was a first move and we should show flexibility, but determination at the same time. That was how negotiations were handled. We had worked long and hard to get to this critical point. A few more exchanges back and forth would allow both sides to feel out the other and reach a compromise.

Briefing Schwartz on these developments, he also noted that a settlement of Pugh in the "two to three times Lockerbie" range had been floated by the Libyans at his meetings, although he was careful not to comment on whether this was a good or bad start to the process. He suggested that my clients carefully consider every step and not lose sight of the time restraints under which the Libyans appeared to be working. He did not mention the time pressure his own bosses, President Bush and Secretary of State Condoleezza Rice, were under as their term rushed to its end. But he did say that the Libyans were insisting that whatever deal President Bush was able to approve must also involve Congress, to make sure Libya was no longer subject to the type of litigation pressure I was putting on them every day. That seemed reasonable to me, since I assumed any settlement might be part of a treaty or international agreement blessed by Congress.

I promised Schwartz that we would move fast and do our best to negotiate a quick resolution. All it took was good faith on both sides and a desire to wrap up this dispute as part of a bigger deal. He seemed more on edge than normal—it was clear that the growing pressure to come to terms was falling on the professional shoulders of Schwartz and his boss, Ambassador Welch. I also was nervous as we sensed that a critical moment was approaching, after all the years of delay, frustration and successes, to work out something with Libya.

Unbeknownst to me, that moment was at hand.

* * *

SITTING AT MY desk, I can look up from the morning papers, briefs and e-mails to gaze out the windows towards the east, the risen sun and a truly authentic Washington view that never gets old.

On 4 August, at around 10:00 a.m., as I was organizing a bunch of items and getting ready to return the morning's phone messages, I received a call from someone in my firm's small lobbying shop. We were not known as a major lobbying player, but had made our reputation more in the areas of litigation, regulatory and international work. But a few folks worked the halls of Congress for a living, most of them former Hill staffers who could take advantage of long-running relationships and inside information to help guide clients through the legislative maze.

She wanted to know if I had any information about a bill regarding Libyan terrorism issues that had just been introduced into the Senate that morning and immediately enacted by voice vote without objection. This procedure was known as Unanimous Consent or UC and was sometimes employed by the Senate to pass bills that were not controversial, were bipartisan and often were simply procedural fixes for something more important that already had survived the process. I had not heard of anything on this issue so far along in the Senate, although various draft bills were floating around for comment.

My colleague said a friend in a senator's office had called her about the matter since it appeared to be something that was uncontroversial and affected all the pending terrorism cases against Libya. She had not heard about it before and was asking me for any light I could shed. I could not help, since no one had mentioned this specific bill to me in all of my conversations with Schwartz, Welch or anyone else. Obviously, I was quite interested to know what was afoot. She went online and within minutes I was reading the hard-copy version of legislation that the Senate had passed unanimously only minutes before.

Needless to say, I was stunned. Without debate, discussion or even commentary, the entire United States Senate had just passed a bill entitled the Libyan Claims Resolution Act. The name seemed quite familiar, since my global proposal to the Libyans and the Bush Administration had been similarly worded. But the substance was different from my proposal in some very significant ways. It began innocently enough with the "sense of Congress" that typically was at the front of a bill to demonstrate Congress's intent: "Congress supports the President in his efforts to provide fair compensation to all nationals of the United States who have terrorism-related claims against Libya through a comprehensive settlement of claims by such nationals against Libya pursuant to an international agreement between the United States and Libya as a part of the process of restoring normal relations between Libya and the United States." I read on with intense interest.

The bill authorized the Secretary of State to designate an "entity" to assist in providing compensation to US nationals "pursuant to a claims agreement." But I did not see any such "claims agreement" in the bill, nor did it provide for such a thing.

The next section shed some light on where this was headed. Stating that "notwithstanding any other provision of law"—a sweeping revocation of anything Congress had enacted into law in previous bills—the legislation just passed by the Senate by "unanimous consent" provided that "Libya ... shall not be subject to the exceptions to immunity from jurisdiction, liens, attachment, and execution contained in" the 1996 terrorism exceptions to the Foreign Sovereign Immunities Act. This was the very law we and all other victims—and Judge Kennedy—had relied on for all these years to pursue Libya for its terrorist acts.

The only condition for restoring Libya's immunity to lawsuits—after twelve years of such cases—was that the lawsuits would be void and all cases, including my Pugh judgment, dismissed when the Secretary of State provided Congress with a certification that "the United States Government has received funds pursuant to the claims agreement that are sufficient to ensure ... (i) payment of the settlements" in the Lockerbie and La Belle Disco cases, and "(ii) fair compensation of claims of nationals of the United States for wrongful death or physical injury" under the terrorism exception of the FSIA.

Short and to the point, and without even two minutes' debate or comment. With a unanimous voice vote, the Senate had agreed to help President Bush close a global deal with the Libyans even before an unidentified "settlement" had been signed between the countries. Clearly, the Libyans had played their cards with Bush by insisting that no global deal could be consummated until Congress voided all the laws on the books that allowed victims to go to court and hold Libya responsible for blowing up airplanes, killing innocent civilians, holding hostages or attacking airports. The vote had taken less time than the UTA victims took to fall to their deaths. The Senate had handed Bush half of what he needed to make Qaddafi happy.

After a quick call to Matthews, who had some of his own contacts in the Senate, we marshaled our law firm's resources to find out what was going on and, more importantly, what the schedule might be for the House of Representatives to consider the bill already approved by the Senate. Unlike an international treaty with another country— where the US Senate alone provides the "advice and consent" to the President—this bill was directed at stripping the federal courts of any and all authority to hear a single terrorism case against Libya if it paid to the US government an unidentified amount in an unidentified settlement to an unidentified claims facility. The bill just passed by the Senate would have to be approved by the House.

A few calls and e-mails later quickly revealed to us that this deal had been "hot-wired" by the White House and the bipartisan leadership of the Congress, in both houses. The House of Representatives was already scheduled to conduct a voice vote and all that was required was a simple majority. Apparently the speaker of the House, Nancy Pelosi, and the leaders of the US Senate, major figures such as Lautenberg, Joe Biden and others, had been personally lobbied by President Bush to enact this bill quickly and quietly to provide the President with what he needed to close a deal with Qaddafi.

In addition, the bill provided that the remaining amounts still unpaid in the Lockerbie settlement—$2 million per family, amounting to over $532 million—as well as a tentative settlement in the La Belle Disco Berlin bombing—$10 million each for the families of the three Americans who were killed, $3 million for all those injured, totaling over $260 million—would be paid as soon as monies were received. It was ironic that Congress had blessed these two "settlements" since they were actually not enforceable against Libya and courts had so held. Libya did not actually owe these two cases any more funds under the strict terms of their deals. Nevertheless, this bill would bless those "settlements" as if they were enforceable—a very nice gift by Congress to these two cases and the deserving victims of those attacks. The other dozen or so pending cases against Libya would receive some unidentified "fair compensation" for dismissal of their cases—pretty good work, considering that they had not advanced their cases to anything approaching our Pugh judgment. Indeed, many of these other cases faced serious legal and evidentiary hurdles that might allow Libya and its new legal teams actually to prevail.

The House of Representatives pushed through a unanimous voice vote within twenty-four hours, the deal in place at the highest levels of the government without any debate or discussion. No committee hearings, no mark-up sessions, no comments from affected persons—this was the most rapid and uncontroversial legislation one could imagine in the world's greatest democracy. On the face of it, it looked like a very good deal for American victims of Libyan terrorism. Qaddafi would finally be rid of the annoying lawsuits that had plagued his bid to rejoin the world, and greatly expand his commercial ties with the United States and its oil and gas firms.

I sat pondering this new law that had put us into an unexplored twilight zone. As my team evaluated the situation and Matthews called every twenty minutes for updates, one question was burning through my mind. What about our Pugh judgment? Where would it fit into this surprising and extraordinary new landscape? And where exactly was President Bush and his State Department in negotiating this unidentified and still-not-final settlement? Not to mention the Libyans?

I had a lot of very anxious clients who wanted answers I could not yet provide. The press was calling for comment on the legislation, since the lawyers and families for the Lockerbie and La Belle Disco attacks were enthusiastically praising the move as a significant and positive step to bring closure to their long ordeals. The *Wall Street Journal* ran a story on its law blog pointing out the overall positive message from other victims of Libyan terrorism. Except for the Pugh families, whose hard-earned and unique judgment had held Libya accountable and made clear that the consequences for premeditated mass murder would be very high, even by the standards of an oil-rich state.

I waited anxiously for Schwartz to return my calls. Clearly, we had urgent business to discuss.

Chapter 19

Espousal

ONLY DAYS AFTER Congress had so quickly enacted the Libya Claims Resolution Act (LCRA), President Bush signed it into law. Clearly, this was a tightly controlled and closely held plan coordinated by the President and Congress.

Schwartz finally called me back right after the President had signed the rushed legislation. He was quite aware of the urgency in my voice messages and e-mails and immediately apologized for his lack of contact. He had been under strict orders from the White House to maintain radio silence with certain folks, especially me, who might disrupt the President's carefully orchestrated plan to advance US–Libya relations through this emerging deal. He readily conceded that I might well have been able to slow down, and thus derail, this secret deal between President Bush, the bipartisan leadership of Congress, and the Lockerbie and La Belle Disco families who stood to benefit directly from this arrangement. But he went out of his way to acknowledge that Pugh, and its court judgment, were different from any other case or claim, and that the State Department hoped to respect that difference when it came time to distribute funds from what he hoped would be an eventual final settlement and payment by Libya.

Obviously, I was trying to understand how our Pugh case would fit into this emerging arrangement. Schwartz was vague about the Administration's plan, but he suggested that the Pugh families and Interlease still could wind up with "two or three times" what the Lockerbie families had received—meaning two or three times the $10 million for each family set by that case. This was a remarkable revelation, since that was the amount Curran had floated to me about a possible resolution. Schwartz repeated his view that the Pugh judgment had played a significant role in bringing Qaddafi to the negotiating table, in coordination with enactment of the Lautenberg Amendment. In addition to providing President Bush a significant diplomatic weapon, it also had been an anchor dragging down the discussions between the two countries. Judge Kennedy had simply awarded too much money, despite the fact that he had done so based on a solid record, first-class expert opinions and firmly established legal precedents. To put it another way, Judge Kennedy had properly performed his job as a federal judge, and done exactly what Congress and the President had authorized him to do.

The Rule of Law had been imposed on Qaddafi and his regime for an unspeakable act of premeditated mass murder, and then it had been voided as part of a political and diplomatic settlement that could not accommodate an outcome that all three branches of the United States government had specifically intended to occur. It was a great irony. To make it even more painful for my Pugh clients, the Pugh judgment had been a major force in convincing the Libyans to pay the remaining $2 million to the Lockerbie families. They had been frustrated by the fact that Libya had only been required to pay $8 million per family (over $2 billion total to date) because President Bush had not removed Libya from the list of state sponsors of terrorism within the time period called for in their settlement agreement. Thus, over $500 million in additional Libyan money would soon flow to the Lockerbie families for a settlement that did not even require such a payment. Libya would pay that extra amount gratis as part of a political deal, notwithstanding that it was not legally required to pay another dollar.

The same held true with the La Belle cases. There had been a tentative settlement between Libya and those families with death and personal injury claims for approximately $250 million. But a federal judge in Washington had specifically ruled that the settlement was not final or enforceable. And yet, the anticipated deal with Libya would pay that settlement in full. As with Lockerbie, politics was more powerful than law.

Thus, two other cases that could not succeed in court or advance further were, pursuant to political decisions by President Bush and Congress, now to receive a full and immediate payment if the deal could be closed soon. The case that had gone to trial, with Libya and its counsel fighting at every turn, and had resulted in detailed findings of Libya's responsibility for a notorious bombing that killed 170 innocent people as well as a historic damages award under federal law, would be pushed aside, subject only to the whims of the President. Having used the Pugh families and their historic achievement in court to hold Libya accountable, President Bush then made a decision that, in his view, was more important to United States foreign policy.

In short, the President of the United States cut a deal with Qaddafi before he left office and this diplomatic deal took priority over the Pugh case. It was that simple. Power politics and a President's legacy. So much for the Rule of Law.

I knew Schwartz was only the messenger, so I did not take out my frustration on him. His client was the United States government, and he was dealing directly with the President and Secretary of State on these issues. That is the harsh reality of high-stakes play in the major leagues.

Trying his best to keep me informed, subject to the strict confidence he was sworn to uphold, Schwartz promised to brief me in more detail, but was in a rush to catch a flight. He and Ambassador Welch were headed to Tripoli to finalize the deal that Congress had just authorized their boss to negotiate.

* * *

JUST A FEW days later, on 14 August 2008, the President's emissary to the Great Leader, Ambassador David Welch, put his signature on what is known as a "bilateral agreement" between the United States and

Libya. Unlike a treaty, such agreements are entered between heads of state as a sort of "international contract." They are self-executing and, unlike a treaty, do not require the "advice and consent" of two-thirds of the US Senate to become effective. Besides, Congress already had provided President Bush with the necessary vehicle to enter into such an agreement without being bothered by the pesky details of lawsuits, federal judges and court judgments. The undebated and break-neck hasty Libya Claims Resolution Act had made that quite clear.

In what was a relatively short document, the Claims Settlement Agreement between the two countries proclaimed that they had reached this deal "in order to further the process of normalization of relations on the basis of equality and mutual benefit." Beyond this boilerplate diplomatic language, the Agreement's objectives were stated loud and clear: (1) to reach a "final settlement" between the countries and their nationals, (2) to "terminate permanently all pending suits (including suits with judgments that are still subject to appeal)" and (3) "preclude any future suits that may be taken to their courts." Lest there be any doubt which lawsuits the Agreement was designed to "terminate," it spelled out that "any claim or suit" against either country by its nationals that "arises from" death, personal injury or property loss caused by "an act of torture, extrajudicial killing, aircraft sabotage, hostage taking" or even "military measures" was barred. This covered any terrorist acts by Libya occurring prior to 30 June 2006.

With the stroke of a pen, President Bush had absolved Qaddafi and his government, agents and officials from any accountability for acts of terrorism covering what was close to thirty years of violence and murder around the world. Once Libya paid the United States an agreed-upon lump sum, all civil cases against Libya in the federal courts were required by Presidential power and Congressional blessing to be dismissed, and Libya would once again enjoy the immunity from lawsuits that had been lifted in 1996. The Agreement even required the President to have his own Department of Justice make sure that any civil cases against Libya were terminated and its immunity restored in full.

The Annex to the Agreement spelled out the price Qaddafi had agreed to pay for this diplomatic absolution for killing, kidnapping, torturing and injuring American citizens. The sum of $1.5 billion would be paid by the Libyan government itself to the United States Treasury, to be released by the US government when the court cases had been dismissed, and not before.

Unlike the French settlement, this was not a private agreement between the Qaddafi Foundation and private citizens. This was a binding international contract between two sovereign nations, with all the legal and diplomatic force such an agreement carried. But the Annex had an additional provision that the Libyans had insisted be put in separate from the monies to settle the American cases. Another $300 million would be "paid" to the Libyan Treasury to compensate Libyans who might have claims against the United States government, especially arising from the April 1986 military attacks ordered by President Ronald Reagan. Qaddafi needed political cover domestically if he was to turn over monies to compensate for the death of Americans at the hands of his agents. So this separate amount would be made available as part of the deal to enable eligible Libyans to receive a compensation payment, as determined by the Libyan government. Of course, the source of funds for this second settlement fund was the same as the one that would fund the American settlement—the Libyan Treasury. Such sleight-of-hand maneuvers were typical of Qaddafi—he could have his propaganda machine tout how he had "forced" the United States to "respect" Libya and its citizens by paying for their pain and loss as well.

It was a complete charade, just another transparent device for a dictator to retain his domestic authority and to fill the Libyan newspapers with falsehoods so that the Great Leader did not appear weak or intimidated by the American lawsuits and political power.

* * *

WHEN SCHWARTZ RETURNED from Tripoli and reported to me on the Agreement, we spoke at length about the state of play, especially how the settlement might impact Pugh and my other cases. Once again, Schwartz made clear that the judgment issued by Judge Kennedy back in January—what seemed like years ago, but was only eight months— had played a significant role in the Bush Administration's leverage on Libya, but would also be a diplomatic casualty given that the dollars were simply too big for Libya to swallow. The language in the Agreement regarding "suits with judgments that are still subject to appeal" obviously was directed at a single case—our judgment in Pugh, which Libya had taken up to the DC Circuit Court of Appeals. The requirement that such cases, even judgments, must be terminated in order to receive anything from the settlement fund left nothing to the imagination. Our Pugh judgment was as good as dead for the sake of President Bush's legacy. This was a bitter pill for Matthews and the Pugh families to swallow.

But a lawyer cannot throw in the towel before the game clock has counted down. Schwartz acknowledged that Pugh was special, and had played a unique role in compelling Qaddafi to enter into this historic, albeit unfair to my clients, settlement agreement. He implied that the "most senior levels" of the Administration concurred in that view, which I understood meant the President and his Secretary of State. And he encouraged my law firm to submit any proposals we could dream up to expedite the payment process, and perhaps provide the Pugh families and Interlease something extra. My partner Cliff Elgarten and I got to work.

Moving quickly, we submitted a detailed letter to Schwartz just a few days after the Settlement Agreement was signed in Tripoli. Once again, as with our earlier proposals, we presented our ideas for a "global" payment scheme, not limited to our law firm's cases and clients. Schwartz had always welcomed our ideas for his own consideration, and this was no exception. Our historic court judgment had been derailed, but we still had an opening to advocate for our clients that they receive the maximum share of the settlement funds that they were entitled to under the President's deal.

Critical to our proposal was the fact that the Department of State had just made several statements to Congress at the behest of several Senators who wanted to understand how the Pugh judgment would fit into the new settlement agreement. In an 11 August letter to the Senate from Ambassador John Negroponte, the Deputy Secretary of State, he made clear that "as a matter of equity" President Bush had decided that all the Americans with death claims should receive the same $10 million Lockerbie payment. But for the Pugh claimants, he continued, they would "have an opportunity to apply for additional compensation in light of the special circumstances surrounding their claim ... and will be able to seek additional compensation to take account of the stage their litigation had reached in the US courts."

Speaking frankly to the senators, Negroponte's letter set out the realpolitik conducted by President Bush: "It will be impossible to reach a comprehensive settlement with Libya without covering all the pending cases in the US courts," and "if the Pugh case were to be excluded simply because it was more advanced in our courts (but potentially years from resolution), the hundreds of other claimants would not receive any compensation, since we would have no settlement." With the promise of "$10 million off the top" plus "unprecedented recoveries" for the Pugh families under the President's settlement, Negroponte assured the United States Senate that the Administration had struck the right balance between diplomatic necessity and the pursuit of justice under the Rule of Law.

We hammered at this point in our proposal, convinced that the White House and State Department would follow through on this commitment to treat Pugh as a special case deserving additional recoveries from the President's settlement fund. We asked State to make sure that the Pugh families would receive something akin to the amount of their actual judgments. If so, they would wind up with the "two or three times Lockerbie" amounts that Schwartz and Curran had floated by me.

But the process was out of our hands—and the federal court's—as the political forces quickly swept towards a conclusion that was nothing like we had imagined back in January.

* * *

ON 5 SEPTEMBER 2008 Qaddafi finally received the most important gift which President Bush could provide him as part of his plan to re-emerge on the world stage as a statesman. Secretary of State Condoleezza Rice and her Air Force jet touched down at Tripoli's airport for the first visit by a US Secretary of State to Libya since John Foster Dulles briefly stopped there in 1953. The only other US official to visit was Vice

President Richard Nixon in 1957. It had been decades since the North African country had been paid such respect by its former enemy. This was Qaddafi's reward, complete with photo opportunities to be flashed around the world.

Stepping onto the tarmac and into the bright desert sunlight, Secretary Rice made clear in her remarks that Libya and the United States had affirmed their desire to "move forward in a positive way," making "difficult decisions" on a variety of issues. Looking around a city that once had been bombed by American planes in an effort to kill the Leader who was now her host, Rice observed to the press that "the United States does not have permanent enemies."

Later that night, as she met with Qaddafi in his tent, Rice might have had second thoughts about the whole visit. Although Qaddafi refused to shake her hand, as devout Muslims must observe, he did make clear his own personal satisfaction regarding the Secretary's historic visit.

"I support my darling black African woman," Qaddafi said in Arabic. "I admire and am very proud of the way she leans back and gives orders to the Arab leaders. Yes Leeza, Leeza, Leeza, I love her very much."

But with all the hoopla surrounding Rice's visit, which was broadcast around the world as a triumph of Qaddafi's resilience, there was one item that the Leader would not confirm. When would Libya wire the $1.5 billion to Washington to close the deal? Apparently the Secretary of State was unable to get her host to say much more than a diplomatic version of "the check is in the mail." She left Tripoli after her short visit without a commitment to a firm payment date. Of course, Qaddafi had obtained what he desired most of all things—the United States Secretary of State paying homage to him in his own country—and he still had not paid any of the money promised in his deal with President Bush. Here was another demonstration to his people of how he was handling the Americans.

* * *

BY THE END of October, the Libyans finally had sent the money to the United States Treasury. On 31 October the State Department sent to Congress a letter certifying that it had received funds "sufficient to ensure payments" described in the Libya Resolution Claims Act and the Bilateral Claims Agreement between the two countries. As promised, State told Congress that the payment would cover the Lockerbie and La Belle Disco settlements as well as provide "fair compensation" for all the other pending cases, including Pugh. For the first time, the Department of State now spelled out exactly how the $1.5 billion would be allocated, at least in the first instance.

For the Pan Am 103 Lockerbie final payment—the last $2 million per family, to total $10 million each—$536 million would be paid immediately by State to close out the most famous terrorist case in the Libyan file. As for the La Belle Disco settlements, which had been ruled by the courts as not being settled at all, $283 million would be paid immediately by State. That would leave $681 million for all the other Libya cases, including Pugh. How that last pile of cash would be divided was not explained in the State Department's note to Congress. Clearly, we still had more work to do with State on that front.

But with the monies in hand, the United States government had one more piece of business of which to take care. It was critical that there be no loose ends remaining that might allow our case to slip through the cracks and continue to cause headaches for Qaddafi.

Down the street from my offices, at 1600 Pennsylvania Avenue, President Bush issued an Executive Order declaring, under his constitutional powers, that "in order to continue the process of normalizing relations between the United States and Libya" he had "settled" the claims of his fellow Americans against the Libyan government. Of course, the Executive Order made clear that "any pending suit"— including any suit with a judgment that is still subject to appeal—"shall be terminated."

The authority for President Bush to terminate our judgment was not only supported by the Libya Claim Resolution Act and the Bilateral Claims Agreement. Under the United States Constitution, and for over two hundred years, the President has enjoyed the absolute power to settle international claims its citizens pursued against other countries. The entire basis for this power is the President's and Congress's authority to conduct the nation's foreign policy. The federal courts simply play no role in that function. Except, of course, when Congress and the

President hand that power to the federal courts, as they did in 1996 when terrorist states such as Libya were expressly declared a legitimate target for Americans who sought to hold them accountable and recover damages for terrorist attacks.

But what Congress and the President giveth, they also have the power to taketh away. This power is traditionally known as espousal and essentially allows the President to stop a lawsuit in its tracks if it is required by an international agreement. That is what President Bush did to the Pugh judgment—and all the other Libya cases—on 31 October 2008. By issuing his Executive Order, President Bush espoused our clients' rights to sue Libya or anyone else for the UTA 772 attack.

By his signature on the Order, President Bush wiped out our Pugh judgment. Nothing Judge Kennedy, or the Court of Appeals, had done in the case would survive if it violated the Agreement with Libya. For me and my law firm, six years of hard work, worldwide negotiations, collection of critical evidence, an emotional trial, unprecedented judicial findings and a historic judgment were gone in a flash. Nineteen years after Qaddafi and his regime blew up the DC-10, murdering 170 people, the last legal case arising from the terrorist bombing of UTA Flight 772 was finally concluded.

* * *

MATTHEWS AND THE seven Pugh families certainly were very disappointed and angered by the President's decision to espouse their judgment. They were now forced to accept a settlement that they had not agreed to and which appeared to benefit everyone—Bush, Qaddafi, the oil companies, and especially all the other Libya cases. Benefited everyone except, of course, the group that had obtained the critical court judgment that had helped persuade the Libyans to resolve their global disputes with the United States.

By January 2009 the US Department of Justice, President Bush's lawyers, had filed the appropriate papers with the DC Circuit Court of Appeals and Judge Kennedy and in a flash the Pugh case was dismissed and the judgment vacated. Within a few months we received directly from State the $10 million "minimum payment" for each of the

American victims of the UTA 772 flight. In addition, my other clients with claims against Libya, including the Kilburn family, also received similar payments from State.

The Pugh families drew some solace from the fact that the Libyan government itself had paid the money for this settlement and that every other American victim of Libyan terrorism who had been killed in other attacks also received a similar payment. State then decided to refer the remaining claims—including Interlease's claim for the loss of the DC-10 and the "extra" monies for the Pugh families that Ambassador Negroponte had suggested to Congress could come from the remaining funds—to a small, obscure federal agency called the Foreign Claims Settlement Commission.

Indeed, State created a special "Category C" in its referral to the FCSC that focused exclusively on the seven Pugh families and their judgment against Libya. We were encouraged to see this special category and worked hard during the several years of FCSC proceedings to persuade the Commissioners to award the Pugh families what we and our clients believed was a special additional amount of money from the Settlement Fund.

The FCSC would sort out the details of how the remaining funds would be distributed, thus relieving State of a job it did not want to handle itself. Ultimately, it would take until 2013 for the FCSC to complete that arduous task, after countless hearings, delays, written submissions and awards. Ultimately, Interlease would receive over $20 million from the Settlement Fund for the destruction of the DC-10, a small vindication for all of Doug Matthews' efforts. And the seven Pugh families would receive a small amount of additional funds as well—but nothing close to the "two or three times Lockerbie" amount that had been dangled by the Bush Administration's representations to Congress in 2008.

Money aside, the FCSC also issued a ruling that was particularly difficult for us to swallow. It actually ruled that the Pugh judgment was not anything special at all, since the role of that administrative body was to resolve issues under international law and international settlement agreements—not domestic US law. And federal court judgments, even those arising from the special 1996 FSIA amendment authorizing these very cases, did not carry any weight under international law.

So much for the hard-fought, unprecedented courtroom victory we had obtained against Libya. So much for the intent of Congress in 1996 allowing such lawsuits to be pursued in order to hold terrorist states accountable and "make terrorism expensive." So much for the special and unique assistance the State Department had provided to us in obtaining the court judgment that Libya was responsible for the UTA 772 bombing. Shockingly, the FCSC ruled that the Pugh judgment, which had compelled Qaddafi to settle all his disputes with the United States once and for all, was not worth the paper on which Judge Kennedy had written it.

Of course, the Pugh judgment had even played a major role in providing President Bush a last-minute legacy in his "war on terror" in the final throes of his eight years in office. But even that did not count at the FCSC. As far as that agency was concerned, the fact that Judge Kennedy had issued this judgment did not have any legal effect whatsoever when it came to distributing the remaining Libya Settlement funds.

Obviously, ending our long and arduous legal journey on this note brought more disappointment and anguish for Matthews, the Pugh families and my law firm. It appeared that President Bush had been in such a hurry to close his deal with Qaddafi that our own efforts, and accomplishments, had been thrown under the political and diplomatic bus, at least as far as the representations made to Congress in 2008 by Ambassador Negroponte, and the later "Category C" referral to the FCSC, that the Pugh families would have the opportunity to obtain two or three times the amount recovered by the Lockerbie families. In the end, those representations proved lacking, and clearly had been made at our clients' expense.

But, looking back on the experience as I drafted this story, I strongly believe that we nevertheless had accomplished something that no one else had achieved in the saga of Qaddafi and his worldwide campaign of terrorism. Only the Pugh families and Interlease had gone the distance with Libya and obtained a federal court judgment, formally and legally establishing that Qaddafi and his agents had blown up the DC-10 and committed mass murder. Clearly, not even the Pan Am 103 Lockerbie families had been able to hold Libya responsible, or even have their "day in court." Their frustration was expressed in newspaper articles, books and even testimony to Congress.

The diplomatic settlement that Bush and Qaddafi had put together was simply about money. Lots of it, for sure, but simply money. The President of the United States had decided at the very end of his term that he needed to clear the decks for Libya to do business with the United States oil companies. A financial payment—one that Bush determined was fair and sufficient, notwithstanding the people who had been killed and injured, or the thoughtful judgment of an independent federal judge—was Qaddafi's ticket to his new life as a statesman.

Certainly, President Bush had obtained more than simply money. Libya had ceased supporting terrorism, turned over its nuclear program and was providing support in the fight against radical Islamic groups such as Al Qaeda. All of these were factors in the President's decision, and no one questioned their importance to the interests of the United States. But the lawsuits had been intended by Congress to hold countries such as Libya accountable for their despicable conduct. Paying people a check to avoid accountability was not what Congress had in mind when it allowed such cases to be prosecuted in 1996. Passing another law to shut down the very cases that had changed Qaddafi's conduct also was not what the law had been intended to do. And having the President require that all such cases be terminated—especially our judgment in Pugh—seemed to reward Qaddafi far beyond the price he was paying for admission back into the world's theater.

Significantly, our clients in Pugh had also achieved something that no one, not even the Pan Am 103 Lockerbie families, had been able to accomplish. By coming to Washington to testify in the federal court, with Libya defending the case and the full force of the law supporting their claim, the Pugh families had achieved a significant level of closure on their own personal journeys of pain and loss. Losing a daughter, or husband, or wife is a devastating experience. Losing them suddenly in a terrorist attack at 35,000 feet over the North African desert is unimaginable, as their compelling testimony at the trial made clear.

No one had ever done this before. And because Congress and the President had closed the door forever against pursuing terrorism suits against Libya, no one would ever attempt to accomplish such a thing in the future. And for that, Ambassador Pugh and the other six American families of UTA Flight 772, along with Doug Matthews, achieved the ultimate victory over terror and violence. They had ensured by their bravery and perseverance that the last flight of the DC-10 would never be forgotten.

Epilogue

Memorial

EVEN WITH THE historic settlement between Libya and the United States in 2008, the subject of Qaddafi and his prolific sponsorship of terrorism continued to make news on a regular and prominent basis. As the world knows, in 2011, the mercurial ruler's reign ultimately reached its nadir.

As always had been the case, any issues or developments regarding the Pan Am 103 Lockerbie case were bound to be front-page news around the world. One of the legacies of that case was the frustration, disappointment and anger many of the Lockerbie families continued to experience notwithstanding the completion of the $10 million per-family payment as a result of the Bush–Qaddafi settlement agreement. Those final payments, of course, were only made possible by the diplomacy and political decisions that the Pugh court judgment had helped enable. It seemed to many that a true sense of closure for the deserving Lockerbie families was always out of reach.

To their great annoyance, the settlement with President Bush had made Qaddafi's regime one of the richest in the world. The "success" they had achieved in their own pursuit of justice against Libya had mostly been in the form of a large monetary payment. Even that success was effectively unraveled by the very same criminal justice system in

Scotland that they had relied on to obtain a sense of justice. Just as they were receiving the last payments from the State Department's distribution of funds from the diplomatic deal—made possible by the pressure raised by our judgment in Pugh—the only man convicted of blowing up the Boeing 747 jumbo jet over Scotland was set free.

On 10 August 2009, Abdelbaset Ali Mohmed al-Megrahi walked out of his Scottish prison, boarded a private jet at Glasgow Airport and flew directly to Tripoli. As he stepped out of the plane and put his feet down onto his native soil, hundreds of Libyan children cheered him as a returning hero, waving green Libyan flags and throwing flowers. He was kissed on both cheeks by Saif al-Islam Qaddafi, the Leader's Western-educated son and architect of the various settlements with the UK and United States. He was also greeted by Lamin Khalifa Fhimah, his acquitted co-defendant at the infamous trial at Camp Zeist. They had not seen each other for over eight years. Later that evening, the Leader himself welcomed al-Megrahi at his tent, a homecoming and honor that was broadcast on Libyan television.

Despite his conviction by the special Scottish court for committing a notorious act of mass murder, the Cabinet Secretary for Justice in Scotland, Kenny MacAskill, had granted al-Megrahi's request for early release from prison. The stated reason was that he was dying of prostate cancer and had less than three months to live. Relying on compassionate and "humanitarian" grounds for his decision, the Scottish official explained that he was bound by the tradition of allowing a prisoner to die at home.

The Lockerbie families were outraged. They could not determine how such an insult to their murdered loved ones and total disregard for the criminal justice system had come about. The leaders of the British government insisted that the decision was a "local" one made by the Scottish authorities without regard to the growing bilateral relationship between the UK and Libya. The fact that Britain's largest company, British Petroleum, had been able to sign huge energy development concessions with Libya was simply a coincidence, certainly not a *quid pro quo* for the convicted killer's release. BP executives vigorously denied that they had lobbied the UK government for al-Megrahi's release. He was a dying man, they insisted, and it was consistent with the norms of Scottish justice to allow him to spend his last few days at home.

But to the surprise of no one, al-Megrahi did not die within the predicted three-month period. Instead, he remained quite alive and active in his comfortable villa on the Mediterranean, a national hero to his fellow Libyans. As of 2011, he was still quite alive, and did not die until later that year. To rub salt even more deeply into their wounds, the only man convicted of killing their loved ones told the British paper *The Times* right after his release that he had "new evidence" that would exonerate him of responsibility for the Lockerbie bombing. At the time of my writing, no such evidence has been put forward.

Despite repeated requests from the Lockerbie families, the Scottish authorities have refused to release al-Megrahi's medical files upon which they based the decision to release him back to Libya. Apparently, his ability to survive cancer for over two years after his release was something of a medical miracle.

* * *

ANOTHER PERSON OFTEN implicated in the bombings of both Pan Am 103 and UTA 772 also made the front pages on a regular basis. Moussa Koussa, the Libyan intelligence chief interviewed by Bruguière in Tripoli and the subject of an Interpol arrest bulletin—but never charged with either bombing—ultimately was appointed by Qaddafi to act as Libya's Foreign Minister. The man who had been expelled from London in 1980 for making death threats on Libyan dissidents had emerged as Qaddafi's essential diplomat with the United States and Great Britain. After the attacks of 11 September 2001, Moussa Koussa had been the point man for providing intelligence to the CIA and MI6 to hunt down Islamic extremists in Al Qaeda, one of the triggering events in allowing Libya to emerge from isolation.

Ironically, the man who had played such a critical role in carrying out the Lockerbie and UTA attacks had come to London to seek the release of his fellow Libyan al-Megrahi on humanitarian grounds. Free to travel around the world under the protection of a diplomatic passport, Moussa Koussa was the smiling public face of a former terrorist state—another painful reminder to the Lockerbie families of their loss as well as the lack of accountability for the murderers.

* * *

A FEW WEEKS after al-Megrahi's triumphant return to Tripoli, the Leader himself completed the march back to worldwide respectability with his own remarkable travel itinerary. For the first time in his forty-year reign, Qaddafi flew to New York to address the United Nations General Assembly at its annual meeting in the Grand Hall next to the East River. The world body that had, through its Security Council in the same building, imposed severe sanctions on Libya for blowing up the Pan Am 103 and UTA 772 flights was now officially hosting the Colonel as an honored guest and speaker.

The Leader's introduction was more suitable to a political function in Tripoli than the world's diplomatic forum for debate and assembly. After listening to himself described as "leader of the revolution, the president of the African Union, the king of kings of Africa," Qaddafi proceeded to deliver a rambling ninety-minute speech, seventy-five minutes beyond his allotted time. Most of the delegates yawned or were annoyed by the disruption to their schedules. The speech, delivered in Arabic, was carried live on CNN around the world.

Dressed in his traditional Arab robe, Africa-shaped pin on his chest, Qaddafi rambled through a series of unrelated stream-of-consciousness thoughts, touching on the causes of swine flu, the assassination of John F. Kennedy, the need to create a combined state of Israelis and Palestinians, and his open invitation to move the entire United Nations to his own country to escape the dangerous venue of New York. For dramatic flair, he tore up a copy of the United Nations Charter to demonstrate his point that the Security Council and its permanent members were treating Libya and others as "second-class citizens."

But no one took him up on these points, and the speech was widely reported not for its substance, but for the fact that one of the world's outcasts was now back in the fold. For every family of every victim of Libyan terrorism over the prior twenty-five years, Qaddafi's appearance on the podium at the United Nations—and on international television—was a painful indignity. It appeared that the man who had ordered so many murders and terrorist attacks was, in the end, allowed to take an honored place at the table of international order. But this honor was not to last very long.

* * *

IN FEBRUARY 2011 a strong wind of change blew across North Africa and the Middle East. Characterized as an "Arab Spring," it carried away several long-time dictators and rulers. When those winds reached Libya, several decades of despotic rule finally saw the Great Leader swept up and away.

In Benghazi, protesting Libyans caught up in the events broadcast on their televisions rushed into the streets and expressed their frustration with the years of Qaddafi patronage, corruption and widespread unemployment. Not willing, or able, to tolerate any domestic criticism, the Leader ordered his army to open fire on their fellow citizens marching in the streets, killing hundreds and only adding fuel to the inferno. Over the next few months, a new organization of rebellious Libyans calling themselves the National Transitional Council (NTC) organized an open revolt, which quickly spread to all the cities along the coast, where most Libyans lived.

By August, Qaddafi's army and security services had disintegrated, NATO had announced its support for the rebellion, and the Arab League once again distanced itself from the dictator who had long prided himself on being independent and unique. The United Nations Security Council, which years before had imposed and then withdrawn the sanctions that had forced Qaddafi back into the civilized world, once again took a role in the future of Libya when it authorized the military assistance that ultimately ousted the Leader.

With his government dissolved and the NTC taking control of the major cities, Qaddafi fled Tripoli in an armed convoy and headed for the vast interior desert where he had retreated on many occasions for security and comfort. But the desert could no longer protect him from the wrath of his own people or the accuracy of NATO military jets.

With his convoy caught in an attack from the air, the man who had addressed the United Nations in triumph and taken on the world's powers was forced to hide in the drainage pipe of a construction site as his last remaining bodyguards attempted in vain to fend off rebel fighters. Overpowered and then captured, the rebels began to beat and stab Qaddafi without mercy. Once he was dead, his lifeless body was thrown on the hood of a pick-up truck and displayed as a trophy. The scene was captured on video by rebels using cell phones. Qaddafi's final public appearance—a humiliation—also was broadcast around the world on CNN.

Not wanting to create a memorial that might serve as a rallying point for his few remaining followers, the new NTC government had the former Leader buried in an unmarked grave in the desert. There would be no marker for the former dictator's remains.

As President Barack Obama declared at the time, the shadow of tyranny over Libya had been lifted forever.

* * *

WITH THE LEADER brutally killed by his own enraged people and buried in an unmarked desert grave, his former chief of intelligence and brother-in-law was brought to justice using more civilized methods.

Abdallah al-Senoussi, convicted in absentia by the French courts for the UTA 772 attack, managed to slip out of Libya just as Qaddafi met his violent demise. Eventually, he bribed his way to the African nation of Mauritania, but even his fat wallet could not prevent his extradition back to Libya to stand trial for hundreds of murders of Libyan citizens.

In 2015 al-Senoussi was convicted by a Libyan court of multiple counts of murder and sentenced to be hanged. At the time of the publication of this book he sat in a Tripoli jail pursuing a final appeal. The British government was apparently trying to interview him to determine with certainty Libya's role in the Pan Am 103 Lockerbie bombing, in which he would have been a principal participant. The French government still has an outstanding request to extradite him to Paris to face justice for his leading role in the UTA 772 attack. Given his prominent role in Qaddafi's brutal regime, and his death sentence, it is unlikely al-Senoussi will ever leave Libya alive.

* * *

ALTHOUGH THERE WOULD be no memorial or marker for Qaddafi's remains, and his chief aides faced justice in the new Libyan dynamic, another project had been launched in the North African desert that would serve a very different purpose. French film director Jerome Carret had been hired by the French victims of UTA 772, Les Familles du DC-10 d'UTA, to document their plan to erect a lasting memorial for the victims of the attack near the actual crash site in the Ténéré desert. Unlike the crash of the Pan Am 103 747 jumbo jet in Lockerbie, the crash site in the remote African desert had never been cleaned up or even monitored. The only exceptions were that the French authorities had removed the remains of the victims to Paris right after the crash to conduct autopsies and burials, and Bruguière's investigators later had brought back to Paris the pieces of the aircraft that were needed to reconstruct the fuselage around the baggage compartment. The rest of the pieces of the huge DC-10 and its debris had been left in the blowing sands of the Ténéré for almost twenty years, like a shipwreck on a remote island.

The French documentary film is a sober and quiet piece. It follows a group of UTA 772 family members read each of the 170 names and nationalities of the victims at the memorial in Paris outside Les Invalides, where I had stood with Madame Rudetzki. The leader of the group and the Foundation established with the second Libyan settlement payments stands with his fellow mourners: Guillaume Denoix de Saint Marc had also taken the lead in the struggle to construct the memorial in the desert.

Brief video interviews with Judge Bruguière help explain some of the background to his remarkable investigation and detective work. The documentary includes some photos of the reconstructed fuselage section in Paris that clearly highlights the hole blasted by the Libyan suitcase bomb. There is even footage of Qaddafi's triumphant state visit to Paris, where French President Sarkozy greeted him with full honors at the Élysée Palace as victims of the Leader's terrorist attacks protested outside its walls.

But much of the film tracks the long, harsh ride in SUVs hundreds of miles into the desert, over sand dunes and dry lake beds, to the crash site. Over one hundred local workers were enlisted to assist the mechanics and designers who had made it to the desolate site. Camels and local Bedouins passing on the horizon no longer notice the wind-blown remains of the DC-10 that have littered their path for the past two decades.

Given the site's isolation, the materials for the memorial had to be trucked in from mountains seventy kilometers away. The workers lift fifty-pound boulders out of the trucks and carry them to the site under a brutal desert sun, the heat and blowing sand forcing them to remain wrapped in Bedouin headgear and face scarves. They form the two-hundred-foot-diameter circle of smooth black rocks, placing them in precise order, according to a drawing brought from Paris and using surveyor's tools. The 170 panes of cracked glass, set in concrete, are tributes to each of the victims whose lives were brought to a sudden and violent end on 19 September 1989.

Finally, the Bedouin workers haul the long, lonely section of the DC-10's right wing several miles across the desert from its twenty-year sleep in the sand. Lying in a flat-bed truck, the plane's wing resembles a hunter's prey, hauled back as a trophy. It is set in the landscape, standing outside the circle of rocks and cracked panes, standing on its thick end as a tall monument bearing a bronze plaque listing the victims' names.

The 170 who lost their lives on UTA Flight 772 will be remembered by Le Memorial du Ténéré for all time, only a short distance from where they perished. The final resting place of flight UTA 772 is visible for all the world to see from outer space, and, through this extraordinary tribute, the forgotten flight will forever be remembered.

A satellite mapping the surface of the earth takes a clear photograph of the memorial. The careful placing of the rocks outlines the DC-10, in full authentic size, its flight path frozen north-by-northwest towards its home in Paris.

The coordinates are clear.

16 degrees 51′ 54″ north.

11 degrees 57′ 13″ east.

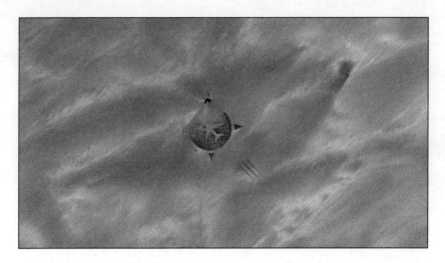

The UTA Memorial, 3 April 2011 (courtesy of DigitalGlobe)

Author's Note on Sources

THE FORGOTTEN FLIGHT is the story of my representation of the seven Americans who were killed in the 19 September 1989 UTA 772 terrorist attack as well as the owner of the wide-body DC-10 that was destroyed during its routine flight from North Africa to Paris. As the reader learns, the book relies on the extensive documentation, information and interviews that supported my work as an advocate seeking justice against the Libyan State.

As part of the UTA 772 litigation and diplomacy, along with the many other terrorism cases I have handled against Libya, Iran, Sudan and other countries (some of which I discuss in the book), I acquired more than the typical lawyer's "inch-wide/mile-deep" knowledge of the facts affecting my clients' case. Instead, I became deeply immersed in a broad range of issues from the early history of Colonel Qaddafi's political strategy to engage in state-sponsorship of global terror—an essential part of his foreign policy—to how a number of particular terrorist attacks carried out by Libya and its agents fitted into the bigger picture of his global conflict with the West.

On this basis, my book is not intended to be a detached case study or comparison of the notorious December 1988 bombing of Pan Am

103 over Lockerbie, Scotland, and the relatively forgotten but similar suitcase bombing of UTA 772 over North Africa nine months later. Of course, these two aircraft attacks were the specific reason that the United Nations Security Council imposed a series of sanctions on the Qaddafi regime, sanctions that ultimately compelled him to change his violent ways. My own role as an advocate in the UTA 772 portion of this history is the window through which I acquired much of the material for this story, and through which I attempt to provide the reader with a context for the wider narrative of Qaddafi's legacy as the Osama bin Laden of his time.

For this reason, and because the story (especially Part II) is put forward as a mostly first-person narrative, this book is not conducive to a scholar's usage of detailed footnotes to describe sources. Much of what I describe is told from my first-hand experience, observations and advocacy, as well as the extensive files and evidence I compiled and acquired during the course of the work.

As described in the book, much of the material was acquired directly from those persons in France, the United States, Libya and elsewhere who played important roles in the narrative. The knowledge came from multiple interviews, meetings, review of court and government documents, expert forensic reports and my own law firm's files. I absorbed this information in my job as an advocate and employed much of it to seek a positive result for the clients.

Given the broader implications of the story beyond the UTA 772 litigation against Libya, it is helpful for the reader to understand some of the sources that I relied on, both for my work as counsel as well as an author telling a story long after the legal work was completed.

Of particular importance to the case, and this narrative, were the thirty-three thick binders of original paper files my law firm was able to copy from Madame Rudetzki's office at Les Invalides, the grand gold-domed building on the Left Bank of Paris. These files are the complete, original and authorized version of the official court records supporting the French criminal investigation and prosecution in absentia of the six Libyan officials and agents found guilty of the murder of the 170 persons killed on the UTA 772 flight.

Those files, mostly in French and translated by native French-speaking lawyers in my law firm's Brussels office, provided much of the factual and forensic support for the French criminal proceedings as well as the parallel civil proceedings I pursued against Libya in the federal court case in Washington, DC.

As noted, these files are not normally available to the public in French criminal courts, but many sections are now a part of the public record (in English and French) in the Washington federal court case, despite Libya's objections to their admissibility during the proceedings before Judge Kennedy. I also maintain a full and unabridged set in my law firm's Washington offices.

To better understand these files, as well as the extraordinary French investigation of the UTA 772 terrorist attack, I spent many hours, over several years, meeting with Judge Bruguière. I needed to understand his own recollections and observations of what he considered one of his greatest achievements as a detective. The story of how his French team connected the Libyan State, at the highest levels, to the destruction of the DC-10 over the remote Ténéré desert must rank as one of the greatest detective stories of all time. Indeed, the French investigators' success in literally putting pieces of the DC-10 back together in a hangar outside Paris—after an exhaustive investigation that spanned the globe—provided my clients with the solid evidence upon which to hold Libya responsible in the contested civil suit in Washington. In addition to many hours spent in his office discussing the case, Bruguière's autobiography, in French, *Ce Que Je N'ai Pas Pu Dire* (*What I Could Not Say*), has some interesting anecdotes that also were helpful in writing this book.

To supplement the French criminal case files and Judge Bruguière's interviews, my team at Crowell & Moring compiled a large file of publicly available, declassified documents and reports from the US Department of State, especially its Report on Global Terrorism (published annually and available at www.state.gov), as well as documents declassified by the Central Intelligence Agency, the US Department of Defense, the Federal Aviation Administration and other agencies. Much of that documentation was submitted as evidence before Judge Kennedy.

The detailed history of the Pugh litigation itself, as well as the related Kilburn, Dammarell and other cases discussed in the book, are publicly available in the Federal Reporter case law books, which also are accessible by internet search. These include Judge Kennedy's summary judgment ruling that the Libyan State was directly responsible for the UTA 772 bombing, his remarkable damages award and the various appellate rulings by the DC Circuit Court of Appeals.

As discussed in the book, a critical part of our legal and diplomatic work in Washington was the preparation and submission of the detailed, written testimony of Ambassador Thomas "Ted" McNamara, the former State Department Director of Counterterrorism during the relevant time frame of the UTA and Lockerbie investigations, the United Nations sanctions and related diplomacy. His first-hand knowledge of the story from the perspective of the highest levels of the United States government provided us, and Judge Kennedy, with even more solid evidence—beyond the extensive French criminal file—to hold Libya responsible for the UTA bombing under US law. The fact that the State Department itself supported our submission of Ambassador McNamara's testimony in federal court on the issue of Libya's responsibility for the attack represented a rare strategic decision by the US government to participate in a type of case that it generally views as a private legal dispute. I am unaware of any other terrorism case against a sovereign state in which the US government played such an important and direct role supporting the victims' case.

Of course, my many conversations, over several years, with State Department Legal Adviser Jonathan Schwartz (as discussed in the book), played a major role in the coordination with the US government in litigating the UTA matter specifically as well as understanding the broader implications of US–Libya diplomatic dynamics. In addition, Schwartz (who recently retired after a distinguished career) wrote a thoughtful article about his own experience handling US–Libya relations, "Dealing With a 'Rogue State': The Libya Precedent," which was published in the *American Journal of International Law*. That article also provides useful background to the broader political picture discussed in this book. Schwartz's views are especially important given his role as the Senior Legal Adviser to the US diplomats working under President George W. Bush who were managing these issues throughout most of the Libya saga.

In a similar vein, the special insights provided by Ambassador Jean Jacques Beaussou—my "private ambassador" to Tripoli—shed light on some of the unique personalities and politics of the Qaddafi era, both in Libya and Paris. Beaussou was more than just a consultant to my law firm and expert on all things Libya. He became a friend and confidant who later returned to the French Diplomatic Corps and served with distinction as the French Ambassador to Peru. His reports to me on his visits and meetings in Tripoli were of immense value to my legal work as well as in writing this book.

I am very thankful to Guillaume Denoix de Saint Marc, who introduced me to Ambassador Beaussou, provided his own insights into the UTA disaster from the perspective of the French victims and their families, and himself played a very significant role in the French–Libyan diplomacy described in the narrative. His own book, in French, *Mon Pere etait dans le DC-10* (*My Father Was on the DC-10*), is, aside from Bruguière's wide-ranging autobiography, the only book I know of by a player in this story that addresses the subject of UTA 772. In contrast to my narrative, it focuses mostly on the French–Libyan diplomatic deal that arose as a result of President Chirac's threat to veto the lifting of the United Nation's Security Council sanctions after the Lockerbie-related agreement was announced. That itself is an interesting dynamic of French–Libyan politics and diplomacy that I describe in the book.

Along these lines, it was mostly because of the efforts of Saint Marc and his Paris-based Foundation for all the UTA victims that the UTA 772 Memorial was constructed in the Ténéré desert, under extremely difficult conditions and in very rough terrain. This haunting memorial to the 170 victims of the UTA 772 terrorist attack is now visible from space on anyone's computer screen via an Internet search engine.

The French television documentary *Le Memorial du Ténéré*, directed by Jerome Carret, follows Saint Marc and the construction of the UTA Memorial in the desert. It provides rare footage of the disaster site and wreckage of the DC-10, much of which still sits in the shifting sands and dunes of this remote, desolate area. I have borrowed liberally from those images, in conjunction with the evidence and reports in the French investigative and forensic files, to portray the crash site in the opening and closing pages of this book.

The chapter describing the Pan Am 103 bombing over Lockerbie is taken mostly from the civil negligence case pursued by the Lockerbie families against Pan American Airways, which resulted in a substantial monetary award paid by Pan Am and its insurance carriers. The federal trial judge on Long Island who heard that case, along with a jury, oversaw a detailed factual and forensic record that was closely reviewed by the US Court of Appeals for the Second Circuit, which affirmed the trial court award against Pan Am. Those official proceedings are presented at length in the Federal Reporter law books, which are publicly available, and upon which I rely to summarize some of the more important evidence. That court verdict and monetary award against Pan Am was the death knell of what had been the most prestigious airline in the United States. In parallel, the case brought by Pan Am's insurers against Libya in the Washington federal court for indemnification of the damages they had paid to the families also is set forth in several publicly available court decisions and pleadings.

In addition, the special Scottish court criminal proceedings that took place in the Netherlands against the two accused Lockerbie bombers is taken from Scottish law reports and other publicly available sources in the UK.

The description of the terrorist attacks at the Rome and Vienna airports are based on records and awards before the US Foreign Claims Settlement Commission (FCSC), which oversaw a number of claims arising from the 2008 settlement between President Bush and Qaddafi. My law firm represented a number of claimants before the FCSC, including clients who were the victims of several of these attacks for which payments were made from the Libyan funds. The FCSC proceedings and awards are publicly available on the FCSC website.

Similarly, the description of the attack on La Belle Disco in Berlin also is taken from FCSC proceedings and awards on the website, although my law firm did not represent any claimants regarding this particular attack.

I also have relied on the trial and appellate records from the federal court in Denver and the US Court of Appeals for the Tenth Circuit (also available in the Federal Reporter law books) to describe the criminal prosecution of Timothy McVeigh for his role in carrying out the bombing of the Murrah Federal Building in Oklahoma City. As discussed in the book, it was this act of domestic terrorism that created, in coordination with the Pan Am 103 Lockerbie attack, a unique bipartisan window through which Congress enacted the 1996 law, allowing victims of state-sponsored terrorism to pursue civil cases in federal court. Without that bipartisan coordination, the federal courthouse doors would have remained shut to my clients—and all other victims of state-sponsored terrorism—and thus we would never have been able to obtain justice against Qaddafi's Libya for the UTA 772 bombing.

For general background on all these events and issues, I have relied on several respected secondary sources to write this book, including contemporaneous articles from the *New York Times*, BBC, *Washington Post*, *Wall Street Journal* and other publicly available media. However, these secondary sources were not relied upon in the legal proceedings in which I was involved, nor are they used in this book other than to confirm dates and statements set forth in the primary sources mentioned above.

Of course, one of the most important sources for this story, and the book, were my clients in the UTA 772 case—Doug Matthews, the owner of the aircraft, and the seven American families who lost their loved ones on 19 September 1989. Their engrossing trial testimony before Judge Kennedy is taken directly from the public court transcripts. In addition to the trial proceedings described in the book, the various other court proceedings in which I acted as counsel before the US Court of Appeals for the DC Circuit also are taken from publicly available briefs, transcripts and court decisions.

Acknowledgments

IT IS NO easy thing to prosecute a complex civil case for terrorism and murder against a rogue sovereign state that has vast resources upon which it can call to mount all sorts of defenses. During my years of legal work on the Libya terrorism cases, I did not anticipate that the story would find its way into a published book. But, upon reflection, the book took shape. I drafted sections, off and on, while still managing a pretty hectic international disputes practice at Crowell & Moring. Outlines, notes and chapters would emerge from my returning to Bruguière's reports, the federal law books reporting on some of the other cases and the extensive case files sitting in my office. I would work on drafting for a while and then get sucked into the vortex of yet another trial on another case, the manuscript on my computer dormant, unedited and un-updated, for months. Eventually, the story emerged, and, with Doug Matthews' review and blessing, I moved ahead with completing a manuscript.

Once the manuscript took shape, I was fortunate to have some wonderful assistance, both in correcting factual mistakes as well as getting the book to publication. Joe Brinley served for many years as Director of the Wilson Press, the publication arm of the Woodrow

Wilson International Center for Scholars in Washington. His support and comments were invaluable, as were the two peer reviews of the manuscript conducted by respected scholars associated with the Wilson Center. My friend and client Kaveh Moussavi, a scholar and human rights lawyer long associated with the Centre for Socio-Legal Studies at Wolfson College, Oxford University, played a major role in helping me get the manuscript into the hands of a world-class publisher. Novin Doostdar, the Publisher of Oneworld in London, made the brave decision to take on the book project and see it to publication. I am grateful to them all, and others who lent their support.

But any acknowledgments of the story told in *The Forgotten Flight* must begin with how Congress opened the court house door for this, and all other, terror victim lawsuits. The 1996 bipartisan federal law enacted by Congress and signed by President Clinton allowed, for the first time, civil suits against sovereign states for supporting terrorist attacks against Americans. It is an extraordinary piece of legislation. Until recently, the United States had the only legal system in the world that authorized such cases—Canada recently enacted a law along the same lines, but the case law is still developing. Other countries mostly deal with terrorism through criminal prosecution and imprisonment of individuals, the traditional legal mechanism for pursuing justice against those who commit murder. When it comes to dealing with "sovereigns," diplomacy is the standard method for resolving disputes, not civil litigation brought by victims and their lawyers in domestic courts.

Moreover, waiving or limiting the scope of sovereign immunity to civil claims against sovereign nations runs against centuries of international law going back to Ancient Rome, to contemporary legal systems of almost every nation on earth. And I have learned this through first-hand experience.

Indeed, I was rebuffed in my own efforts to extend the reach of the 1996 law to the judicial systems of other civilized countries (such as Italy) when attempting to domesticate overseas some of the terrorism judgments against Iran that were issued by the federal court in Washington. Making that task even more challenging, the International Court of Justice in The Hague recently indicated in the case of Germany v. Italy that it views the 1996 US federal law as a violation of international law. It appears that holding sovereign states responsible for notorious acts of state-sponsored terrorism is, for the most part, a uniquely American philosophy.

For example, the case discussed in the book against Iran arising from the April 1983 terrorist attack against the US Embassy in Beirut, Lebanon, is where I first encountered Ambassador Pugh—as a witness, not as a client. The Court of Appeals of Rome, Italy, firmly rejected our efforts to domesticate the Washington civil judgment against Iran (known as the Dammarell case) in the Italian legal system. For more background on the history of this case, the reader also should consult the critically acclaimed book by Kai Bird entitled *The Good Spy: The Life and Death of Robert Ames*. Mr. Ames' estate and surviving widow are two of my clients in the *Dammarell* case.

As for the final chapter of the Pugh case, in the end, even the US legal system itself raised a serious roadblock to justice. As discussed in the Epilogue, the State Department referred the claims of my client families to the Foreign Claims Settlement Commission to sort how much in additional payments they would receive from the Libya Settlement Fund. Their ability to pursue additional amounts was based on representations to Congress made by the State Department when the Libya Claims Resolution Act was enacted in the summer of 2008, as well as the terms of the "Category C" referral by State to the FCSC that was tailored to handle the claims of the seven Pugh families.

The FCSC took several years and two rounds of proceedings ultimately to determine that Judge Kennedy's judgment in Pugh, and judgments generally arising from the 1996 FSIA terrorism law, had no basis in international law. It is certainly ironic that a US agency such as the FCSC would make a ruling that the Pugh judgment was irrelevant under international law despite the express pronouncements of all three branches of the US government that authorized and issued the Pugh judgment under US federal law. That irony has never been addressed by Congress, which might find it curious that its own statutes have no legal force when it comes to claims before the FCSC. The rulings of the FCSC denied the Pugh families any additional substantial payments from the 2008 settlement between President Bush and Colonel Qaddafi, despite the history and record discussed in the book. As noted above, the FCSC's decisions are set forth in written awards publicly available on the FCSC website, www.justice.gov/fcsc.

But beyond the cases that have been brought pursuant to the 1996 legislation, there is a more nuanced administrative device that remains in the hands of the Secretary of State, and thus the President, and therefore also beyond the authority of the federal courts. This device ensures that, notwithstanding the ability of some victims to pursue claims in court against certain countries, the President and the Secretary of State ultimately decide how the United States will conduct this critical aspect of its foreign policy. The reader should have some basic appreciation of that scheme to understand further the background and challenges we faced in litigating the Pugh case.

In particular, the Secretary of State has sole discretion, by federal statute, to decide which sovereign nations will be designated "State Sponsors of Terrorism." This designation is a necessary prerequisite not only to the lawsuits by victims against a particular country such as Libya, but also a broad range of financial, regulatory and even criminal penalties and sanctions that are purposely designed to influence the conduct of a terrorist state. This "listing" is based on the Secretary's finding that a particular state has "repeatedly provided support for acts of terrorism," pursuant to a regulatory scheme more fully described in the State Department's website at www.state.gov.

The Secretary first issued this state sponsor list in December 1979, with Qaddafi's Libya a charter member. Other nations placed on this list—and some taken off in due course—included the wild country formerly known as South Yemen, Saddam Hussein's Iraq, the senior Assad's Syria, Castro's Cuba (added in 1982), the Ayatollah's Iran (added in 1984 after the devastating attacks in April and October 1983, respectively, in Beirut against the US Embassy and the US Marine Barracks), Kim Jong-il's North Korea (in 1988) and Bashir's Sudan (in 1993). This rogue's gallery is important because each tyrant was governing a sovereign state that is a full member of the United Nations. The state sponsor list is unique because it is separate from a number of other lists of individuals and organizations—such as Al Qaeda, ISIS and Abu Nidal—that are deemed "terrorists" by the US and other governments. This uniqueness carries several important consequences.

The most important consequence of being placed on the "state sponsor list" is that it automatically implicates a broad range of economic and legal restrictions on how, and to what extent, US companies and individuals may engage in commerce with such a state. There are various limits on using the US banking system to send dollars to such countries, limitations on travel and a variety of penalties for violating such restrictions. And, of course, these various sanctions are separate from the type of sanctions imposed by international bodies such as the United Nations Security Council. Moreover, all these devices are separate from the criminal prosecution of individuals—or even military actions—by the United States and many other countries.

As described at various points in the book, Qaddafi desperately sought to have Libya removed from this list, in parallel to the lifting of severe sanctions. His historic, multi-billion-dollar settlement agreement with the Pan Am 103 Lockerbie families (discussed in this book) opened the door to this strategy at the United Nations and with the United States government. At the same time, that same settlement agreement caused serious tensions and uneasiness with many of the Lockerbie families. Many were very uncomfortable with a deal that even remotely aligned their pursuit of justice with the cold-blooded calculations of the brutal dictator who had ordered the murder of their loved ones. For very different reasons, American diplomats also were very uncomfortable with the "private" Lockerbie settlement agreement that essentially forced their hand on the issue of how to deal with Qaddafi and his terrorist state. Schwartz's thoughtful article on this subject discusses this dilemma at some length.

This is one of the principal differences regarding how these two aircraft disasters were handled in the US legal system. Pan Am 103 Lockerbie was settled without any sense of closure or justice for the families, while the American families in Pugh took the UTA 772 issues all the way to trial and obtained a detailed judgment on liability and damages. As described in my book, the intangible benefits of pursuing justice and obtaining a federal court judgment—even one suddenly snatched away by the President of the United States and Congress—were something Qaddafi could not take away from my clients simply by writing a very large check.

Of course, Qaddafi had very practical reasons for pursuing this strategy. So long as Libya remained on the state sponsor list and was the subject of economic sanctions, American and European energy firms could not easily return to Libya to do business and thus replenish the Libyan treasury with billions of dollars in oil revenues. And certainly Qaddafi sought and obtained these measures from the Bush Administration because being sued by American victims—and then having to worry that their large court judgments could interfere with billions in commerce—is bad for business. Not to mention his desire to restore some measure of respectability to a nation long known for its terrorist policies and actions.

But another substantial factor in Qaddafi's desire to be removed from the state sponsor list and lift the economic sanctions was to buttress his domestic standing. He wanted to convince his people that only he could lead them out of the wilderness and solve the complex problems that, for the most part, were his own creation. Dictators actually want and need to build domestic support—whether by consensus or coercion—or else they will not remain long in their position. With that support would come acceptance by the international community. His strategy culminated in Qaddafi's "victory tour" to many European capitals and his grandiose, internationally broadcast speech at the United Nations General Assembly in New York, described towards the end of the book.

In the end, Qaddafi was able to achieve all these goals, have his nation removed from the terrorism sponsor list and lift the UN's draconian sanctions. He accomplished this through the intertwined legal/diplomatic/economic measures described. Despite this achievement and his worldwide victory tour, however, it did not take long for the rule of this despot to come to an inglorious end at the hands of his own enraged people.

Libya may now be off the terrorism list, and energy firms have returned in force. But it has many serious challenges ahead if it is to become a stable country. Whatever the future holds for Libya, Qaddafi will go down in history as the dictator who used the Libyan State, and its resources, to murder hundreds of innocent people on Pan Am 103 and UTA 772, as well as in many other attacks. None of his "achievements" for Libya can erase that legacy. And thus, the legislation enacted by Congress in 1996, combined with Libya's earlier placement on the state sponsor list, opened the door for my clients and the courts to write that history for all time. Nothing can change this historical record—not even the combined authority of President Bush and Congress, or the tensions between international and US federal law.

In reviewing this story and the wide range of sources that supported my legal work as well as the writing of this book, it is critical not to forget that the case against Libya for the UTA 772 attack was always about getting justice for the victims and their families. As noted, one of the benefits of the 1996 federal law that opened up the courthouse doors was to provide the victims and their families something that almost no other legal system in the world provides—a sense of closure and compensation against the perpetrator of the terror. These cases allow victims to publicly prove in a court of law how terror affects normal people.

I have handled many cases arising from terrorist attacks in all sorts of situations and for all types of victims. What we have learned from them is that terrorism knows no boundaries and has terrible consequences for innocent people, which can last for many years. This is the real meaning of terror. And that is why handling these cases is so challenging, and rewarding, for an attorney.

For this reason, I owe Doug Matthews a debt that cannot be repaid. He sought me out to handle this matter and brought the American Pugh families together in a sensitive and effective manner. Without Doug, we could never have put forward the compelling case to hold Libya responsible for blowing up his DC-10 and murdering not just my seven clients, but 170 innocent people. He organized the early coordination with Judge Bruguière, Madame Rudetzki and the French authorities, protected the interests of the seven families at all turns and supported my law firm's work throughout this extraordinary adventure. Without Doug, this case would not have happened, justice would not have been served and this book would never have been written. *The*

Forgotten Flight is dedicated to Doug Matthews, the seven American Pugh families I had the honor of representing, and to all the 170 victims who lost their lives on 19 September 1989.

May they finally rest in peace.

Washington, DC
August 2016

Index